HOW TO
DESIGN
AND WRITE
WEB PAGES
TODAY

HOW TO DESIGN AND WRITE WEB PAGES TODAY

Karl Stolley

Writing Today

 GREENWOOD

AN IMPRINT OF ABC-CLIO, LLC
Santa Barbara, California • Denver, Colorado • Oxford, England

Library of Congress Cataloging-in-Publication Data

Stolley, Karl.
   How to design and write web pages today / Karl Stolley.
     p. cm. — (Writing today)
   Includes bibliographical references and index.
   ISBN 978-0-313-38038-9 (hardback) — ISBN 978-0-313-38039-6 (ebook)
  1. Web sites—Design. I. Title. II. Series.
  TK5105.888.S76   2011
  006.7—dc22   2010051317

ISBN: 978-0-313-38038-9
EISBN: 978-0-313-38039-6

15   14   13   4   5

This book is also available on the World Wide Web as an eBook.
Visit www.abc-clio.com for details.

Greenwood
An Imprint of ABC-CLIO, LLC

ABC-CLIO, LLC
130 Cremona Drive, P.O. Box 1911
Santa Barbara, California 93116-1911

This book is printed on acid-free paper ∞

Manufactured in the United States of America

To Patricia Sullivan

CONTENTS

PART III. STRATEGIES FOR SUCCESS

PART IV. PROBLEMS AND SOLUTIONS

SERIES FOREWORD

Writing is an essential skill. Students need to write well for their coursework. Business people need to express goals and strategies clearly and effectively to staff and clients. Grant writers need to target their proposals to their funding sources. Corporate communications professionals need to convey essential information to shareholders, the media, and other interested parties. There are many different types of writing, and many particular situations in which writing is fundamental to success. The guides in this series help students, professionals, and general readers write effectively for a range of audiences and purposes.

Some books in the series cover topics of wide interest, such as how to design and write Web pages and how to write persuasively. Others look more closely at particular topics, such as how to write about the media. Each book in the series begins with an overview of the types of writing common to a practice or profession. This is followed by a study of the issues and challenges central to that type of writing. Each book then looks at general strategies for successfully addressing those issues, and it presents examples of specific problems and corresponding solutions. Finally, each volume closes with a bibliography of print and electronic resources for further consultation.

Concise and accessible, the books in this series offer a wealth of practical information for anyone who needs to write well. Students at all levels will find the advice presented helpful in writing papers; business professionals will value the practical guidance offered by these handbooks; and anyone who needs to express a complaint, opinion, question, or idea will welcome the methods conveyed in these texts.

PREFACE

The arts are made great, not by those who are without scruple in
boasting about them, but by those who are able to discover all of
the resources which each art affords.

—Isocrates, ca. 390 B.C.[1]

First, a disclaimer. This book will not teach you everything you need to
know about writing and designing for the Web.

No single book can.

But what this book will do is provide you with just about everything
you need in order to *learn* everything you need to know to write and
design for the Web.

The Web is unique among all forms of digital communication, in
that top to bottom, the Web is language. Language that you can learn
to read and write. From the visual designs of your pages, to the structure
of your pages, to the Web servers that deliver your pages to readers, the
Web is nothing but language. And those who wish to be rhetorically
successful on the Web must command the languages and accompany-
ing concepts behind the languages in order to best communicate with
the unique audience for any given Web site.

Contrary to how software companies market their products, the
ability to write and design and communicate effectively on the Web
is not determined by how much money you have, the software you
can afford to buy, or the whims of a particular computer company.

It is determined by how well you can command the languages of the Web to best communicate with the audience you are hoping to reach through your Web site and other forms of digital identity that you establish on the Web.

RHETORIC AND TECHNOLOGY

Even though, for most of us, the Web is a commonplace technology, it is still tempting to think of it as an entirely new form of communication. But the challenges of writing for the Web are just a recent development in the more than 2,500-year-old tradition known as the art of rhetoric. And it is rhetoric—not technology alone—that has informed and guided the writing and design advice in this book.

Now, you are probably more familiar with the word "rhetoric" in its popular, negative usage: politicians in particular thoroughly enjoy attacking one another for spouting "empty rhetoric" or "heated rhetoric." My PhD is in rhetoric, and I often tell my family and friends that it's the dirtiest word for which you can get a PhD. All joking aside though, the popular usage of the word "rhetoric" is unfortunate, and there are interesting historical reasons for why that negative sense of rhetoric is so common, but suffice it to say that there are also positive meanings of "rhetoric."

Rhetoric, in its better sense, is a productive, generative art of communicating with other human beings. The art of rhetoric enables people to discover, as it is expressed in Aristotle's *Rhetoric*, the available means for developing something to say, and for supporting what they say.[2] Rhetoric also suggests how to establish the best form to say something in, and to deliver the form appropriately for a particular audience in a particular context of time, values, and beliefs.

All of these issues—development, form, audience, and context—are central to maximizing the affordances, or available means, of Web communication. And all of the Web's affordances are derived from language: the language of the content you post to the Web (your text, images, multimedia, even page design), of course. But the Web also has its own languages, including the Extensible Hypertext Markup Language (XHTML), Cascading Style Sheets (CSS), and ECMAScript, better known as JavaScript. You can even use language to control Apache, the world's most popular Web server,[3] to better deliver your content across the Web.

DON'T CALL THEM, THEY'LL CALL YOU

But here's the trick with the Web: you rarely get to actively contact your audience, the way you do with an email or an instant message. Most of the time, your audience has to find you—usually through a search engine, such as Google. But they might also find you via your Twitter account or a bookmark of your site that someone has posted to Diigo. On the Web, we have to write so as to make sure that we are found. And that means writing for other computers, like search engines, in addition to writing for, and connecting with, human beings.

Once a human being has found your site, though, your rhetorical work has only just begun. You've been able to attract your audience's attention, but now you must work to maintain their attention: not just for the length of their visit to your site, but for as long as you continue to maintain your site. And that's where the long-term challenge of Web design lies. Anyone can post a site, and anyone can draw people to that site; but providing an experience that merits return visits (or job offers, or admission to school, or more customers for your business or members of your club) is a matter of good content, good design, and masterful use of the technologies that make up the Web.

In other words, it's all a matter of good rhetoric.

But learning technologies apart from rhetoric will gain you nothing more than technical proficiency. Learning the rhetoric apart from the technologies and languages will leave you at the mercy of whatever technology you can afford (or person you can afford to hire) to build your Web pages for you.

KNOWLEDGE AND VOCABULARY

Writing and designing for the Web is an important end in itself. But the techniques and approaches that this book offers are also grounded in a particular view of human relationships to technology: writing and designing for the Web is not just about helping you to work differently with Web technologies, but about deepening your understanding of them to change how you think, learn, and talk about them, too.

One thing you will notice about this book is that it does not shy away from the technical knowledge and vocabulary surrounding Web writing and design. There is a very good reason for this: more than any other form of digital writing, writing for the Web is a community activity. People work together to establish new practices and technologies for communicating on the Web. Two examples of that are open-source blogging software such as WordPress[4] and the Microformats.org[5] community, which is helping to make the information on Web pages easier to share and use away from the Web.

But in order to join or even simply benefit from the knowledge of any community—whether photographers, football fans, carpenters, knitters, poker players, medical doctors, or Web designers—you have to know or be willing to learn the words that that community uses *in addition to* engaging in photography, carpentry, poker, or whatever activity the community is known for. Think for a moment about your hobbies, your college major, or classes you have taken: in each of those areas, you have acquired specialized knowledge and technical words to talk about different subjects in ways that are more sophisticated than someone outside of your hobby, college major, or classroom.

Writing for the Web is no different: its terms may be unfamiliar and technical, but you know technical terms from other domains already. Web design and development is just another domain of knowledge. This book does not expect that you know these terms already, but it will help you learn them, search the Web for them, and use them to talk and collaborate with others on Web projects.

ESSENTIAL TOOLS AND TECHNOLOGY

In addition to the knowledge and words, you have to know the tools that a community uses: in the Web's case, the tools are the languages—particularly XHTML, CSS, and JavaScript—that people write with when they write for the Web, and a few generic pieces of software: a text editor, a search engine, and a Web browser.

However, this book does not teach Web writing according to one particular piece of software, and it outright discourages the use of what-you-see-is-what-you-get (WYSIWYG) software packages, such as Microsoft FrontPage or Adobe Dreamweaver, because WYSIWYGs fail Web writers at three important things:

- First, WYSIWYGs fail at supporting revisions to pages. Writing must always be revised. It never comes out perfectly the first time. And on the Web, things other than writing will also need revision: for example, your design might work in one Web browser, but not another. Web page creation is relatively easy; Web page revision is not—unless you understand how you wrote the page initially.
- Second, software packages for creating Web pages fail to prepare you for other, more advanced forms of Web production. If you want, for example, to build a custom template for a WordPress site, you have to understand how to write with the Web's languages; there is no WYSIWYG system for WordPress templates. (True, you can download a WordPress template of someone else's design, but that diminishes the rhetorical impact your site would otherwise have if it featured your own unique design.)
- Third, if you learn how to create Web pages only according to one piece of software, then your abilities will be dependent on the continued existence of that software. And even if the software's brand name continues to exist, the company behind it may radically restructure the software's interface and features—and you'll find yourself a beginner all over again.

It was exactly those three problems that I encountered in my own Web design work that led me to develop new methods to teach my students to design Web pages the way I write about in this book.

That said, my philosophy toward learning digital communication technologies is simple: learn them right and learn them well the first time. If you know or are willing to learn the languages of the Web—XHTML, CSS, JavaScript—then you will always know how to build Web pages, regardless of what software you have available. Learning the languages of the Web, coupled with the concepts for thinking and talking about them, will make it even easier for you to pick up other languages, or changes to existing ones, in the future.

The only tools you absolutely have to have to build a Web site are a Web-friendly text editor, a search engine, and a good Web browser, all of which are available as free downloads. There are suggestions for each later in this book.

- **A Web-friendly text editor** is where you do your writing; it is the view of your Web page where you do your work. But not only are you writing the content of a page that someone else will read, you are also writing, in the Web's languages, about your content. And when you learn to write in the Web's languages, you can then begin to shape not just what but *how* someone will read your pages. You may also find, as I have, that writing about your content in XHTML and CSS even helps you refine the content itself to better reach your audience.
- **A search engine** is your portal to XHTML, CSS, and JavaScript references and guides (so you don't have to memorize everything about those languages) and your means of discovering the many communities of people who are devoted to the art of writing and designing for the Web. A chapter toward the end of this book lists some trustworthy references and helpful communities to get you started.
- And finally, **a good Web browser**—I recommend Mozilla Firefox—is the last essential piece of technology you need. As a solid development browser, Firefox will provide an initial real-world view of your Web pages and, with the help of some add-ons (also free), will help you to refine your page's construction and design before you test them on as many other browsers and devices as you can. (However, the approaches to Web writing and design suggested in this book will help you to minimize differences from browser to browser.)

I have also created a Rapid Prototyping Kit (RPK) that is available as a free download from this book's companion Web site. The RPK will help you start building your site and its pages with confidence, while

still giving you plenty of flexibility to tailor your site for the specific
needs of your audience.

ORGANIZATION OF THIS BOOK

This book is a complete approach to Web writing and design: it takes
you from learning to read the Web like a writer and designer, up through
posting a complete, customized Web site—even a custom-designed
WordPress blog, if you're interested. The book itself is organized into a
few key sections:

- "What Am I Writing?" looks at the rhetorical situation of the
  Web, particularly why an online identity that you develop and
  control is essential to have—and possible to establish even before you begin to build your Web site.
- "Issues and Challenges" presents the guiding principles for
  making informed decisions about every component of your
  site—from bits of text and images on individual pages to the
  navigation and architecture of your entire site—with regard to
  the issues of accessibility, usability, and sustainability. All three
  issues are key to building a site that reaches the widest possible
  audience while giving you the freedom to constantly revise and
  improve (rather than simply maintain) your site over time.
- "Strategies for Success" covers essential techniques and strategies that you need to write and design individual Web pages.
  Because a Web site is basically a collection of pages, any successful Web site will depend on the solid construction of individual pages, including page elements such as branding, text
  and media content, and navigation.
- "Problems and Solutions" moves to the challenges surrounding construction and maintenance of an entire Web site, such
  as developing a site architecture and employing methods to
  display repeated content (such as branding and navigation)
  over multiple pages from a single file. It also looks at setting
  up and customizing a popular open-source blog package, Word-
  Press, to power your site. This section concludes with a chapter
  on tracking visitors, using site statistics packages, and making

material that you post to your site easier to share with others on
Facebook and elsewhere, so as to broaden your identity across
the Web.

- And finally, "Resources for the Future" provides a topical list of
  additional print and digital publications to consult to extend
  your knowledge of writing and designing for the Web. It also
  lists links to galleries of Web design to peruse for inspiration,
  and some suggested Google search terms to help you discover
  even more resources.

Because this book is about Web design, it will necessarily cover many
technical topics and terms. A glossary is provided to help you manage
the book's many technical words and concepts.

A NOTE ABOUT SCREEN CAPTURES

To add visual interest and to illustrate certain concepts or techniques, I
have included screen captures of different views of Web pages throughout the book. These are all of my own making, because I subscribe to
graphic designer Paul Rand's view that

> words about art and design are best explained in the presence of
> the artist's work. The reader, then, can more readily understand
> what the writer is talking about, and whether opinions expressed
> are based on empirical or theoretical values.[6]

The examples I've provided from my work are not necessarily great. In
fact, I'm just as likely to showcase something that I've done previously
that was bad design as I am to show off an example that was good. But
in all cases, because the examples are of my own making, I can talk
honestly and accurately about how they were made, and why.

The limitations of print being what they are, I encourage you to look
at the live versions of all screen captures, which are available via this
book's companion Web site. In the "Resources for the Future" section,
as well as on the companion site, there are links to some amazing Web
design galleries that you should browse for examples that are far more
inspiring than mine.

HOW (AND WHERE) TO READ THIS BOOK

I have written this book in an environment similar to what I hope you'll read it in: near the computer, with Web editor and Web site handy, browser open, and ready to try new things, learning at every step. You will also want to use your browser to open this book's illustration- and example-rich companion Web site at `http://sustainableweb` `design.com/book/`. The companion site features

- a Rapid Prototyping Kit (RPK) for building your Web site,
- live versions of the examples in this book (plus others),
- up-to-date instructions for working with different technologies, and
- notes about any corrections or modifications to the content of this book.

You can, of course, read this book straight through. But I suggest you begin with the "What Am I Writing?" section. Next, read quickly through the "Issues and Challenges" section, so that you at least expose yourself to some of the key concerns of Web writing and design. Then, download the RPK and, with your text editor and Web browser handy, start working through the "Strategies for Success" section, planning and building your own basic pages, fixing any mistakes (we all make them!), and sketching out page designs for your Web site. You might want to revisit the "Issues and Challenges" section before moving on to the early chapters of "Problems and Solutions."

As you get down to the work of building your site, work through Chapter 20 to learn how to develop an organized architecture for your site. Refer also to the Web-available instructions mentioned in that chapter for getting your own local Web server set up on a USB drive, so that you can better test and design your pages before going live.

If you're enthusiastic about the idea of running your own WordPress-driven site, read through Chapters 21 and 22; otherwise, save those for later and look at Chapter 23 and how to go about publishing your Web site to the open Web. Finally, Chapter 24 will guide you in ways to both technologically and legally simplify how others may share your content, extending your identity and reach across the Web.

NOTES

1. Isocrates, "Against the Sophists," in vol. 2 of *Isocrates*, trans. G. Nordlin, Loeb Classical Library (Cambridge: Harvard University Press, 1929), 169.

2. Aristotle, *Rhetoric*, in *The Rhetoric and Poetics of Aristotle*, trans. W. R. Roberts (New York: The Modern Library, 1984).

3. "September 2009 Web Server Survey," Netcraft.com (September 23, 2009), http://news.netcraft.com/archives/2009/09/23/september_2009_web_server_survey.html

4. WordPress.org, http://wordpress.org

5. Microformats.org, http://microformats.org

6. Paul Rand, *Design, Form, and Chaos* (New Haven, CT: Yale University Press, 1993), xii.

ACKNOWLEDGMENTS

This book is largely the product of teaching students who put an incredible amount of trust in the unorthodox thing I encourage them to do: abandon the constraints of software and learn to write the Web by hand; not as programmers, but as writers and designers.

I am still grateful, many years later, to the first group of undergraduate students to whom I taught standards-based Web design in a multimedia writing course—and to David Blakesley, who encouraged me to teach the course while I was a graduate student at Purdue University. And I am also grateful to the graduate students in technical communication and information architecture at Illinois Institute of Technology, who expressed enthusiasm and encouragement while reading the draft form of this book in our Web design class. In particular, I offer special thanks to Laurie Riley, Kelly Schaefer, and April Wedekind, who offered thoughtful responses to this book's earliest draft chapters, and to Erica Dekker and Susan Mallgrave for their comments and corrections when the book was nearly complete. I also thank my graduate assistant, Freddrick Logan, for his work on this project.

Many thanks to the Mozilla Foundation for its policy allowing writers to reproduce screen captures of the Firefox Web browser and to Frank Hecker for answering my questions about the Mozilla Foundation's policies. Thank you also to Chris Pederick (chrispederick.com) for creating and maintaining the Web Developer Add-on for Firefox and for permitting me to showcase it in screen shots throughout this book. Many thanks also to Don Ho for his work on Notepad++ and for likewise permitting me to use screen shots of Notepad++ to illustrate Web writing.

I am grateful for the support of all of my colleagues at Illinois Institute of Technology in the Lewis Department of Humanities. And this book would not have taken the shape it has without my many colleagues and friends across the fields of rhetoric, computers and writing, and technical communication. Any list of names risks being incomplete, but you know who you are. See you on Facebook or Twitter.

I express my sincere thanks to George Butler, my editor at Greenwood/ABC-CLIO, who approached me to write this book for Greenwood's Writing Today series and who was receptive to the idea of a book that would take a rhetorical, software-neutral approach to Web design. I am also grateful to Bill Hart-Davidson and Janice Walker, who served as the manuscript's reviewers, for their thoughtful criticisms and encouraging feedback.

I am forever indebted to my mentor Patricia Sullivan, whose pioneering work in digital writing and rhetoric continues to inspire me to pursue the line of research that led to this book. More than that, Pat is a dear friend whose wisdom is matched only by her generosity and unwavering dedication to her students, past and present.

Nancy DeJoy has my profound gratitude for her constant encouragement and friendship. More than a few of this book's chapters were drafted in Nancy's kitchen, where we both worked on our separate projects, punctuating periods of quiet with spirited conversation as we shared and responded to each other's writing.

I also thank my brother, Colin Stolley, who answered my questions about both computer science and the law and the intersection of the two and offered invaluable suggestions and guidance throughout this project.

I reserve my deepest thanks and gratitude to my wife, Amy, for her love and her seemingly boundless capacity for patience and understanding as both a partner and a collaborator.

PART I

WHAT AM I WRITING?

This section prepares you to begin writing on the Web. As with all other parts of this book, you will stand to benefit most if you read with a computer nearby so you can try some things out and learn in a more hands-on way.

On the Web, we write to be found—an idea the first chapter explores in depth, along with simple things you can do to immediately begin establishing or improving your Web presence. Reading is the counterpart of writing, and the second chapter suggests approaches and tools for reading the Web like a writer and designer.

The remainder of this section involves preparing content for your Web site, including a chapter with a brief history of how Web pages were made in the past, and how they are made now according to what are called *Web standards*, which guide the design advice in this book.

Finally, this section concludes with a chapter about setting up your own custom environment to write, design, and test your pages. As we will see, building great Web pages is more than what any one piece of software can do, and some of the best software for building Web pages is available for free on the Web—thanks to many thousands of volunteers devoting their time and effort to building quality free and open-source software.

CHAPTER 1

Why Write for the Web?

The fact that you are holding this book in your hands (or displaying it on your screen) might tempt you to skip this chapter. You probably already have reasons for writing for the Web. But this chapter offers some ideas about writing for the Web that will help you strengthen and clarify your own sense of purpose in establishing or improving your Web presence.

WRITING TO BE FOUND

Whether you are building a Web site for yourself, or for a business or organization, there is no more important reason to write for the Web than to build a stable, custom online identity that you control. It is no secret that schools and employers search the Web for their applicants' names as part of their admissions or hiring process. And yet for many people, the results that show up in Google and other Web search results are far from ideal in conveying an accurate, well-rounded identity.

Do a Google search for yourself right now (also known as ego surfing). Be sure and try variations on your name. If your name is Catherine, for example, but you sometimes go by Cathy, search for both (with your last name, of course!). You might even want to search for alternate spellings of your name: in Catherine's case, Katherine and Kathy. When I ego surf, I also routinely search Google and Google's Blog Search for combinations such as:

- `Karl Stolley`
- `"Karl Stolley"` (with quotation marks, to search first and last names appearing in sequence)

- "Stolley, Karl" (with quotes, to search last name first, as some pages list names that way)

What kinds of results appear for you? People with common names, like Jim Smith, may see results for dozens, even hundreds of so-called **Googlegängers:** people with the same name, but vastly different (and sometimes morally suspect) interests and backgrounds.

People with multiple Googlegängers will want to whittle down the results. Try adding to your name the city where you live, your employer, job title, occupation or professional field, or perhaps the school you attend. For example, I will search for these variations:

- Dr Stolley technical communication
- Professor Stolley Illinois Institute of Technology

Even for people with uncommon names, the search results may not be encouraging. There may be no results for your name at all. And if there are results, they may be scattered, confusing, and downright goofy: perhaps you were quoted in a story for a school or local newspaper. You might find yourself on a missing classmates page in the alumni area of a college or university Web site. Or perhaps you used your real name when replying to an online forum about troubles with the type of car you drive. You might even find that some well-meaning relative tagged you in an unflattering photograph on Flickr.

In all of those cases, the results do not point positively to one page or another that fully and accurately represents you. As you look at the list appearing with your name, ask yourself: "What would a potential employer, a potential college or graduate school think of these results?" If you're working on a Web site for a business or a club, and searching the Web for its name, ask yourself what potential customers or members would think.

Scattered, random results are frustrating. And if you have your own Web site already, it might be even more frustrating to discover that it does not appear as the number one ranking for your name search on Google, or even in the top ten.

The methods for writing and designing Web pages presented in this book will help you to establish your Web presence and likely improve your site's ranking in Google and other search engines.

STAYING SAFE ONLINE

Everyone's heard news stories of identity theft, stalking, and other horrors of life on the Web. There's no need to recount them here, or to let them act as a deterrent for building a Web presence. But there are some simple things you should do to establish an online presence while keeping yourself safe:

- Never post or reveal anything online that you wouldn't want to appear on a billboard next to a busy highway. (If that doesn't bother you, then reword it as "Never post or reveal anything that you wouldn't want your mother to see.")
- Even more important, **never post or reveal anything online about** *others*—**your friends, family, coworkers, colleagues—that they wouldn't want on a billboard or seen by their mothers.** Just because Uncle Jimmy willingly posed for that wacky picture at the family reunion doesn't mean that he wants his coworkers to see it on Facebook (and then print it and hang it up all over the break room at work).
- **Don't reveal information about yourself (or others) in Tweets or Facebook status messages that could endanger you, your family, or your property:** "Walking home alone late at night along Lincoln Ave"; "Left the kids at home by themselves"; or "New computer was left at the back door of the house. Too bad I'm at work."
- Many sites—from banks to email providers—feature "security questions" meant to aid you in accessing your account should you forget your username or password. **Be very careful about choosing security questions whose answers are available online.** If you have listed your hometown or high school in an online profile, avoid security questions like "What is your city of birth?" or "What is your high school mascot?" If a site allows you to write your own security questions, choose that option, and keep them obscure: "What was your family language word for milk?" or "Where do you think you lost your favorite toy in third grade?"
- Visit `http://www.onguardonline.gov` to learn more about online and computer safety.

WRITING TO ESTABLISH AN ONLINE IDENTITY

Whether you have a Web site or not, one of the best first steps for establishing an online identity is to begin microblogging. There are a few sites that support this activity, although perhaps the most popular is Twitter.[1] Twitter will help you to establish a Web presence by frequently answering the question "What's happening?" in 140 characters or less. You can post to Twitter via its Web site, special add-ons to your Web browser, or stand-alone clients like TweetDeck.[2] It is also possible to post to your Twitter account from just about any kind of mobile phone. In Twitter-speak, to post is to tweet.

Registration on Twitter is quick and free (see the "Controlling Your Name" sidebar for help choosing a Twitter username). But Twitter might seem ridiculous to those who haven't tried it: What possible good can 140-character microblog posts do for establishing an online

USERNAMES AND PASSWORDS

One problem with using `yourname` for your usernames is that it's not terribly hard for anyone to guess (then again, neither are usernames that become part of URLs, as they do on Twitter).

To keep your accounts secure, then, you need to use very strong passwords. It's now conventional wisdom to avoid using dictionary words, the username itself, or an all-number password. Here, though, is a strategy for creating rock-solid passwords:

- Use an acronym derived from song lyrics, a line in a poem, or some other phrase that you'll remember easily. "Yankee Doodle came to town, riding on a pony" becomes `ydcttroap`.
- Unlike usernames, which I prefer to keep all lowercase, mix in some uppercase letters (I prefer to do this at the beginning or end of a password); "Yankee Doodle" has uppercase built in: `YDcttroap`.
- Swap out letters with numbers and symbols (note that some services disallow certain characters; adjust accordingly). `YDcttroap` might become `YDc++r0ap`, with plus signs replacing the Ts, and a zero replacing the lowercase O.
- If you have no other nonalphanumeric symbols, throw in an exclamation mark at the beginning or end: `!YDcttr0ap`

The acronym will make the password easy to remember; but only time and your own consistency (e.g., treating letter Os as zeros) will make number- and symbol-swapping memorable. This technique works well not only for Web services like Twitter, but for securing online bank accounts, home wireless networks, and computer account logins, too. Remember, too, that the longer the password, the better.

identity? The answer lies in many little lessons that Twitter teaches about Web writing in general:

- **Be interesting.** Yes, you can announce to Twitter that you're eating a sandwich or walking the dog. But that's not terribly interesting. It's much better to post your perspective on issues you care about, or share the thinking side of your professional work or even your hobbies.

- **Frequent activity is essential to any Web presence.** Nothing is more important to Web audiences than fresh content and signs of life, or what I call living content. Pages that appear not to have been updated for some time are suspect to Web audiences and might seem to have been abandoned. With Twitter's 140-character limit, it is easy to update often and without the extended efforts required of full-on blogs or Web sites.

- **Get to the point, because no one has time.** Brevity is key to Web writing. No one has time, so maximum rhetorical impact has to be achieved in few words. Frequent use of Twitter will help you learn the art of minimal expression.

- **Write once, publish (just about) everywhere and often.** Some people use their Twitter account to update their Facebook status, and many others use Twitter's RSS feeds to publish their latest Tweets to their own custom Web sites. Updating Twitter, in other words, causes multiple sites to update simultaneously for these individuals. A single act of writing keeps multiple online presences fresh with living content.

- **There is more to connecting on the Web than linking to pages.** An essential part of Twitter is following others' tweets and, by posting interesting things, others following yours. Building networks of connections with other humans, and not just their Web pages, is an essential part of being found on the Web and establishing an identity that is not an island unto itself.

In addition to Twitter, you might also consider establishing a Facebook account.[3] Both Twitter and Facebook will make it easy for you to announce your new or redesigned Web site when the time is right.

CONTROLLING YOUR NAME

Control as many accounts and register as many domain names of your name or your organization's name as possible, even if they go unused. Sites like Namechk* let you check the availability of usernames over hundreds of sites and services all at once, but here is a starter list (I use `yourname` as an example; in my case it would be `karlstolley`):

- The .com, .org, and .net Top Level Domains (TLD) of your name (e.g., `yourname.com`, `yourname.org`, `yourname.net`; see Chapter 5)
- Twitter (e.g., `twitter.com/yourname`)
- Diigo (e.g., `diigo.com/yourname`)
- Facebook (e.g., `facebook.com/yourname`)
- Google (used with Gmail and other Google services, e.g., `your.name@gmail.com`)
- Yahoo! (used with Flickr and other Yahoo! services, e.g., `flickr.com/yourname`; note that Flickr and other services may require additional steps to claim URLs/usernames)
- MySpace, particularly "My URL" (e.g., `myspace.com/yourname`)

Of course, if your name is common enough, `yourname` may not be available. Consider these alternatives with the example name of Jane Amy Smith:

- `jane-smith` (addition of a hyphen)
- `jane-a-smith` (middle initial plus hyphens to improve readability)
- `jane-amy-smith` (middle name plus hyphens)

Notice that in all of those examples, "Jane" and "Smith" were parts of the URLs/usernames. The reason is simple: a Web search for a particular person is going to include a first and last name; having both in the URL or username may very well improve the ranking in search.

Here are other guidelines for those unable to register `yourname`:

- Don't add numbers corresponding to your birthday or birth month/year (see the "Staying Safe Online" sidebar).
- Don't include the place where you live (people move, after all).
- For some, professions or job titles might makes sense (e.g., `jane-smith-plumber`), but career changes are commonplace, too.

Whatever variation you make, keep it readable and memorable.

*Namechk, http://namechk.com

But Twitter will allow you to start establishing a presence in Google search results immediately (provided you do not elect to protect your Tweets).

Beyond microblogging, there are other general categories of Web sites where you can begin to establish your online presence by registering and using an account:

- **Social bookmarking sites,** such as Diigo, let you share bookmarks to things you find on the Web
- **Social networking sites,** such as LinkedIn, MySpace, in addition to Twitter and Facebook
- **Photo sharing sites,** such as Picasa and Flickr
- **Video sharing sites,** such as YouTube and Viddler

WRITING TO CONNECT WITH PEOPLE

A central idea in this book is that you write and design for the Web in order to be found. But being found requires more than good search rankings. You need to go out and find others, too. Twitter, Facebook,

DO UNTO OTHERS . . .

Simply stated, **Don't let your Web site or social media account (Twitter, Flickr, MySpace) come to shape the identities of others who have not established their own Web presence.**

Once you begin to write and design for the Web, you may find yourself referring to friends and colleagues by name. I have a simple rule about this: **never refer by full name to someone who does not have a Web site, or who is not a public figure or published author.** If someone blogs or Tweets under an alias, refer to her by her alias, not her full name.

It is also good practice to **avoid referring to conflicts or sensitive situations in your family, school, or workplace, even if you withhold names.** My own preference is to avoid referring to family, school, or workplace entirely—unless it's the kind of news that someone could be given an award for and that has been announced elsewhere first.

At the same time, if someone does have a Web site and you are positively referring to him by name, be sure to link to his site. This helps strengthen the other person's Web presence; with luck, and your own kind treatment of others, they will link back and do the same for you.

and other social Web sites allow you to do this through direct "follow" or "friend" relationships.

There are less structured ways of connecting with others, too. Just as you searched for your own name in Google and other search engines above, you can search for the names of your friends, peers, and colleagues, too. Some of them may have Web sites and blogs. Finding new people is as simple as searching for interests, professions, or careers and the words "personal Web site" or "blog."

Blogs, in particular, present terrific opportunities for connecting with others, particularly through comment functions available in most blogging software. Comments allow readers to add reactions and indicate interest in others' writing, and on many blogs, to share the address to their own Web sites.

If you don't yet have a Web site that you control, you can always share your Twitter address when you comment on a blog post. When you do have your own URL, add it to your Twitter profile. Readers intrigued by your comment on someone's blog, and interested by your Tweets, could easily follow the link in your profile to your Web site.

And once you have your own Web site, particularly if it includes a blog component (see Chapter 22), regularly linking to others' sites or blog posts and portfolio items helps you to establish even more connections with other people. (Chapter 24 will talk about server statistics and other means for getting a sense of who is visiting and linking to your site.)

NEXT STEPS

On the Web, we write to be found. Twitter is a great first step to establishing an online presence, as are other social media sites that allow you to connect with other people. But such sites are just a start; a custom Web site is still a crucial component of your online identity and presence. Once you have a custom Web site, your many other online presences—Twitter, Facebook, Diigo—can be used for lifestreaming:[4] announcing new content, site changes, and so on at your Web site, to audiences you share a closer connection with already.

The next chapter will address the important rhetorical skill of reading the Web, which will help you see how others have worked to establish an identity for themselves.

NOTES

1. Twitter, http://twitter.com
2. TweetDeck, http://tweetdeck.com
3. Facebook, http://www.facebook.com
4. Paul McFedries, "Lifestreaming," Word Spy, http://www.wordspy.com/words/lifestreaming.asp

CHAPTER 2

Reading the Web

Every view of the Web is unique, depending on such technological conditions as the type of computer, the fonts it has installed, the resolution of its screen, and certainly its Web browser. Someone viewing a Web site on an Apple computer with the Safari Web browser will see a very different view of a Web page compared to someone on a Windows computer using Internet Explorer. Someone using a mobile phone to view the Web will see still another view. And a person with low vision might not even see the Web, but will hear it read aloud instead.

For new and seasoned Web writers and designers alike, this is the most important lesson to learn: every view of the Web is unique, and every view of the Web *should* be unique. This is not a failure of the Web, but rather one of its strengths. The goal of every Web writer and designer should be to capitalize on the differences and needs of a wide range of readers to make each unique view as great as possible. (That means abandoning any attempts to make all experiences of a Web site exactly the same.)

Much of this book consists of guidance for writing and designing to those differences. But the purpose of this chapter is to help you learn to view and read the Web not as a casual user, but as a writer and designer. It is important that Web writers and designers appreciate just how differently a page may appear under certain circumstances. Understanding these differences from a reader's perspective will make you a much more effective writer and designer when it comes to creating pages that work optimally in many different browsing environments.

READING WITH MULTIPLE BROWSERS AND DEVICES

Many people access the Web using the browser that came installed on their computers: for Windows users, this means Microsoft Internet Explorer; for Mac users, Safari. But Web writers and designers need to go beyond their own habitual browser use and look at the Web in many different ways, using multiple browsers (see the sidebar "A Web-Reading Toolkit").

A WEB-READING TOOLKIT

To read the Web (and later to test your own designs) in as many ways as possible, install some or all of the following free browsers and tools:

All Users (Windows, Mac, and Linux)
- Mozilla Firefox (http://www.mozilla.com/firefox)
- Chris Pederick's Web Developer Add-on for Firefox (https://addons.mozilla.org/firefox/addon/60)
- Google Chrome (http://www.google.com/chrome/)
- Opera browser (http://www.opera.com/)

Windows Users
- Internet Explorer 8 or above (IE)
- Microsoft Expression Web SuperPreview (For testing multiple versions of IE) (http://expression.microsoft.com/en-us/dd565874.aspx)
- Safari for Windows (http://www.apple.com/safari/download/)
- Lynx for Windows (http://home.pacific.net.sg/~kennethkwok/lynx/)

Mac Users
- Lynx for OS X (http://www.apple.com/downloads/macosx/unix _ open _ source/lynxtextwebbrowser.html)

If you cannot install software, try a Google search for "browser emulator" to find sites that offer approximations of the views provided by different browsers.

Try making yourself use a different browser every day for a week or so. Try alternating between, say, Mozilla Firefox, Google Chrome, Opera, and Internet Explorer, particularly with sites you visit every day. You may even find that different browsers are better for different activities. On Windows computers, I prefer Chrome for most of my daily use: reading my Gmail account, posting to Twitter, and managing my Web sites. On Mac, I prefer Safari (whose WebKit engine is also used in Chrome). And on all computers, I rely on Firefox for Web design and development. Because Firefox is open source, people have built many excellent Web design add-ons for it, such as Chris Pederick's Web Developer Add-on that's used throughout this book.

Many Browsers, Few Engines, One Web

There are dozens and dozens of Web browsers available: Mozilla Firefox and Opera are two browsers that can be used on Windows, Mac OS X, and Linux operating systems. Mozilla Firefox is also what is known as an open-source browser: Firefox's source code is openly available to everyone. It is also developed and tested by a large group of volunteers and a smaller group of paid individuals working for the Mozilla Foundation. Opera, like Microsoft's Internet Explorer and Apple's Safari browser, is a proprietary browser, meaning that most of its code is kept secret and is developed almost exclusively by each company's employees.

But unlike Firefox and Opera, some browsers are designed for only one or two operating systems. Internet Explorer has only been available on Windows machines since its version 6. Konqueror is a Linux-only browser. Safari has both its native Mac OS X version and a Windows version. A look at the Wikipedia page that lists Web browsers will give you a rough idea of just how many browsers there are, and which are unique to different operating systems and mobile devices.[1]

The good news for adventurous readers of the Web is even better news for Web designers: most Web browsers use one of three rendering engines: Mozilla's Gecko engine,[2] the WebKit engine (used in Apple Safari and Google Chrome),[3] and Microsoft's Trident engine. In many respects, browsers based on Gecko and KHTML/WebKit generally display Web pages very similarly. Firefox and Chrome, for example, tend to display pages the same way; although depending on the operating system (Windows, Mac OS X, Linux), each browser will have access to different fonts (see Chapter 10). The Trident engine, which tends to be the most unpredictable, is used in Internet Explorer and AOL Explorer.

If you regularly change up your browser use, you will see that some Web sites take a hostile approach to readers who aren't using a specific browser. It's not uncommon to encounter Web sites ranging from banking sites to university and corporate intranet/Web portals that demand that visitors use a specific Web browser. People attempting to view the site with the "wrong" browser may be greeted with nothing more than a message stating, "Your browser is not supported." Gee, thanks.

The approaches to Web design in this book emphasize designing in a browser-neutral way. The technology and standards exist for browser-neutral design (see Chapter 4), but it is an eye-opening experience to see just how many Web sites are still designed to work only on specific browsers.

ASSESSING PURPOSE AND CONTEXT

Like any other piece of writing (or design), successful Web sites have some type of general, controlling purpose. The purpose of a portfolio Web site, for example, is to promote its creator's work. A collaboratively written blog may have the purpose of advancing views on a particular topic, from graphic design to a specific political position or issue.

Yet as obvious as a site's controlling purpose might be, there are often other purposes at work. The controlling purpose of the Gmail or Hotmail sites is to enable people to access and read their email accounts. But such sites also have the purpose of generating ad revenue and alerting users of other services on the site. A personal blog may have the controlling purpose of offering its author a platform for expressing her views, but it also, through links to blogs that she reads, has the purpose of establishing her as part of a particular community on the Web.

A site's purpose is always situated in many contexts: a charitable organization's Web site is situated in a broad context of interested supporters and of other Web sites maintained by similar organizations. Sometimes a site's authors deliberately inject their site into a particular context, even through design. For example, if a particular charity

KEEPING A DESIGN JOURNAL

It's a good idea to maintain a record of sites that you've visited and found to be instructive and inspiring. But design ideas and inspiration can come from many places. Magazines, billboards, even DVD menus and title sequences to movies and television shows can all be sources of ideas. Consider keeping one or more of the following kinds of design journals as you read and, later, as you design and write:

- **A blank, bound sketchbook.** These can be found for cheap at most bookstores. They're very useful for cutting and pasting ideas from printed matter, sketching out your own ideas, and keeping notes about designs that you find.
- **A Diigo or other social bookmarking account.** This is great for keeping track of inspiring sites. I use a dedicated "design inspiration" tag in my account. The short notes area that Diigo offers for posts is a good way to briefly summarize why the site is enjoyable or inspiring.
- **An HTML or word processor file stored on your computer.** I never post negative comments about people's sites on Diigo, but I'm brutally honest in the HTML file that I store on my computer. A digital file helps you keep notes about ideas that didn't work, including screenshots and clickable links back to the site, when that is helpful.

supports high school athletes from underprivileged backgrounds, it might design its site to look something like ESPN.com. Such a design choice would help to put the organization in the context of sports and sport Web sites. (Whether that design choice would increase donations is another matter. An overly lavish Web site design could conceivably hurt a charitable organization if it appears that donations are all spent on Web design!)

When reading a Web site, challenge yourself to identify its purpose and context. Sometimes the purpose is expressed in the site's content: writing, images, and other media. Design also plays a role in conveying purpose and context, as does the performance of the site. The next sections offer lists of questions to consider for reading according to content, design, and performance.

Reading for Content

Reading for content is the most obvious way to read the Web. It's probably how you read it already. Content is the most important aspect of any site; readers may tolerate terribly designed Web sites if the site's content is still good. Here are some more specific questions to guide you in thinking about the effectiveness of different Web sites' writing and design choices:

- **Text:** How long are the chunks of text on the site? Does the site make use of headings and bulleted or numbered lists? Are the sentences punchy and direct, long and complex, or some mixture of the two? Does the site offer contextual links in its text? Are the links to other places in the site? Or to external sites?

- **Photographs:** What kinds of photographs or other images are presented on the site? Do the photographs appear to be part of the site's content? Or are they part of the overall design? If the photographs are meant as content, are they presented in a way that makes their content clear or interesting? Are they highly compressed? Pixelated? Distorted? Do small, thumbnail-sized photographs link to larger versions of the same image?

- **Video and Media:** If a site includes video or animations and other media, consider the same questions as for the photographs above. Also, does the video or animation run smoothly, or does it appear choppy? Is it paced in such a way that it can be read (if it includes text) or comprehended? If the media includes sound, does the sound sync with the moving image? Is the sound too loud or too soft? Distorted or crystal clear?

- **Controls:** Are the labels on the site's navigation area(s) accurately descriptive of the pages they link to? Are the functions of other page controls, such as those for printing or emailing the page, made clear? Does the site use icons or text links for controls, or both?

- **Layout and Design:** Layout and design are a kind of content, too. Are text, photos, and media arranged in a way that makes sense for the site's purpose and context? What impressions do the site's colors convey? Does the design seem to support the content of the site—or to contradict it? Does the design affect how credible you believe its author/designer to be?

Reading for Design

Effective Web sites carefully knit their designs and content together. On such sites, the design is clearly much more than a simple container for holding content. Rather, it reinforces or adds interest to the site's content. Users might tolerate sites with solid content but poor design, but they will love well-designed sites with great content.

- **Text:** Are pieces of text presented in a way that is inviting, that makes you want to read? Are fonts sized and colored appropriately to ensure the text is readable? Does the text stretch across large areas of the screen? Or is it contained to narrower columns?
- **Photographs:** Are photographs and other art part of the site's design? Do they compete for attention with the rest of the site's content? Are the photographs presented in true-to-life color? Or are they monochromatic? Do colors in the photographs appear in other site design elements—font colors, borders, shaded areas?
- **Video and Media:** Have the edges of video and media been integrated with the design of the site? Or are they simply placed on the page with a stark border between the video/media content and the page design? Are there buttons for pausing/playing the media? Do they match the rest of the site design in terms of their shape and color?
- **Controls:** What is it about the site's controls that make them clear (or not) as navigation? Do the site's controls stand out from the rest of the design and content, or are they integrated? If there are icons or buttons on the site, do their colors, shape, and texture seem to fit with the rest of the design?
- **Layout and Design:** Is the design inviting? Does it encourage you to explore the site's other content? Would you estimate that the design is original or a template taken from somewhere else? Does it seem like the site's designer had content in mind while making the design? If the design appears to be custom, do you think that its creator spent a great deal of time on it?

Reading for Performance

Some sites are absolutely striking to gaze at on the screen. But where they reveal their weaknesses is often in performance: pages and/or images that take a long time to load, navigation and other controls that behave unpredictably, or slow-moving animations that seem to stop time itself and make the whole site feel like it's made of molasses. High performance rarely reveals itself the way poor performance does, simply because readers expect pages to load quickly, text to be readable, and so on.

- **Text:** Is the text readable, both in length and in screen presentation? Has the text been overstyled with bold, italic, and underline all at once? Are there typos or plain old bad writing that slow down your reading? Do contextual links take you to misleading places?
- **Photographs:** Are photographs sized appropriately? Are they worth the download time? Does the site have physically small photographs that seem to take forever to load? Do the photographs have an appropriate amount of detail and clarity for the subject matter that they convey?
- **Video and Media:** Do video and media elements stream? Or must you wait for the whole file to download before it begins to play? Do Flash movies contain some sort of preloader to indicate download activity while you wait for the movie? Are there any media elements, particularly sounds, that play automatically when you load a page? Are there controls for starting, stopping, or skipping any media elements? Does the presence of media elements make other actions, like scrolling down the page, seem choppy or slow?
- **Controls:** Do site navigation controls behave predictably? If there are any movements or pop-ups involved, is it easy to control them with your mouse? Are the movements or pop-ups distracting? Or do they clarify events that are happening as you use the site? Do links open up in new windows, or the same window?
- **Layout and Design:** How quickly does the page content appear with its full layout? As the page loads, do items appear one place on the screen, and then jump into place elsewhere?

As you move from one page to another in the same site, does it take a long time for the page to be "redrawn," or does the design appear to be almost static, with only the content changing?

Reading by Breaking

In addition to looking at sites in modern, graphical browsers like Firefox, Safari, and Opera, it is instructive to view sites in the Lynx browser or a Lynx emulator, which provide text-only views of a site. Viewing a site as text only will give you a sense of what will be read aloud to low-vision readers, and in what order, when they visit a site. Lynx will also reveal what some mobile phone browsers may render.

For a more nuanced way of looking at a site with certain features disabled, install the Web Developer Add-on for Firefox. With it, you can choose to disable any JavaScript on a site, disable the display of images, and even disable the page's CSS.

"Breaking" a page in those ways gives you more than a view similar to users without JavaScript, image display, or CSS. It also gives you hints as to how a page has been made: if you turn off CSS, for example, and the page's design barely changes, it means the page's author used outdated, HTML-based methods for designing the pages (see Figures 2.1 and 2.2). With CSS off, there should be no design other than default browser styles (see Figures 2.3 and 2.4). If JavaScript is disabled and content disappears, the site's author probably uses JavaScript to generate content rather than placing the content directly in the HTML where it belongs.

- **Text:** Do the site's headings and lists still appear to be headings and lists in default styling in Lynx or with CSS disabled? Are all contextual links still clickable and usable in the absence of JavaScript? Does the text refer to any missing photographic or media content in a way that makes the site confusing or unusable?
- **Photographs:** Does alternate text appear for missing photographs? Is the text a meaningful alternative, one that would be useful to someone without the ability to view the site's images?
- **Video and Media:** Is there any alternate content offered for video and other media, particularly when the site is viewed

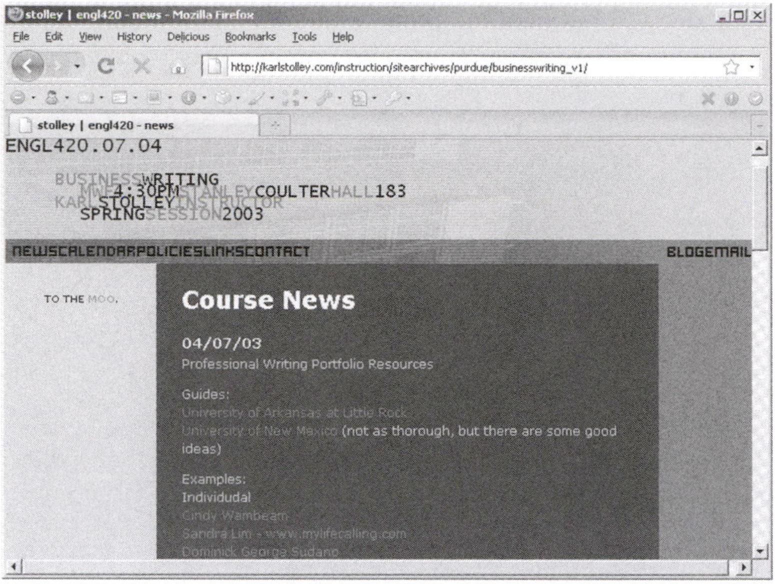

Figure 2.1. An old course Web site that I created with HTML-based design. Figure 2.2 has CSS disabled, but the design is basically the same.

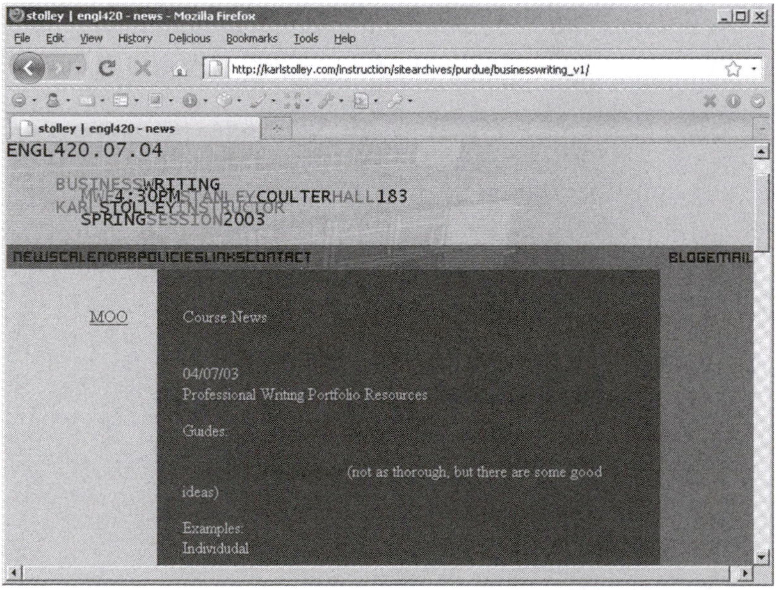

Figure 2.2. The same design as Figure 2.1, but with CSS disabled. Because the design used outdated HTML properties, it is virtually identical when CSS is disabled.

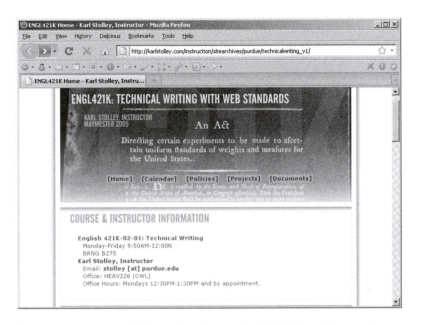

Figure 2.3 A course Web site that I created with CSS-based design, about a year after the one in Figures 2.1 and 2.2. Figure 2.4 has CSS disabled, leaving no traces of the design.

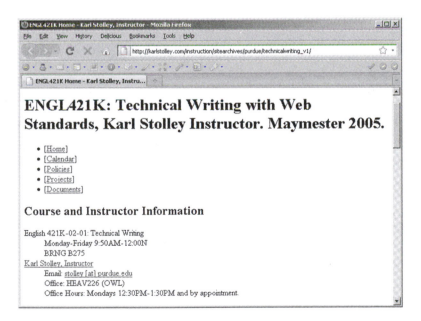

Figure 2.4. The same design as Figure 2.3, but with CSS disabled. All that is left is the default browser styling—evidence of a modern, CSS-based design.

in Lynx? Does disabling JavaScript cause Flash movies to no longer display/load? Are there links to download the media for viewing/hearing outside of the browser?

- **Controls:** If JavaScript is disabled, is it still possible to navigate the site? Do any page functions cease to operate in terms of printing, sharing, and so on? Are image galleries still browse-able? If images are disabled, do you see alternate text for buttons or other controls?
- **Layout and Design:** Even in Lynx, are headings, paragraphs, and lists clear? Or does text run together or seem to be spaced in strange ways? When disabling CSS, is a page still useful in terms of the order the content appears in? Is the page useful/navigable in mobile devices, or when using the "Small-Screen Rendering" in the Web Developer Add-on (found under the Miscellaneous menu)?

NEXT STEPS

There is no one best way to write a site's content, create its design, or ensure its performance. But reading a variety of Web sites—the ones you use everyday, plus some of the gallery sites suggested at the end of this book—will help you to develop a sense of the range of approaches to building Web sites. Reading a variety of sites for design and performance will also help you get inspired to start working on your own design.

But content is still the most important aspect of a site. In the next chapter, we will look at how you can begin gathering and creating content for your Web site while you begin to learn the Web writing and design technologies covered in "Strategies for Success."

NOTES

1. Wikipedia, "List of Web Browsers," http://en.wikipedia.org/wiki/List_of_web_browsers
2. Mozilla Developer Center, "Gecko," https://developer.mozilla.org/en/gecko
3. The WebKit Open Source Project, http://webkit.org/

CHAPTER 3

Creating Web Content

The content for your site is essential to have on hand when designing Web pages. Although you can work with dummy content, such as *Lorem ipsum* text,[1] stock photographs, and so on, site designs emerge more organically from their real content. Designs, in turn, will shape how your content is prepared: if you have a content area that is a certain number of pixels wide, that will guide the dimensions for sizing your images.

This chapter is an overview to preparing content for the Web. Specific aspects of content creation and revision will be explored in greater detail throughout the rest of the book. But the ideas here will help you to start gathering, creating, and preparing the written, photographic, audio, and video content for your Web site immediately, in formats that are Web friendly.

WRITTEN CONTENT

The written content of your site is crucial to your site being found and accessible. Even if you are a photographer or a visual artist, search engines index and allow people to search the writing of your page. Image searches aren't image searches at all, but rather searches on "captions, descriptions, and other contextual information."[2] Written content can also be read aloud or presented as Braille, and therefore made accessible to readers requiring assistive technologies. That is why all media elements—image, audio, and video—should have text equivalents.

OPEN-SOURCE SOFTWARE FOR IMAGES, AUDIO, AND VIDEO

Software for editing photos, audio, and video can cost hundreds, even thousands, of dollars. The good news is that there are many good free and open-source alternatives to expensive software. All of the software listed here rival or best commercial-grade software, and work on Windows, Mac, and Linux:

- **Image editing with GIMP:** The unfortunately named GIMP stands for GNU Image Manipulation Program. It is a solid, surprisingly feature-rich and customizable graphics package. (http://www.gimp.org/)
- **Audio editing with Audacity:** A fully featured audio editor. I personally prefer Audacity to all but professional-grade audio products. It requires a plugin to output audio to MP3, but otherwise has everything necessary for preparing audio for the Web. (http://audacity.sourceforge.net)
- **Video editing with Avidemux:** A simple, straightforward video editor. While it doesn't have a lot of effects or bells and whistles, that can be a plus if you're just learning to cut and edit video. (http://fixounet.free.fr/avidemux/). (Your computer may also come with video editing software, such as Windows Movie Maker or Apple's iMovie.)

A Google search for these and other open-source media applications will also point you to portable versions that can be run on a USB drive, if you don't have your own computer.

Web audiences typically expect a Web site's written content to be direct and to the point, with plenty of headings and lists to make the content navigable. Posting to Twitter is a great way to learn to write more directly: How expressive can you be in 140 characters or less? In addition to a direct style, written content should be rich with keywords that you think your intended audience might plug in to search engines. Writing teachers always teach students to write with thick, rich description. That approach to writing pays big dividends on the Web: it helps your ranking in Web searches on key terms, while also helping you to better communicate with your readers.

Although I prefer to compose most Web content directly in my text editor, there is nothing wrong with composing your text (but not your XHTML or CSS) in a word processor. (Just be sure that you use the Unicode character set, UTF-8, in your XHTML; see Chapter 9.)

Keep in mind the following if you decide to write in your word processor:

- **Do not waste time doing a lot of formatting in the word processor.** You'll be pasting your text directly into XHTML, which has no visual properties of its own, so any formatting is going to be lost anyway. An empty line of space between headings, paragraphs, and lists is more than enough formatting.
- **Separate headings and list items with extra lines of empty space by using the Enter key.** Lines of white space will be useful when you go to add your XHTML markup later. If the visual formatting in the word processor helps you write, use it. But be careful of copying bulleted lists from word processors, though, as the bullet itself often gets translated to an asterisk (*) when it's pasted into a text-only environment, like a Web editor.
- **Paste any word processor text into the "code view," if you are using a WYSIWYG Web editor.** Some WYSIWYGs try to be helpful by retaining markup to the text copied from word processor documents, but that markup can be a real pain to edit later.
- **Do not import images into your word processor documents.** Images must be treated in a particular way for the Web (see Chapter 18). However, if you know of an image you want to accompany your text, you might make a note of it in your word processor file for future reference.
- **Do not post word processor documents on your site.** If you are creating a portfolio or thinking of posting forms for a small business Web site, you might be tempted to post and link directly to a word processor document. In most cases, it is better to publish word processor documents in Portable Document Format (PDF), and then post the PDF to your Web site. Mac users can create PDFs using the built-in features of the OS X operating system; Windows users need either the full Adobe Acrobat software, or an open-source alternative like PDFCreator.[3] (See Chapter 6 for more information about accessible Web file formats.)

Regardless of where you write, prefer direct sentences and paragraphs and make good use of headings and lists. Headings and lists help readers navigate a page quickly to get a sense of its content, or help them find the specific content returned by a Google search.

CONTENT IMAGES

Content images, including photographs, scans, and illustrations, can help a Web site's content spring to life. Like all media content, images must be prepared for the Web in particular ways.

Preparing images for the Web is a compromise between the size, in **bytes,** of an image file and its quality. Image quality is a matter of the

---

ESSENTIAL EQUIPMENT

Capturing images and perhaps audio and video is key to developing original media content for your Web site. Here is a list of essential equipment that you should consider purchasing. You may even discover that your school or public library has some of this equipment available for your use:

- **A digital camera.** The quality that even cheap digital cameras provide is often more than enough for Web purposes. Look for cameras that have a high optical zoom (3× or above; digital zoom is not terribly useful), a recharge-able battery, and removable memory cards. But in a pinch, even a cell phone camera or a Web cam can get you started.
- **A scanner.** Good scanners are available for around $100, especially if they aren't bundled with a printer/fax machine. For Web purposes, a low-quality scanner is more than enough for scanning in artwork and printed matter. If you only have a few things to scan, try to find a scanner at your school or library.
- **A digital video camera.** Many digital still cameras come with some sort of limited video capability. There are also inexpensive video cameras available, some of which plug directly into your computer with an onboard USB connection.
- **A good quality microphone.** Computers are very good at capturing audio that sounds great, provided you have a quality microphone. Stores that cater to musicians usually have a better selection of microphones available than electronics retailers. For recording the human voice, look into purchasing a condenser microphone that comes with its own power source, usually an on-board battery (just remember to power it off when you're done recording).

dimensions (in **pixels**) of an image and in the case of JPEG (. jpg) images, a matter of image compression, which removes some data from an
image to reduce its file size.

Always keep copies of your original photographs and scans. Photographs and images that come off of a digital camera or scanner are
almost never Web ready; they must be resized, compressed, and otherwise edited first. But keep all of the original image files, in case you ever
need to re-edit them.

Here are some basic approaches to preparing your images for the
Web, which should be saved in either JPEG or PNG format (see Chapter 18 for more about loading media onto your pages):

- **Learn to use the crop and resize functions in your image
  editor.** Most image editors have filters for all sorts of visual
  effects, and all of them have controls for adjusting the contrast, brightness, and other visual properties of images. But
  to start, the two most important features you should learn are
  cropping, which helps you cut off the edges of a photograph,
  and resizing (sometimes called resampling), which reduces the
  dimensions of an image to Web-appropriate sizes.
- **Images for the Web display according to their actual pixel dimensions, so coordinate those with your layout.** Most image
  editors have dots per inch (DPI) or pixels per inch (PPI) settings
  alongside their resize function. But Web images display indepen-
  dently of any DPI or PPI setting: 72dpi or 96dpi are both common settings for Web images, but the setting only has an effect
  when the image is printed. What matters in the screen display
  of Web images is actual pixel dimensions: an 800-pixel-wide by
  600-pixel-tall image will display in a Web browser as 800 by 600
  regardless of whether the file's DPI is set to 300 or even 1.
- **Different photographs will look best at different compression rates.** When you go to save your image, most image editors offer some type of slider that varies the compression of
  JPEG images. High compression means lighter files and faster
  downloads, but at the expense of image quality. And image
  quality varies under the same compression rate: a picture of the
  sky, which has a large area of roughly the same color, will get
  ugly, rectangular splotches at high compression rates. Images

with high contrast details, like black letters on a white street sign, will get little "sparklies" and other compression artifacts around the high-contrast area. Get to know your image editor and the way it compresses different images.

You can find examples of image treatment at the book's companion Web site, http://sustainablewebdesign.com/book/.

MEDIA CONTENT: AUDIO AND VIDEO

The focus on this book is textual content and images; however, here are some rough guidelines for working with audio and video. See the book's companion Web site for recommended reading about audio and video.

Audio Content

Audio content destined for the Web should be prepared in MP3 format; while MP3 is a proprietary file format, it is also widely used in all sorts of desktop and portable digital audio players.

Preparing MP3 audio files is a complex matter, but here are some basic settings that you should use: output your files as 8-bit stereo sound. Perhaps the most important setting on MP3 files is their bit rate; for voice applications, 64 kilobits per second (kbs) will provide adequate sound quality, although 128 kbs often sounds noticeably better. However, the higher the bit rate, the larger the sound file.

Be sure also to record and prepare your MP3 audio at a 44.1 kHz sample rate, simply because that sample rate is supported by Flash and other players, and there are no savings in file size with MP3s when you lower the sample rate. For a technical but all-in-one discussion of this, see http://www.blogarithms.com/index.php/mp3secrets/.

Video Content

Video content is the most complicated material to prepare for the Web. In addition to shooting and editing your video, it is essential that sound syncs with motion. For most purposes, posting video on YouTube is an ideal solution (Chapter 18 lists other, similar sites for video hosting). First, the videos are stored and transferred from YouTube's servers, not yours. This keeps you from expending large amounts of bandwidth, or the amount of data your server can serve at any one time, on your own server. YouTube also does a generally outstanding job of behind-the-scenes compression and resizing of video, though be sure to consult their documentation on making and posting videos.[4] Finally, maintaining a YouTube account is yet another way to establish your presence on the Web. Because YouTube allows you to set up a profile that can include a link to your Web site, you may be able to attract YouTube users to your site.

The only problem with YouTube is that the code it provides for embedding videos on your Web site does not adhere to Web standards. (See Chapter 18's discussion of JavaScript and the SWFObject 2.0, which addresses this issue.) For testing purposes, though, there is nothing wrong with cutting and pasting the YouTube code. You can swap it out with the JavaScript-based solution before your site goes live, or as a future improvement.

NEXT STEPS

The work of writing and designing your pages depends on the real content of your site. Now that you have some idea of how to prepare for the Web the content you should be gathering and writing, it's time to look at what a Web page is, the history of how pages have been made, and why standards for Web writing and design are so important.

NOTES

1. Lorem ipsum, http://www.lipsum.com/
2. Google Web Search Help, "Getting Started: About Google Images," http://www.google.com/support/websearch/bin/answer.py?answer=112512
3. PDFCreator, http://sourceforge.net/projects/pdfcreator/
4. YouTube.com, "Making and Optimizing Your Videos," http://www.youtube.com/t/howto_makevideo

CHAPTER 4

Standards-Based Web Pages

So far we've looked at reasons for writing on the Web and a few approaches to reading the Web with a designer/writer mindset. In Chapter 3 we covered some of the basics of creating and gathering content for your site.

This chapter covers the guiding principles behind well-built pages to deliver your content according to **Web standards**. Web standards are guidelines issued by the World Wide Web Consortium (W3C), an international organization of people associated with technology companies and universities. Its aim is to make the use of Web languages and protocols uniform across different user agents (UAs), a fancy phrase for Web browsers and other devices that access the Web.

Now, the idea of "standards" may seem contradictory to an activity as creative as Web design. If everyone is to follow Web standards, is there any room for creativity?

The answer, of course, is "Yes." In fact, not only do Web standards not stifle creativity, they actually encourage it. Think for a moment about some of the standards that people have come to rely on. You can buy any kind of electronic device you want—a blender, a television set, a guitar amplifier—and not have to worry that its plug won't work in the socket where you live. That one standard frees you to make mojitos or milkshakes, watch trash TV or high-brow documentaries, and play blues or heavy metal.

The design of electrical sockets is standardized, just as are the threads for light bulb fixtures, traffic signals and signage, and the USB connectors on computers. We also have standardized weights and measures, standards for television and radio signals, and even some standards for

WHAT YOU WON'T LEARN IN THIS BOOK

Here is a brief list of Web design practices that you won't learn in this book. These are practices as outdated as the belief that the sun revolves around Earth; run, don't walk, away from anyone who suggests any of the following:

- **HTML tables to design pages.** Used for their intended, structural purpose, HTML tables are good for one thing: marking up tabular data. Tables for layout present significant accessibility issues and make a page harder to re-purpose or redesign later. Instead of HTML tables, use CSS layout techniques (see Chapter 17).
- **Frames and framesets.** Another accessibility nightmare, frames are artifacts from an era before Web servers could easily include content shared over multiple pages. Instead of frames, use server-side includes (see Chapter 21).
- **Invisible GIF image spacers.** Often used in tandem with HTML tables, invisible GIF spacers are the chewing gum and chicken wire of shoddy Web design. Instead of image spacers, use CSS layout techniques (see Chapter 17).
- **"Save As HTML . . ." in a word processor.** Just because the option is there doesn't mean it should be used. Word processors are great for their intended purpose of word processing, but they are as appropriate for building Web pages as chainsaws are for fixing eyeglasses.
- **Adobe Flash for site design.** Treat Flash like a chef treats an extremely hot chili pepper: used in moderation in the right dishes for the right people, it adds layers of excitement and complexity. But always give people the option to omit it, and never allow the Flash chili pepper to be eaten by itself (see Chapter 18).

For a crash course in these and other problem practices on the Web, visit `http://www.webpagesthatsuck.com/`.

spoken and written language: *This is a standard sentence. Standard this sentence is not (unless Yoda you are).*

If you had to install a different kind of electrical outlet for every device you own, learn different traffic-signal patterns from city to city, or learn to speak a different language for each individual human in your neighborhood, you'd probably be a hermit who'd never leave the solitary, candlelit comforts of home.

WEB PAGES ARE SETS OF INSTRUCTIONS

Like many digital formats, Web pages are made up of content and sets of instructions for presenting content.

However, writers and designers don't often have to think about the instructions that present digital content. When you write a word processor document or even an email, the blank box or page you type in lends itself to the impression that what you write is all that there is to your document. Software dubbed as "What You See Is What You Get" reinforces this impression.

But below the deceptively simple surface of a blank email or document is an entirely different kind of writing: computer language. That language does things like ensure that the email address in the To: box is where the email is ultimately sent, or that when you hit the bold button in your word processor, the text displays as bold and is saved and printed that way.

Most of us rarely think about that language beneath the surface. We write our documents, print them out, and hand them off; we send emails or instant messages, or post on Facebook and Twitter, and never give the underlying code a second thought.

Or at least that's what we do until something goes wrong.

Web Design: A Pessimist's View

Everyone has a story about a digital file that gets messed up: a word processor document that mysteriously puts a bullet point next to what ought to be a paragraph. An email message whose punctuation appears as question marks. Although it is tempting and sometimes the most logical thing to assume that the software has simply gone crazy, those errors and thousands like them often originate in the instructions that get passed to a program to read the contents of a digital file.

In the case of most word processors, email programs, photo editors, and many other kinds of software and the files the software generates, there is no hope for a human who wants to fix the file's instructions herself. In many cases, both the software and the document it produces is closed source, meaning that its code cannot be viewed or edited directly by a human being.

By contrast, Web pages in HTML and CSS are all open source: go to your favorite Web browser and chose View > Source, and you will see the instructions that cause any given page to display as it does. And not only can you view open source, but you can edit it, too—although your changes will only appear if the page is yours and you have access to the server where it is stored.

Don't Send a Machine to Do a Human's Work

Unfortunately, choosing View > Source on many Web pages is not a comforting, feel-good experience (see Figure 4.1). It's usually just horrifying: miles and miles of unintelligible code appear on even the simplest-looking Web sites. But in many such cases, the code that makes up a site has been created by a computer, not a human being.

Computers are tireless. They are not unlike the broom in *The Sorcerer's Apprentice*: give computers a set of instructions, and they will continue to carry out those instructions without complaint or sign of fatigue. The trouble is, when computers misbehave or do something that someone does not intend (like adding mysterious bullet points to a document), digital writers may have no choice other than to start their projects over from the beginning. Open-source, standards-based Web design helps you avoid ever having to start over like that.

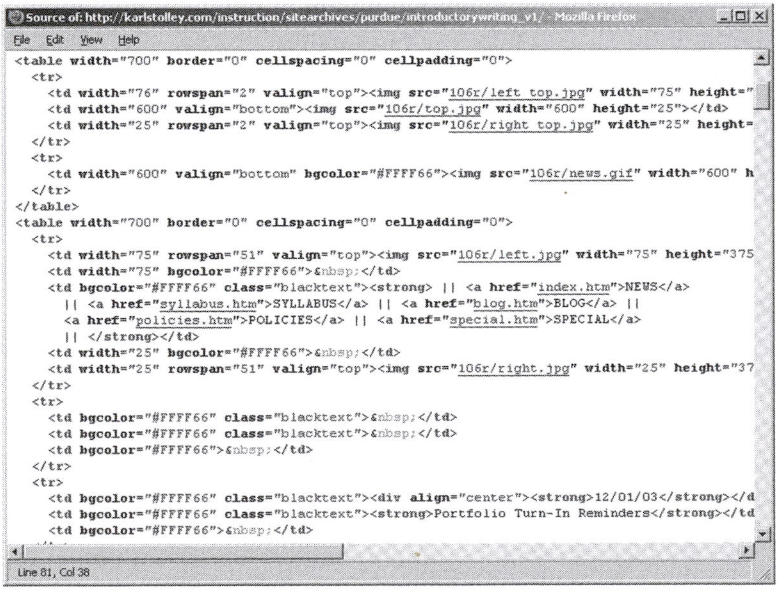

Figure 4.1. Source from an old Web page of the author's. Don't stare at it too long; but take heart: Web pages no longer have to be this complicated.

DESIGNING TO STANDARDS, NOT
SOFTWARE OR BROWSERS

Many of the bad habits that make for poor Web design (see the sidebar "What You Won't Learn in This Book") originated with Web designers designing with bad software or to a specific browser. The rest originated with limited or nonexistent support for Web standards, particularly Cascading Style Sheets (CSS). But these bad habits continue because some Web designers (and their teachers) are unaware of advances in how the Web can now be written and designed.

These advances in Web design fall under the umbrella term of "Web standards," a term promoted by a grassroots movement formed in 1998 called the Web Standards Project (WaSP).[1] WaSP, a group of influential Web designers who had had enough of browser-based design practices, pressured Netscape and Microsoft to adopt the W3C's specifications for the Web's many languages and protocols in the design of their browsers. The idea behind Web standards is that no one company or browser manufacturer controls XHTML, CSS, or any other Web language. At the same time, all browser manufacturers should support those standards in their browsers (and all modern browsers do, to varying degrees). That means a Web page can be authored in a browser-neutral way, and designers can be relatively certain that their pages will display and function acceptably in any browser. Note that "acceptably" is very different from "exactly the same," which will be an important distinction when you begin to work with CSS.

Certain standards have been well supported since the beginning of the Web, including the Hypertext Transfer Protocol (HTTP) behind the `http://` string that appears with Web addresses. Without HTTP, it would be impossible to reliably transmit a Web page from a server to a Web browser. The trouble is that what the WaSP calls "standards" are actually issued under the term "recommendations" by the W3C. In the heated battle between Microsoft and Netscape in the 1990s known as the "browser wars" (see Berners-Lee for a history[2]), the term "recommendation" had limited influence. Representatives from both Netscape and Microsoft served on the committees, or "working groups," that wrote the W3C "recommendations" for XHTML, CSS, and other key standards.[3] Yet both companies often ignored the standard specifications that they had helped to write.

VALIDATE THIS!

One interesting benefit to designing your pages according to Web standards is that there is an external, nonvisual method of assessing just how compliant your Web pages are with the standards. This method is known as validation, which involves using a **validator** to check the code of your Web pages against the rules for the languages you have used, including XHTML and CSS. There are two validators that you should use throughout your project's development:

- **The W3C Markup Validation Service** (`http://validator.w3.org/`). This service, offered by the W3C, allows you to validate your HTML either by inputting a URL, uploading an HTML file, or even copying and pasting your HTML directly into the validator.
- **The W3C CSS Validation Service** (`http://jigsaw.w3.org/css-validator/`). As with the Markup Validation Service, the CSS Validation Service gives you multiple options for checking your CSS.

As you are writing and designing, if something strange or unexpected happens when viewing your Web pages in a browser, the first thing you should do is validate your XHTML (even if you suspect a problem with your CSS). If the XHTML is valid, then validate the CSS. You will learn more about working with the validators in the "Strategies for Success" portion of this book.

WaSP changed all of that through years of tireless activism. With the stable releases of Internet Explorer 6 (IE6, in 2001) and Netscape Navigator 6 (NN6, in 2002), both leading browsers provided viable support for W3C standards, including XHTML and CSS, among other standards. Web designers could begin to design and write Web pages to the "recommendations" of the W3C. That is not to say that IE6 and NN6 implemented Web standards precisely. (Even now, no browser follows all W3C standards to the letter, though some browsers are more standards compliant than others.) But by 2002, both browsers followed the W3C's specifications for HTML and CSS closely enough that browser targeting and browser-specific pages should have become a thing of the past. *Should have.* Unfortunately, despite improvements in Web browsers' standards compliance, some Web designers continued to rely on old-fashioned practices (see the sidebar "What You Won't Learn in This Book" for examples).

WEB STANDARDS: A THREE-PART APPROACH

Later in the book, you will learn exactly what the rules of XHTML are, and how CSS works to add striking designs to structured content. But for now, it is only necessary that you understand that standards-based Web design consists of three primary components. Web standards guru Jeffrey Zeldman describes these components as structure (XHTML), presentation (CSS), and behavior (JavaScript).[4] JavaScript is formally known as ECMAScript, as the standard is issued by ECMA (formerly the European Computer Manufacturers Association, but which now goes only by the acronym ECMA). But JavaScript is the generic name that Web designers use (also, people confuse this point often: "Java" is not short for JavaScript, but an entirely different language).

A standards-based Web page, then, is made up of three separate parts:

- Structured content in pure XHTML (e.g., a hyperlink in a site's navigation)
- Visual (and even audible) design in CSS (e.g., the styling of the hyperlink in the site's navigation)
- Advanced functionality and enhancement in JavaScript (e.g., providing a short preview of the page the navigation hyperlink links to)

The JavaScript component that Zeldman labels "behavior" I prefer to call "performance." I do this because how a Web page performs, both with and without JavaScript, is an essential part of solid Web design. And page performance includes factors such as user viewing preferences and computer speeds, which tend to fall outside of what would normally be considered "behavior." So the three-pronged approach to Web design described in subsequent chapters emphasizes structure, presentation, and performance.

Structure: The XML Recommendation and the Birth of XHTML

In February 1998, the W3C issued the first recommendation for Extensible Markup Language (XML).[5] XML is one of the more widely

HTML5

There is a new specification for HTML in development, called HTML5.* It is intended to be the successor to HTML 4.01. What is interesting about HTML5 is that its specification originated in 2004 outside of the W3C by a group that dubbed itself the Web Hypertext Application Technology Working Group (or WHATWG). Although it is possible to write pages in HTML5, the specification is still largely in development.** Learning XHTML 1.0, as this book advocates, will prepare you to pick up HTML5 later, if you decide to use it rather than XHTML 1.0. There are also HTML5 resources on this book's companion site, `http://sustain ablewebdesign.com/book/`.

*W3C, "HTML5: A Vocabulary and Associated APIs for HTML and XHTML," http://www.w3.org/TR/html5/
**WHATWG, "FAQ," http://wiki.whatwg.org/wiki/FAQ

supported standard Web languages in existence. But despite being called a language, XML is actually a standard set of rules for creating other languages (called "applications," in XML-speak) that enable people and computer applications to share structured content with one another.

The most important XML application for Web purposes is XHTML 1.0, which appeared as a W3C recommendation in January 2000.[6] XHTML is the HTML language rewritten according to XML's rules. In many ways, HTML and XHTML are the same language. But XML's rules are much simpler and more consistent than SGML's, the language from which the original HTML was created.

This book promotes the use of XHTML (specifically, XHTML 1.0 Strict) and only refers to "HTML" in historical senses (although see the sidebar "HTML5").

In addition to drawing upon XML's simplicity and consistency, XHTML also reflects the spirit of XML, which is to provide structured information, free from any visual presentation. Old practices in writing HTML resulted in messes like:

```
<FONT face="Arial, Helvetica, sans-serif"
color=#cc6600 size=7>
     The World Wide Web
</FONT>
```

Here it is, rewritten according to the rules of XHTML:

```
<h1>
     The World Wide Web
</h1>
```

XHTML is used to do nothing more than provide meaningful structure to all of a page's text content and any media elements such as images, audio, and video. The "Strategies for Success" portion of this book offers guidance in building structured content in XHTML.

Presentation: Widespread Browser Support for CSS

Visual design used to be handled in nonstandard HTML "tag soup," as seen above. To add the fonts, color, and size from the old "tag soup" HTML, Web designers now write with the CSS design language, often in a separate file:

```
h1 {
     color: #C60;
     font-family: Arial, Helvetica, sans-serif;
     font-size: x-large;
}
```

One thing that makes CSS a better alternative to HTML-based design is that CSS can completely change the look of a site without a designer having to rewrite the site's XHTML. The most famous demonstration of this is the CSS Zen Garden.[7] The Zen Garden is a showcase of CSS-based designs, all of which use the exact same XHTML. Have a look; you'll be amazed.

CSS also allows you to control the look of your entire site from one CSS file. Changes to that file—for example, changing headings to appear in purple rather than red—are instantly reflected across your entire site. To redesign a site involves nothing more than changing the CSS file. This also makes sites load faster: the CSS instructions only have to be downloaded once, which helps Web browsers build your pages in the browser window very quickly.

And CSS can change more than just the visual design of a page on screen. CSS can also be used to specify how a page looks when printed, removing needless items like site navigation or making visible detailed copyright information. CSS can be used for assistive technologies, too.

Special CSS properties exist for changing how a Web page sounds when it is read aloud. That is why CSS can be said to handle "presentation," which includes the more specific term "visual design." However, in this book, CSS is limited primarily to visual design for screen and print. For more on CSS, see Chapter 10.

Performance: JavaScript and the DOM

In standards-based Web design, JavaScript works primarily with the Document Object Model (DOM) to change what happens when a link is clicked, to reveal hidden parts of a navigation bar, or even to change a page design for extremely widescreen views of pages. JavaScript coupled with the DOM is often called "DOM Scripting," a term that this book will use. For more about JavaScript and the DOM, see Chapter 19.

NEXT STEPS

Now that you have some sense of where Web standards came from and why they are necessary for Web designers to know, the next chapter prepares you to write and design by helping you set up a custom writing, design, and publishing environment that supports writing and designing with Web standards.

NOTES

1. The Web Standards Project, http://webstandards.org

2. Tim Berners-Lee with Mark Fischetti, "Competition and Consensus," *Weaving the Web: The Original Design and Ultimate Destiny of the World Wide Web* (New York: HarperBusiness, 2000), 103–21.

3. Berners-Lee, *Weaving the Web*, 91–93.

4. Jeffrey Zeldman, *Designing with Web Standards*, 2nd ed. (Berkeley, CA: New Riders, 2007), 53–57.

5. W3C, "Extensible Markup Language (XML) 1.0," http://www.w3.org/TR/1998/REC-xml-19980210

6. W3C, "XHTML™ 1.0 The Extensible HyperText Markup Language (Second Edition): A Reformulation of HTML 4 in XML 1.0," http://www.w3.org/TR/xhtml1/

7. CSS Zen Garden, "The Beauty in CSS Design," http://www.csszengarden.com/

CHAPTER 5

Preparing to Write and Design

Designing and writing Web pages isn't a job for one piece of software; instead, you will want to set up an entire environment for building your site. Although you will have to purchase a domain name and Web hosting, almost everything else you need to start writing and designing Web pages can be downloaded from the Internet for free.

But don't let the free price tag fool you into thinking that "free" means lower quality than expensive software. Some of the best Web development tools—such as the Firefox Web Developer Add-on,[1] the Notepad++ editor,[2] and the XAMPP Web server,[3] all of which you can run on a USB drive—are available for free and are better than their for-pay counterparts. Or, as with the Web Developer Add-on, simply have no for-pay counterparts.

SELECTING A WEB-FRIENDLY TEXT EDITOR

To write text content and XHTML, CSS, JavaScript, and later PHP requires nothing more than a text editor. Windows comes with a text editor called WordPad (it has Notepad, too, but never use this to edit files for the Web), just as Mac OS X comes with its own editor, TextEdit. Although either of these can be used in a pinch, they are not well suited to writing XHTML and CSS, mostly because WordPad and TextEdit lack **syntax highlighting,** meaning that they display all text in black.

Here, then, are features to look for when choosing a Web-friendly text editor; there is also a list of editors that I recommend at the end of this section.

PORTABLE APPLICATIONS

If you work with different computers at home and at work, or even if you have no computer of your own but rely on school or public libraries for computer access, portable applications enable you to use the same applications wherever you go. Portable applications are software programs that you can run on a USB drive (sometimes called a "thumb" or "jump" drive) or even an iPod. A 2GB or larger USB drive provides sufficient space to install your own set of applications and take them wherever you go.

There are numerous Web sites that list portable applications that you can download, but these two sites offer extensive lists:

- For **Windows,** PortableApps.com (http://portableapps.com/) lets you download an entire suite of applications, or via the Applications page, download individual applications. PortableApps.com lists portable versions of just about every kind of software you need to do Web development: image editors, audio editors, text editors, and so on.
- For **Mac,** the best collection of portable applications that I have found is housed at FreeSMUG.org (http://www.freesmug.org/portableapps/).

(Note that if you switch between Mac and Windows computers, you might have to keep two copies of each application, one for each operating system.)

- **Syntax highlighting,** or functionality that recognizes XHTML tags and other language features, and colors them according to their purpose. Different editors highlight XHTML and CSS in different ways, using different colors. The colors do not matter, but the coloring does: it makes XHTML and CSS easier to read, and much easier to find errors in your code.
- **Line numbering,** which displays a line number next to each line in your XHTML and CSS (note that the numbers are not part of your XHTML and CSS files, though). This feature is very useful for correcting errors discovered in XHTML and CSS validators, which report errors by the line they appear on.
- **Function reference/completion** is a feature not available in all Web editors, but it suggests XHTML tags and CSS properties as you type or on a particular key command. Note, however,

that some Web editors with this feature may suggest nonstandard tags, so always have a Web-available language reference with you as you work (see Chapters 9, 10, and 19).

- **A built-in File Transfer Protocol (FTP) or Secure File Transfer Protocol (SFTP) client** makes it easier to move files from your computer or USB drive to your hosted Web space. Not all editors have an FTP client built in, but there are plenty of stand-alone FTP/SFTP clients available.

With those features in mind, here are the free and open-source Web editors and FTP/SFTP clients I recommend to my students:

- **Windows:** Notepad++ makes writing XHTML and CSS very simple through syntax highlighting and other features. It has a built-in FTP client, but if your Web host requires SFTP, try WinSCP.[4] If you plan to use the lunch hour at work to do Web development and/or if you want to use the program on a public computer in a library or a cyber cafe, Notepad++ can be run from your USB drive (see the "Portable Applications" sidebar).
- **Mac OS X:** TextWrangler is a great free editor, also with a built-in FTP client.[5] A solid stand-alone FTP/SFTP program for Mac is CyberDuck.[6]

You are not limited to these, of course; there are hundreds more that a Google search for *Web text editor* and *SFTP client* will turn up. Just keep in mind the features listed above if you choose to use a different one.

NAMING AND ORGANIZING FILES AND FOLDERS

File naming and organization is essential to keep yourself sane while developing your Web site, and to make sure that you have meaningful URLs on your site that are easy to share. Follow these rules to make your files and folders Web ready:

- **Show file extensions in your operating system.** This is critical. Many operating systems (Windows, Mac, and Linux) hide file extensions by default. So rather than seeing `myfile.htm` listed in your folder, you'll see only `myfile`. You might also think you're saving a file as `myfile.htm`, when in reality it's been saved as `myfile.htm.txt`! Do a Google search for "show file extensions" and the name of your operating system to learn how to reveal file extensions on your computer.

- **Use only lowercase letters, numbers, and the hyphen.** Most Web servers are case-sensitive, meaning that `MyFile.htm` is different from `myfile.htm`. By always using lowercase letters, you and your audience never have to guess the capitalization on your site's URLs: there is none. Numbers are safe, as are hyphens. Do not use any other symbols or punctuation in your file names, as almost all of them (?, &, +, =, etc.) have special meaning to Web servers.

- **Never use spaces in file and folder names.** All operating systems allow spaces in file and folder names. But spaces cause trouble on the Web. A file saved as `research interests.htm` on a computer translates to `research%20interests.htm` in a Web browser. Instead of spaces, use hyphens: `research-interests.htm`

- **Make file and folder names as short, direct, and memorable as possible.** `resume.htm` is preferable to `my-complete-resume.htm` or even `my-resume.htm`. You want to be able to tell someone, *My resume is at myname dot com slash resume dot htm.*

- **Never use "new," "old," "current," or other references to time or versions in file names.** `new-photos.htm` will one day not be new.

- **Use numbers with one or more leading zeros.** Serialized file or folder names should begin with one leading zero (e.g., `photo01.jpg`, `photo02.jpg`) if you expect less than 100 items, or two leading zeros (e.g., `photo001.jpg`) if you expect less than 1,000 items. That helps organize the listing of serialized files in FTP clients and other file and folder views on your computer.

- **Use `.htm` or `.html` file extension, but not both.** Consistency is key to staying sane. I recommend using `.htm` on XHTML

ESSENTIAL FOLDERS

Keeping organized is essential to managing the many components of a Web site. The Rapid Prototyping Kit (see Chapter 11) uses these folders:

- `css`: A folder for storing all of your site's `.css` files.
- `gfx`: A folder inside of css, which is for storing all of the graphics for your site. By "graphics," I mean images that are part of the design and referred to in the CSS. Photographs and other content images are stored in the media folder (below).
- `js`: A folder for storing all of the JavaScript files for your site.
- `media`: A folder for storing all of the media content on your site. The media folder contains five different folders to help you keep your content organized, specifically:

  - `audio`: A folder for storing any audio content for your site.
  - `img`: A folder for storing any photographs and other content images. The folder is called `img` as a reminder to you that these are images used with the XHTML `<img />` (image) tag (see Chapter 18).
  - `pdf`: A folder for storing any PDF files that your site's pages link to.
  - `swf`: A folder for storing any published Flash movies that appear on your site.
  - `video`: A folder for storing any video content that appears on your site.

files, but if you opt to use `.html`, always use `.html`. CSS files should all end in `.css`; JavaScript files should all end in `.js`. Again, set your operating system to show file extensions.

Be sure to follow those rules for your XHTML and CSS files and your image, audio, and other media files, too. One shorthand summary: name files and folders as though you have no shift key or space bar.

SELECTING A BASELINE DEVELOPMENT BROWSER

The next most important piece of equipment in your custom Web design setup is a baseline development browser. I recommend Mozilla Firefox. Because Mozilla Firefox runs on Windows, Mac, and Linux systems, it is available to everyone. It doesn't have more advanced

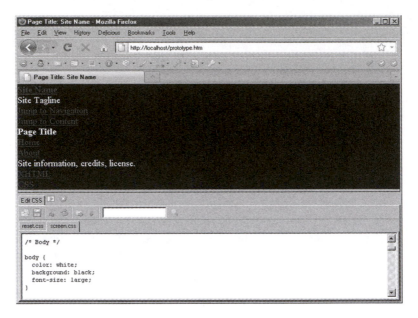

Figure 5.1. Pederick's Web Developer Add-on lets you do things like edit CSS and see your changes instantly in the browser.

standards support, particularly for CSS3, that Mac's Safari has, but it is free of the odd bugs that Microsoft's Internet Explorer is notorious for (see QuirksMode.org[7]).

And because Firefox is an open-source Web browser, a large developer community has developed all kinds of add-ons for Firefox. Many of these add-ons, like Chris Pederick's Web Developer Add-on, are tailored specifically for Web development (see Figure 5.1).

Note that using Firefox as a baseline development browser does not mean a return to designing for one specific browser. Rather, Firefox is the Goldilocks choice: not too advanced, not too buggy, but just right. Web development is a complex activity; limiting early development to one good browser is a wise choice. My experience has been that Safari will handle everything that Firefox will, in terms of CSS and DOM Scripting. Internet Explorer's oddities are easily and sustainably fixed using conditional comments to load a few additional CSS styles (see Chapter 23).

SETTING UP MULTIPLE BROWSERS FOR TESTING

Although Firefox's popularity is growing (with about 24% market share compared to IE's 60% share in 2010, according to Net Applications' *Net Market Share* statistics[8]), there are many other browsers in the world. Once your site is almost ready for posting to the Web, you will want to have multiple browsers available to check your site in. (See the sidebar "A Web-Reading Toolkit" in Chapter 2.)

The one key problem for Web designers who use Macs is that there is no way, short of running Windows on the Mac itself, to test Internet Explorer. However, Windows computers are everywhere. Check with your local library or even your friends and family. Someone is bound to have a Windows machine. In a pinch, you can look into certain browser-compatibility services, which provide a snapshot of how your page appears in IE browsers. While most services cost money, there are a few free ones, such as IE NetRenderer.[9]

BUYING A DOMAIN NAME AND WEB HOSTING

The last key component of a Web setup is your domain and Web hosting. These are two very different things, but they are often confused.

- Your domain name is sort of like a welcome mat for a house. Anyone can go to the hardware store and order a mat that reads "The Smiths." But throwing it in front of a random door doesn't get you the house!
- Your Web hosting, then, is more like the house. It is the actual server space where your files are stored and perhaps where you run blogging software like WordPress. With most hosts, your site is located at a numeric address, or perhaps a URL created by the hosting company. Neither a numeric address nor a hosting company's URL is particularly memorable, though, so that is why it's important to buy the "welcome mat"—the domain name—that you want to use to direct people to your "house"—the contents of your Web site.

SCHOOL/BUSINESS WEB ACCOUNTS

Many colleges and universities, and even some high schools and businesses, provide free Web accounts to students and employees. Avoid these. Thank the school or business for their generosity, but buy your own domain and hosting. Here's why:

- **Your Web identity should be independent of your school or employer.** People graduate or change schools, and they certainly leave their jobs. When that happens, your identity should no longer be associated with the school or employer (they will probably delete your account and along with it, the identity you've established in search engines). When you own your own domain name and your own hosting, changing schools or jobs will not impact your Web identity.
- **Free Web accounts rarely have advanced Web server features.** You can usually only store XHTML, CSS, JavaScript, and media files on free accounts (and sometimes, only a few megabytes' worth); most do not make a database available to you, and many do not even allow you to run PHP or other server-side scripts.
- **The URLs are ugly and are a pain to work with.** The URLs of free Web accounts tend to be something like `http://example.edu/~yourusername/`. That makes using root-relative paths impossible (see Chapter 20), and sometimes the tilde (~) gets encoded by other Web sites or email programs as `%7E`, making the URL even uglier, e.g, `http://example.edu/%7Eyourusername/`.
- **Universities may change the URL structure for accounts at a moment's notice, or disable certain features.** This happened to me when I was in graduate school; my university one day stopped supporting certain features that I'd been suggesting to colleagues and students, all of whom had their sites break. When you purchase hosting, the host wants to keep your business, so those types of unpleasant surprises are almost unheard of.

If you do anything with a free account, limit yourself to posting a nice standards-compliant page linking to the site you host at your own domain.

There are numerous domain name registration sites on the Web. I will not recommend one particular site over another, but do consider the following cautions when choosing a company to register your domain name:

- **Never pay much more than $10 a year** for each of the `.com`, `.org`, or `.net` top-level domains (TLDs) that you buy—and do buy all three of those TLDs together, if you can afford it.
- **Never opt in to any promises of search engine optimization or other services** that registration (or hosting) companies may offer. Register your domain, and that's it.
- **Buy your domain name from one company, and your hosting from another.** Many Web hosting companies invite you to register your domain name with them or to transfer registration for a domain you purchased elsewhere. My suggestion is to avoid this; buying your domain name from your Web host might make it difficult for you to move to other hosts in the future. Keep those two transactions separate, and you will never have to worry about losing your domain name to a bad hosting company.

There are also thousands of Web hosting companies to choose from. Here are some general things to know as you select a Web host:

- **Hosting generally runs between $5 and $20 a month.** Most reputable hosting will be somewhere within that range. Beware of hosting that's cheaper than $5 a month; the old rule of "You get what you pay for" applies.
- **Large or unlimited storage is not necessarily a good thing.** A terabyte of storage might sound like a good thing, but it invites abuse from people posting huge music or photo collections, which may slow down the same server your site is on. Unlimited storage might also be used to deflect customers' attention from less attractive features of the hosting service. Generally, anywhere from 1 to 10 gigabytes (GB) of storage is more than sufficient.
- **Unlimited transfer or traffic can also be a bad thing.** Again, it invites abusive customers; 500GB of transfer a month is plenty for most sites—and find out in advance how much the company charges for overage fees beyond your allotted data transfer.

Most Web hosts showcase Web sites that are hosted on their servers. Look through those sites: note how fast they load in particular. While slow-loading pages on one or two of the sites may not necessarily be the host's fault, if all of their featured sites load slowly, look for hosting elsewhere.

So what features *do* you look for? Here are some baseline hosting features for the long-term growth of your site:

- **Linux or Unix-based servers;** this information can be hard to determine for some hosts, so look hard. A Google search for the hosting company's name and "operating system" can often help you discover this information.
- **MySQL 5.1 database.** Be sure you can have at least three databases. These will be useful if you decide to run blogging or wiki software.
- **Secure Shell access** (also known as SSH). Some hosts enable this by default, but most require you to ask for it. Shell access lets you access your server to run certain commands and is important to have for setting up certain blogging, wiki, or content management system software.
- **SFTP access.** Hosts generally offer FTP access, but FTP transmits your password in the clear (without encryption), which can be a security risk to your site. SFTP stands for "Secure FTP," and is often found with hosts that also grant SSH access.
- **PHP 5.** Watch out for hosts that are still only offering PHP 4; good hosts will offer PHP 4 and 5, but encourage you to use 5.
- **The Apache Web server with support for per-directory configuration files using** `.htaccess`. This feature lets you customize certain aspects of how your Web site and Web server function.

Depending on your needs, you might also consider whether a host offers:

- **Log files and server statistics;** these can help you see who's linking to your site, or what search terms they used to find it (see Chapter 24).
- **Email accounts** (most hosts offer this).

- **Email lists** (essential for business and organizational Web sites).
- **Secure socket layer** (SSL), which is essential for e-commerce.
- **Hosting multiple domain names;** this will allow you to host your own Web site and perhaps another, such as a community organization you belong to.

NEXT STEPS

Now that you have an idea of the basic tools and services required for Web writing and design, know that you'll discover your own preferences as you write and design your pages. The great thing about standards-based Web design is that switching text editors, baseline development browsers, and even Web hosts will not harm your site (although you may have to relearn some things). Finding a setup that works for you and that you're comfortable with is essential. At the same time, give yourself time to learn all about the setup you choose. No one understands these things immediately.

In the next few chapters, we will look at accessibility, usability, and sustainability—a trio of important concerns that everyone writing and designing for the Web needs to consider.

NOTES

1. Chris Pederick, Web Developer Add-on for Firefox, https://addons
.mozilla.org/en-US/firefox/addon/60
2. Notepad++, http://notepad-plus.sourceforge.net/
3. XAMPP, http://www.apachefriends.org/en/xampp.html
4. WinSCP, http://winscp.net/
5. TextWrangler, http://www.barebones.com/products/TextWrangler/
6. CyberDuck, http://cyberduck.ch/
7. QuirksMode.org, http://www.quirksmode.org/
8. Net Applications, *Net Market Share*, "Browser Market Share," http://
marketshare.hitslink.com/browser-market-share.aspx?qprid=0&qptimeframe=Y
9. IE NetRenderer, http://ipinfo.info/netrenderer/

PART II

ISSUES AND CHALLENGES

Accessibility, usability, and sustainability. Those are the three overarching and interrelated issues that largely determine the rhetorical success of a Web site. While having an accessible, usable, and sustainable site is no guarantee of rhetorical success, having an inaccessible, unusable, and/or unsustainable site is usually a recipe for rhetorical disaster.

All three issues are often treated as matters of assessment (is this site accessible? usable? sustainable?) and are therefore considered only after the completion of a site. However, accessibility, usability, and sustainability provide powerful guides to the choices you will have to make throughout the process of Web writing and design. Rather than simple matters of assessment, all three concerns present long-term, ongoing challenges.

The writing and design advice given in this book urges you to consider access, use, and sustainability in every choice that you make, at every step of the process. And as we will see, making a site accessible, usable, and sustainable does not have to be a thankless chore, but can actually help you clarify your work to yourself as you write and design.

Here is a brief overview of each of the three concerns:

- **Accessibility.** Although accessibility is often discussed in terms of addressing only the needs of disabled people, accessibility is about equitable access for all, regardless of physical abilities or means of access. Contemporary Web sites must work on fast and slow Internet connections, on ultra widescreen desktop computers and miniature cell phone screens, with keyboards, touchpads/touchscreens, and mice. Sites must also be accessible to search engines, or your content will never be found or indexed for others to find in a Web search.

- **Usability.** Usability is often associated with "usability testing," where trained experts observe targeted users interacting with a Web site. But usability can also inform your approach to designing for site performance and user expectations. A site that takes forever to load or otherwise performs poorly makes its use difficult or impossible. If user expectations are not met, as when site navigation has confusing or even misleading buttons, users may become frustrated with the site and leave. Beyond simply ensuring that users can complete a task, usability helps you earn the good will and attention of your audience. But usability is not function alone: people like things that function well, but they like fun and pleasing things even more—Web sites included.

- **Sustainability.** A site that is accessible and usable today must continue to be so. Digital technologies change quickly and without much notice, it is true. Still, there are certain design practices and choices that will better future-proof your Web site. Sustainability is also about the access and use of a site as the site grows, or scales. Certain writing and design choices may be accessible and usable on a site of only five pages. But what if the site grows to 50 pages? Or 500?

Each of those issues will be treated in the next three chapters. Refer to them often as you work on the design of your site, and as you work through some of the technical matters in the chapters in "Strategies for Success."

CHAPTER 6

Accessibility

Some Web designers dislike the word *accessibility*, because it can easily be misunderstood as forcing unacceptable limits on artistic creativity or even promoting a bleeding-heart political agenda. But this chapter reframes accessibility in a much broader scope and shows that accessibility can actually encourage creativity, not limit it. We will also see that accessibility is not beholden to any political agenda, but rather a rhetorical one: accessibility maximizes the potential size and range of a Web site's audience.

WHAT IS ACCESSIBILITY?

Accessibility is a Web standard, similar to XHTML and CSS (see Chapter 4). The World Wide Web Consortium has a group dedicated to accessibility: the Web Accessibility Initiative (WAI). The WAI's introduction to accessibility declares that "Web accessibility means that people with disabilities can use the Web."[1]

That's a very limited definition. And if a Web designer believes that disabled people do not use the Web, or that disabled people represent such a small minority of users that their needs aren't worth taking the time to design for, odds are that designer will skip over accessibility matters entirely. But a remarkable study from 2004 found that some 57 percent of working-age adults in the United States benefit from accessible technology, and that this percentage is all but certain to increase as the population ages.[2] The fact is that 57 percent is no minority.

Accessible design addresses the needs of disabled users, yes, but as a product of serving the needs of all people. The accessibility and

ACCESSIBILITY STANDARDS

There are three key resources for accessibility on the Web. Although primarily oriented toward addressing the needs of disabled people, it is worth your time to explore each of these:

- **Web Accessibility Initiative (WAI)** (http://www.w3.org/WAI/): The WAI, an organization that publishes a wealth of information on accessibility, is one of the primary advocates for Web accessibility.
- **Web Content Accessibility Guidelines (WCAG)** (http://www.w3.org/WCAG/): Released as W3C Recommendation WCAG 2.0 in December 2008, WCAG is a very technical document. Because of this, the design community has reacted quite negatively to it, as in Joe Clark's article "To Hell with WCAG 2."*
- **Section 508** (http://www.section508.gov/): "Section 508" refers to a 1998 amendment to the Rehabilitation Act of 1973, which was meant to end discrimination based on physical ability within the federal government and federally funded agencies. Section 508 is specifically about information technologies, such as government Web sites. While Section 508 is not applied as law to nongovernmental Web sites, the Section 508 guidelines and technical standards (http://www.access-board.gov/sec508/standards.htm) are still useful to consider when building an accessible Web site.

*Joe Clark, "To Hell with WCAG 2," *A List Apart: For People Who Make Web Sites*, No. 217 (May 23, 2006), http://www.alistapart.com/articles/tohellwithwcag2

accessible design techniques presented below aim to make sites available to all users, "without special adaptation or modification" and regardless of their computer equipment or physical ability.[3]

Accessible design accounts for the full range of conditions of user access. User access is determined both by human conditions, such as physical or sensory abilities, as well as technological conditions, such as computer equipment, network connection speeds, and so on. In certain cases, human and technological conditions are closely related, as when a particular human condition (such as low vision) necessitates a technological condition in the form of an assistive technology (such as a screen reader).

But in almost all cases, conditions of access—both human and technological—are nonnegotiable. They are states. Web designers, no matter how talented, cannot leverage the technologies of the Web to transform the computer someone uses to read the Web, any more than they can change someone's physical or sensory abilities. Access conditions are states that design should account for, but cannot alter.

ACCESSIBILITY AS UNIVERSAL DESIGN

I prefer to treat accessibility as synonymous with a design approach known as universal design. Universal design, in its best forms, attempts to serve the needs of all users through a single design—rather than through multiple designs tailored to different users. The Center for Universal Design's Universal Design Definition reads:

> The design of products and environments to be usable by all people, to the greatest extent possible, without the need for adaptation or specialized design.[4]

One classic example of universal design is a sidewalk that gently slopes into the curb, down to street level. Not only does that design serve the needs of people in wheelchairs, but also parents pushing strollers, travelers pulling roller luggage, and klutzy people (like me) who tend to trip a lot.

Certain cities enhance sloping sidewalks with special materials that both signal the sloping sidewalk's approach and prevent slipping and falling in icy weather. In Chicago, where I live, reddish cement plates with large round bumps are embedded into the slopes; those bumps are a lifesaver during icy Chicago winters. As an added effect, because of their red color, the plates add a little visual interest to what would otherwise be the drab gray of city sidewalks.

But sidewalks are a physical medium and therefore bound to the limitations of the physical world, where one design serves all and is the same for all. In the digital medium, the Web is in a class by itself in terms of supporting design techniques that lend themselves to universal design: one single page or one site serves the needs of all users, but it serves each user differently. If the sloping sidewalk example were like a universally designed Web site, the sidewalk would actually change its properties, automatically, to best accommodate the needs of each pedestrian.

So while you may encounter advice from accessibility advocates who suggest creating separate, specialized versions of pages that are geared for particular devices, for printing, or for people with specific disabilities, standards-based Web design enables you to create a single page that anticipates and addresses the access conditions of all users.

ACCESSIBLE DESIGN APPROACHES BEGIN WITH FILE FORMATS

The Web is an equal-opportunity storehouse, in that you can post just about any type of digital file you'd like to the Web. But just because you can post any type of file does not mean you shouldn't be thoughtful and selective about what you do post.

What has become known as Postel's Law can guide, among other things, your choice of digital formats for the Web:[5] *Be conservative in what you do, be liberal in what you allow others to do.*[6]

"Be liberal in what you allow others to do" is a foundational user-centered principle for Web writers and designers: people should be able to visit your site with whatever browser or device they choose, using whatever assistive technology they need, and according to any personal preferences (no JavaScript, no Flash plugin, having text enlarged). To be liberal in your treatment of site visitors, though, you as a Web designer must be conservative in how you build your site.

In terms of file formats and content, to be conservative in content construction, build pages with the following:

- **Content structured in XHTML.** On the Web, text presented in well-structured XHTML is the only content that you can rely on to be accessible, because XHTML is the only format that all Web browsers, Web-enabled devices, and assistive technologies can render. That does not mean that designers are limited only to XHTML and text, but rather that any content must be presented in XHTML (or another flavor of HTML).
- **Images presented as JPEGs, PNGs, or GIFs.** Most graphics packages can save images in dozens and dozens of formats. But

there are only three that work reliably in all Web browsers. JPEG and PNG images are generally preferable to GIFs, as GIFs are limited to 256 colors. (See Chapters 3 and 18 for additional information about image formats.) All content images should have alternative text in XHTML, too.

And that is it for the conservative list, as far as content goes.

What's missing from this list? Plenty, including some very popular formats, such as word processor documents and PDFs, sound and video files, and Adobe Flash.

It's not that your site cannot use those formats; countless Web sites do. However, anything beyond XHTML text and the three common image formats must be treated carefully. The challenge is that no content other than XHTML text and common image formats can be viewed directly in most browsers without the use of a plugin (e.g., the Flash Player) or other third-party application (e.g., Adobe Acrobat Reader). If a mobile phone does not have a word processor application on it, it will be unable to access word processor documents posted to the Web. The same problem affects PDFs, Flash, and audio and video files, too: without the appropriate application, or without a certain level of sight or hearing, people may not be able to access those formats.

If you must post PDFs or word processor documents, be sure to alert users which links point to those kinds of files, perhaps by placing the file format in parentheses. You should also include links to download the Flash Player, Acrobat Reader, or other software required to view your files. Remember, though, not all users will be able to install software. So keep your crucial content in XHTML.

BUILD FROM ACCESSIBILITY, NOT BACK TOWARD IT

One of the mistakes both beginning and advanced Web designers make is to delay accessibility considerations until a design is almost completed. I have learned from observing students in my Web design classes that this is probably why some designers see accessibility as such a pain: if addressed only after a design is otherwise in place and ready to go, building back toward accessibility only slows you down and, worse, might force you to scrap design components that represent a significant investment of time and effort.

Particularly among Web designers who work with DOM scripting (see Chapter 19), there are two related concepts that are instructive for building from accessibility, and not back toward it: progressive enhancement and its user counterpart, graceful degradation.[7]

- **Progressive enhancement** is the design approach: each component of a Web page builds on another: rather than putting design instructions directly in XHTML, for example, you build a really solid structure for your content in XHTML. Then the design component, written in CSS and kept in its own separate .css file, is layered by capable Web browsers on top of the XHTML.
- **Graceful degradation** is the corresponding user experience: all browsers read XHTML; most read CSS. Users with CSS-enabled browsers have a progressively enhanced experience. But users with XHTML-only browsers are not punished by the presence of CSS if the site "degrades" to XHTML-only presentation. Note that an XHTML-only device, such as a screen reader, will not provide what seems to a user to be a degraded experience. Rather, graceful degradation enables an optimal experience for an XHTML-only device.

Let me share an example of graceful degradation: After redesigning a major online writing lab Web site, I received an email from a blind student who wished to express her gratitude that the new site contained no design images. (The old site had many, and made it difficult for her to use.) In truth, there were actually plenty of design images on the site; the difference was that the new site presented them in such a way that they would improve the experience of users who can benefit from a graphical display, without punishing users who cannot. That the student thought there were no design images on the site is exactly what she should have thought (content images, however, are a different matter; users must be made aware of those if they cannot view them). Figures 6.1 and 6.2 show how a design-image rich site (Figure 16.1) degrades gracefully for text-only display.

Figure 6.1. A flyer the author created to promote a course. The page makes extensive use of CSS background images.

Rhetoric of Technology

Dr. Karl Stolley, Spring 2010

A Course in Intensive Design Work

   This is a course in designing with cutting-edge
   communication technologies (particularly Ruby and
   git), emphasizing design practices informed by
   rhetorical principles that lead to pleasing and
   useful digital designs.

Rhetoric is Not a Four-Letter Word

   "Rhetoric" is a dirty word in our culture due to its
   frequent use as an insult in politics. But rhetoric
   is much richer and broader than this. Among other
   things, rhetoric is the study of symbols in everyday
-- press space for next page --
 Arrow keys: Up and Down to move. Right to follow a link;
H)elp O)ptions P)rint G)o M)ain screen Q)uit /=search

Figure 6.2. The same page as Figure 6.1, but viewed in Lynx. All of the content is there, with no intrusion by the graphics in 6.1.

Progressive enhancement, then, is how you should design: start with a solid foundation of content marked up in XHTML; add design in CSS; and finally, add any advanced functionality that your site needs using unobtrusive JavaScript (see Chapter 19). Progressive enhancement returns us to Postel's Law from the last section: *Be conservative in what you do, be liberal in what you allow others to do.* In many ways, what I advocate in terms of accessible design is a very conservative approach: it is not about using some trendy method to design pages. But it is a very liberal approach in its view of what users should be able to do: let them view the page in whatever browser or assistive technology they have available.

Once you have designed with progressive enhancement in mind, graceful degradation is what you should test for: view your site in Lynx, or in Firefox with the Web Developer Add-on, which allows you to disable images, CSS, JavaScript, or any combination thereof. (We saw those accessibility tests in action in Chapter 2; apply them to your own site, too.) If the site content and controls are still accessible under all of those conditions, congratulations: your site gracefully degrades, and your visitors should have few problems accessing it. Continue to test your site over time, and consider providing your email address or another means for visitors to contact you in case they encounter accessibility problems.

GOING FURTHER: ACCESSIBLE ENHANCEMENT

So far, this chapter has looked at file formats and a general, progressive enhancement approach to design. While this chapter has discussed them in the abstract, later chapters will treat file formats and progressive enhancement much more concretely. Here, though, are some additional, concrete features you can add to pages to increase their accessibility: in-page navigation, accessibility attributes in XHTML, and accessibility-minded uses of CSS and JavaScript.

In-Page Navigation

For people who routinely browse the Web on desktop and laptop computers, moving through the contents of a single Web page is usually a simple matter of using the scrollbars on the browser, the scrollwheel on a mouse, or in certain cases, the touch pad on a laptop.

On certain devices, such as screen readers and some mobile phones, scrolling down long pages might be difficult or time-consuming. To account for this, it's preferable to design sites that have a short accessible navigation area near the top of each page that allows users to jump to major sections of the page, such as the main content area or the site navigation.

In the Rapid Prototyping Kit (RPK, see Chapter 11), the header area of the XHTML includes an unordered list with a class of `accessibility`. There are two links that allow a device to jump either to the page content or the site navigation. These accessible links save users with screen readers from having to listen to all of a page's content before they can access the navigation or, conversely, to jump to the content without having the navigation read aloud first.

In the RPK, the content area immediately follows the accessible navigation; given that, it might seem silly to have a "Skip to Content" link. However, the idea behind including it is to inspire confidence in users, whether of assistive or mobile devices, that they can control their browsing experience and get right to the part of the page that they seek.

For graphical browsers, CSS can be used to hide the accessible navigation from view, using a technique discussed in Chapter 14. Sites that use that technique enable assistive technologies to read aloud the contents of the accessible navigation, while keeping the page from being cluttered by another navigation element that would be unnecessary for people experiencing the page graphically on a desktop browser.

Accessibility Attributes

The most well-known accessibility attribute in HTML and XHTML is `alt`, which provides alternate text for content images loaded in the image tag, `<img />`. Your XHTML will not validate if you do not have an `alt` attribute on all of your images (attributes and other parts of XHTML are discussed in Chapter 9). However, `alt` text is supposed to be limited to 100 characters.[8] Given the old cliché says that a picture is worth a thousand words, well, you can see the issue here: 100 characters (not words) will not come close. (That's 40 fewer characters than a Twitter post allows.)

There are some different options to addressing the limitation of `alt`; the first is the `title` attribute. It, too, is very limited in length; most browsers will display title attribute text as a tooltip, but some may limit the text to 85 characters. There is another attribute, long description (`longdescrip`), which allows devices to follow a link to a complete Web page with a longer description. Maintaining separate pages of description for each of your images is not a very manageable solution, though, especially given that not all assistive devices support it. Chapter 18 suggests other ways to prepare images and other media with additional text for all users.

The image tag is not the only XHTML tag with special accessibility attributes. There are two attributes that can be added to the anchor tags to assist users in activating page navigation and other important links: `tabindex` and `accesskey`.

- `tabindex` helps change the order in which links are activated by using the Tab key on the keyboard; my preference is to run the tab index on the navigation items, although arguments could be made in favor of eliminating this entirely.
- `accesskey` is an attribute that allows someone to use a keyboard combination to activate a particular link, usually in the navigation area.

See the book's companion Web site at `http://sustainableweb design.com/book/` for examples of using those two attributes to increase the accessibility of your links and navigation.

CSS and JavaScript to Enhance Accessibility

CSS and JavaScript do not have to be stumbling blocks to accessibility. Used appropriately in the right circumstances, CSS and JavaScript can actually enhance the accessibility of a Web page for users with capable browsers. For example, CSS enables you to design text to be far more readable than the default styling Web browsers apply. And JavaScript allows you to add simple mechanisms that, for example, increase the font size on your pages. I use JavaScript in tandem with CSS on my course Web sites for just this purpose (see Figures 6.3 and 6.4): it makes it easy to enlarge the text for projecting during class. But that enhancement also serves any low-vision students who need an easy way to view the site in larger font sizes. It's also possible to refer to alternate CSS files on your pages, a technique that's mentioned in Chapter 10

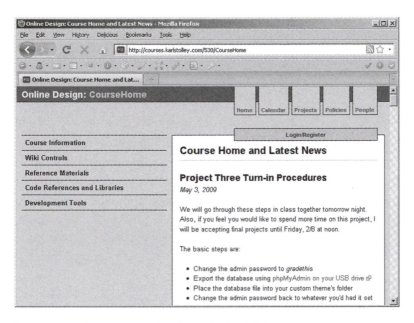

Figure 6.3. The course site for the author's Web design course.

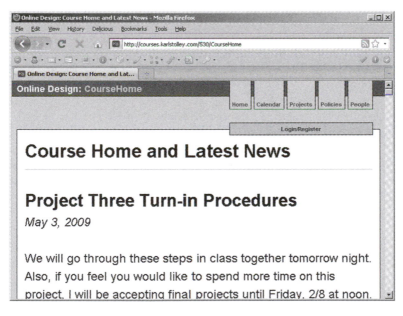

Figure 6.4. DOM Scripting makes the course site more accessible for low-vision visitors, but also aids in projecting content in the classroom. Notice the sidebar disappears in this mode.

and presented with examples at the book's companion site, `http://sustainablewebdesign.com/book/`.

NEXT STEPS

Accessibility and universal design form the foundation for a rhetorically effective Web site, but ensuring equitable access to a site is only the first step. Designers and writers must also be concerned about how and under what conditions users use Web sites, too. In the next chapter, we will look at usability-driven design approaches for creating usable sites.

NOTES

1. W3C Web Accessibility Initiative, "Introduction to Web Accessibility," http://www.w3.org/WAI/intro/accessibility.php

2. Microsoft PressPass, "New Research Shows 57 Percent of Adult Computer Users Can Benefit from Accessible Technology," http://www.microsoft.com/presspass/press/2004/feb04/02-02AdultUserBenefitsPR.mspx

3. William Lidwell, Kritina Holden, and Jill Butler, *Universal Principles of Design* (Gloucester, MA: Rockport Publishers, 2003), 14.

4. The Center for Universal Design, "Universal Design Principles," http://www.design.ncsu.edu/cud/about_ud/udprincipleshtmlformat.html

5. Ironick, "My History of the (Internet) Robustness Principle," *Ironick: Contingency, Irony, and Solidarity* (2005), http://ironick.typepad.com/ironick/2005/05/my_history_of_t.html

6. Information Sciences Institute, *Internet Protocol* (1979), http://www.postel.org/ien/txt/ien111.txt

7. Jeremy Keith, *DOM Scripting: Web Design with JavaScript and the Document Object Model* (Berkeley, CA: Friends of Ed/Apress, 2005), 85–86.

8. W3C, "HTML Test Suite for WCAG 2.0: Test 3—Image Alt Text Is Short" (2005), http://www.w3.org/WAI/GL/WCAG20/tests/test3.html

CHAPTER 7

Usability

In the last chapter, we saw that accessibility is a matter of designing to account for states or conditions of user access. By contrast, usability is a matter of designing to account for user behaviors. But it is futile to design for usability if a site is inaccessible; usability builds on accessibility. For example, an architect might design the rooms of a building to be maximally usable to people in wheelchairs by making wide doorways and placing light switches lower on the wall. But if the only way to get into that building is by a staircase, all of the usability features in the individual rooms are essentially pointless.

Access is about conditions. Usability is about conscious (and unconscious) actions that a user can or might take on a Web page or Web site. Examples of actions are users following links or navigation buttons to find material on your site or even resizing a browser window to view other applications (like an email program) while looking at your site.

However, the primary usability concerns of basic Web sites come down to findability and wayfinding. Findability is a user's ability to find relevant information, whether by a result for your site in a search engine or through your site's navigation and contextual links. Wayfinding enables users to establish a sense of where they are in your site, and how to get to other areas, if necessary.

To determine whether Web sites are usable involves usability testing, where usability specialists observe actual users interacting with a site. For individuals designing Web sites on their own, a formal, extended usability test may not be feasible. But as Steven Krug suggests, testing your site on even one user—a friend, a family member—is better than testing it on none;[1] Jakob Nielsen notes that most serious site usability problems can be discovered by testing on five users.[2] (The end of the chapter will suggest ways for you to conduct your own mini usability tests.)

Testing has its place. However, usability and usable design principles can inform how you write and design for the Web from the very earliest stages.

WHAT IS USABILITY?

Usability, in its most general sense, concerns an interface's ease of use and methods for improving ease of use.[3] The key questions usability experts ask is whether a design is easy for its intended users to use, and whether it does something useful or valuable for those users.

But usability can also include emotional dimensions of a Web site. As usability and emotional design expert Donald Norman has observed, "Usable designs are not necessarily enjoyable to use."[4] Designers should aim to build a site that not only supports the easy accomplishment of a meaningful or valuable action—commenting on a blog post, locating an informational page about a site—but that makes the user's experience of actions enjoyable. Users perceive designs that are beautiful or fun as being easier and faster to use, even if laboratory experiments reveal that a utilitarian design and an emotional design allow people to accomplish the same task in the same amount of time, or the same amount of effort.[5]

DESIGNING FOR ACTIVITIES, ACTIONS, AND OPERATIONS

I'll come right out with an embarrassing truth: Web writers and designers (including me) build sites with a wild fantasy in mind. The fantasy goes something like this: Visitors will open their browsers and go straight to my Web site, maximizing their browser windows to really immerse themselves, experiencing the site as the sole focus of their attention. They will turn off their music and close their instant messenger clients. Nothing will interrupt or otherwise come between them and a pure experience of this incredible Web site. These imaginary visitors will thoughtfully consider the site's craftsmanship, pausing to reflect on the gorgeous photographs and stunning design choices. They will read the pure poetry of every single word, follow every link with deep interest and fascination, and basically spend as much time reading and thinking about the site as I spent writing and designing it.

That never happens. But designing to that fantasy seems to happen a lot, judging by writers and designers who unselectively post tons of content and design poor navigation. Designers operating under that fantasy incorrectly assume that everything on the site will be found eventually, simply because they also assume their users will look at everything.

To develop a more realistic picture of why users visit a site, what they do there and how, we can use a framework that's become popular in human-computer interaction, called activity theory.[6]

A basic component of activity theory is a flexible, three-tiered hierarchy for thinking about user behaviors:

- At the top of the hierarchy is the user's *activity*, which is always motivated by some objective (e.g., using the Web to find the best price on a DVD, a chili recipe for dinner, or Professor Smith's office hours).
- Activities are carried out through the next level of the hierarchy, individual *actions* (searching on Google, exploring relevant results, reading pages on promising sites closely). Actions always have a particular goal: returning search results, clicking a link to explore a result, reading to decide whether the result is relevant.
- And individual actions themselves are often executed in part at the lowest level of the hierarchy, *operations* (typing, clicking, scrolling), which are normally carried out unconsciously.

I have seen many beginning Web designers struggle with thinking about user activity. Most often, beginners are focused only on generating content. They may have a lot of really good ideas for the content they want to present, and some equally interesting ideas for their design and interfaces. But the points they sometimes forget to consider are who their users are, what tasks those users will want to complete, and the broader activity that the users are engaged in that leads them to a particular site.

ACTIVITY: WHO ARE YOUR USERS? WHY ARE THEY AT YOUR SITE?

Users rarely show up at any Web site randomly, unless they're using a site such as StumbleUpon, which exists to show users random but potentially interesting Web sites.[7] And even if they do use such a site, they are still engaged in a specific activity (finding new and interesting Web sites) that might lead them to your site. Activities are defined by the broad objective that people are looking to accomplish when they visit your Web site.

For example, an employer looking to hire qualified candidates in your area of expertise might turn up your resume in a Google search. A potential member of your club might enter your URL from a flyer or postcard. A new customer might find your site by following a link from an online review of your businesses. More randomly, you might have written a blog post about a problem and fix for the mobile phone you own, which attracts the attention of someone else looking to fix the same problem.

In each of those cases, arriving at your Web site is a product of some broader activity: a job search, joining a club, hiring a business professional, or just trying to fix a phone.

To arrive at user activities unique to your site, though, it's essential to develop a realistic list of groups of your site's potential visitors. The more specific the list of people, the better; it'd be great if everyone in the world flocked to your Web site. But they won't. And it would be impossible to design a site that appeals to everyone while still meeting your own goals for the site. So "everyone" is not a useful category of users.

For individual portfolio sites and blogs, more concrete groups of people might include employers, school admission committees, or even fellow hobbyists or colleagues in your profession/field. For businesses, the list would include customers, shareholders, and even employees. Clubs and organizations would list current and potential members, donors, and so on.

From that list, you will want to think about the explicit objective that each kind of visitor might have and develop an action list with items like:

- Potential employers finding my resume
- Like-minded hobbyists contacting me
- School admission committees seeking a list of my recent projects
- Customers viewing how much our business charges for products and services
- New club members printing and mailing membership and payment forms

Just like the "everyone" audience category, it's tempting to say, "Employers looking at every last page of my Web site." But that rarely, if ever, happens. Keep your list to specific and reasonable objectives.

ACTIONS: WHAT ARE YOUR USERS DOING?

Activities are always made up of individual actions. The individual actions a site visitor takes is the primary concern of usability. And the most common actions that occur on a Web site can be broken down into Morville and Rosenfeld's four general types of information-seeking behaviors: finding everything, finding a few quality things, finding a specific thing, and refinding something found before.[8]

Finding Everything That There Is

Again, this type of behavior is pretty rare, like the fantasy scenario above. Google and other search engines are left to handle this type of search, and then individual users search on what the search engines have found. Unless you have a very small site (or a stalker), do not bank on anyone looking at every single thing on every single page.

Some Web sites include a site index page, which is an alphabetical hyperlinked listing of every single page on the site. A site index might be useful as a last resort for someone trying to find something or to see a list of everything. Other sites duplicate the spirit of a site index by linking to every single page from the navigation area. On small sites, linking to every page from the navigation may not be an issue. But on sites with more than a few pages, trying to cram everything into the navigation often results in fly-out or pop-up menus that try (and often fail) to manage the information overload. Chapters 15 and 20 will present approaches to simplifying navigation and building a shallow architecture that make those kinds of workarounds unnecessary.

Besides, because finding everything is such a rare user goal, it is better to concentrate your design efforts to address more common behaviors.

Finding a Few Quality Things

Finding a few quality things is a more typical behavior. Even photography enthusiasts rarely want to see every photograph someone's ever taken—just a few compelling ones. Customers don't have the time or interest to see every single item that an online electronics shop sells, and instead prefer a few that fit their needs and price range. That type of information-seeking behavior is especially common when users are not exactly sure what they're looking for, but have at least a vague idea.

Designing for this kind of user behavior can help determine what to include in your site navigation. For example, you might have a navigation item that links to an overview of your portfolio; rather than listing every item in the portfolio as part of your navigation, you lead users to that particular area of your site. Once there, users might encounter a compelling overview page that uses thumbnail images and persuasive written descriptions that entice users to click. As part of providing wayfinding, which is key to supporting the goals of browsing-like behavior, you might visually highlight the Portfolio item on your site navigation whenever someone is viewing any page related to your portfolio (see Chapter 15).

By providing wayfinding devices such as visual cues in your navigation, you can encourage users to explore other areas of your site simply because they can be confident of where in your site they are. Finding a few quality things is, in large part, an exploratory behavior. But a one- or two-word navigation item, "Resume" or "Design Portfolio," may not be enough to entice otherwise curious users to click. A compelling, hyperlinked image—such as a sample from your design portfolio, if you're a designer—elsewhere on your page might be more appealing, simply because the content of the image may fit better with the vague idea of what a visitor to your site is looking for.

A site with attractive previews and promotional content may even alter a user's actions; visitors to a business's Web site might discover a product or service that they didn't even realize that they wanted or needed previously.

Finding a Specific Thing

Users are sometimes looking for a specific thing. Creating a usable design for that kind of behavior involves helping users to find what they know (or reasonably expect) appears on a given Web site. Web site statistics, which many Web hosts provide (see Chapter 24), sometimes reveal that this behavior begins with a Web search; I often find that people have searched Google for my name plus "vita" or "curriculum vitae," which are the words for an academic resume.

Other examples of known items that users often expect include About and Contact pages. An About page may be a history or biography that offers more information about the person, business, or organization a Web site represents. Users also expect some means for contacting the person or people behind a Web site. Links to these kinds of specific pages should appear in most sites' navigation areas. A home page may even have a brief About Us or About Me blurb that links to the full About page.

Sometimes users will be so moved and interested by site content that they will share it as a link on Twitter or Facebook; that may result in a new user visiting your site on someone else's recommendation. Such a user might want to move back up to your site's overview pages or home page. A site navigation that uses wayfinding devices to indicate the general area of your site that a visitor is in provides a necessary sense of *You are here* (see Chapter 15). A link to your home page on every page, usually in your site's branding (see Chapter 14), may also benefit curious users. The presence of site navigation and home links (and a compelling design) may actually transform visitor behavior from seeking a specific thing, even something recommended by someone else, to finding a few more quality things.

Finding a Thing Found Before

There is a reason that most Web browsers have a bookmarking function, and that sites like Diigo are so popular: when someone finds something useful on the Web, they bookmark it to return for future reference.

Not always, though. We've all had the frustrating experience of vaguely remembering a really interesting page or site, but not having any exact record of what or where it was.

This is where whole-page design and especially site branding comes into play (see Chapters 14 and 17). A strong visual design can help to cue users as to whether they have been to your site or a particular page on your site before. Visual cues, such as a memorable image or color scheme, can also help users to remember a page previously visited. (That is why I advise against things like randomly displaying one of a set of images on a page. It's a fun thing to design, but it is probably more fun for the designer to create than the user to experience on return visits.)

OPERATIONS: HOW DO YOUR USERS DO WHAT THEY DO?

Clicking on contextual links, thumbnail images, and navigation items. Entering text in a text box. Using the Tab key to move through the links on a page. Each of those are examples of the unconscious operations that support actions on a page. Add to that list more passive operations, like being able to comfortably read the text of a page (see Chapter 16), or see an image clearly because it's not overly compressed or run at a dinky size (see Chapters 3 and 18).

When an item is difficult to click or simply not clickable, or when text is difficult to read because it's too small or not run in a high enough contrast with a background color or image, users experience a breakdown. In a breakdown, something that usually happens more or less unconsciously suddenly requires concentration and mental effort. Everyone's had the experience of going to a site whose navigation required very precise mouse positioning and clicking—either to activate a desired link or, because of a densely packed navigation, to avoid clicking the wrong link. Given an information-seeking behavior like finding a few quality things, a difficult-to-click navigation bar might be enough to make a user leave a site.

The easiest way to build a site that's usable on the operational level is to let users be sloppy. Prefer large, clickable areas on links, navigation items, and images. (A test I often do is to see if I can mouse over page controls by moving my mouse with my elbow, which offers less control than my hand.) Provide high-contrast text run in a comfortably large font, with the ability to increase the font size further without breaking the page's layout, perhaps by employing DOM scripting (see Chapter 19). If users can be sloppy—that is, if they aren't constantly encountering breakdowns—they can better focus on their goals and actions.

FOUR QUICK BUT USEFUL MINI USABILITY TESTS

Stephen Krug's book *Don't Make Me Think!* is a great resource for conducting your own basic usability tests (I especially recommend his chapter "Usability on 10 Cents a Day"). One of the things that Krug recommends is iterative testing; don't just test once, but test, make changes, and test again (even if it's on the same friend or colleague who's agreed to help you out).[9] It's also important to test throughout your design process, if possible. With your improvements, a second (and third and fourth) round of testing will reveal other issues that were missed the first time around.

Here are some simple usability tests, which are oriented around the four information-seeking behaviors above:

- **Finding everything that there is.** Most usability tests begin by showing a user the site you want to test. But the usability of a site, particularly for an everything-seeking behavior, actually begins in a search engine. This test, which is only effective on sites that have been indexed by Google and other search engines, asks users to begin from a Web search. Provide a few different scenarios for users: "You're an employer seeking resumes of people in my profession"; "You're a college freshman looking for information about the chess club." Watching what sites they click on, and asking why, can provide insight for how you should structure your pages, and key terms that you should include in your site's text. If you want to limit your test user's results in a Google search, have them add `site:example.com` along with the search terms to limit results to a specific site (e.g., `vita site:karlstolley.com`).

- **Finding a few quality things.** This test begins on your site itself. You might ask a user to find items from your portfolio, or information about your club, its membership, and how to become a member. You can also conduct a more open-ended test, perhaps with a scenario like, "If you were a potential customer, what would you look at to decide whether to buy from us?"

- **Finding a specific thing.** Have your test users locate your resume, an About page, or a Contact page. Have your users find something a little more specific, like a particular item in your portfolio. With this type of test, time might be important, so casually keep an eye on the clock of your computer or phone (do not use a stopwatch, though; its presence might unnecessarily stress your test users, as though taking a long time is their fault—not your site's).

- **Finding a thing found before.** If you're working with someone who tested your site previously, try repeating the test. Otherwise, have your test users find a few different, specific things and then—assuming that first test didn't go disastrously—have them refind the first thing you asked them to.

TIPS FOR YOUR TESTS

- **Explain that your site is a work in progress** (regardless of what stage it's in; sites are always, to some extent, works in progress) and that you need help to improve it. If your test users are close friends or colleagues, they may not want to criticize the site for fear of hurting your feelings. But if you make it clear that you know there are issues to be improved, your test users will likely understand that they can help you more by sharing suggestions and criticisms than by telling you how awesome your site is (although that's nice to hear, too).

- **Modify the tests above to match your specific site.** If yours is a portfolio site, think about your expectations of why users would come to your site in the first place, and what they would do there.

- **Ask the people you have try out your site to talk aloud.** Listen to what they say, but also watch what they're doing. Among usability professionals, it's common knowledge that what users *say* and what they *do* are often quite different. But what they say aloud—"I expected a navigation button for that"; "I'm surprised that image isn't clickable"; "This heading really grabbed my attention, but the writing below it doesn't seem to be what I want"—can be especially helpful for you to reconsider some of your design and writing decisions.

- **Try doing quick revisions while the test users are with you,** at least once you get more skilled writing and designing pages, and have them examine or try out your revised designs. You might even find that some people will share design suggestions as you work. You shouldn't necessarily follow the suggestions exactly, but you might think about their subtext. For example, someone might say, "I really think you should have a big photograph of yourself on your site." Unless you're a model, a theater major, or a newscaster, that's probably not essential, but what your test user might be implying is that your site needs to be more personal somehow, more uniquely you. A photograph may or may not be the way to achieve that particular goal. Regardless, asking test users one question—"Why?"—can usually help you determine why they're offering the advice that they are.

To do a certain kind of long-term, anonymous usability testing of all of your site's users, have a look at some of the sections on click tracking and other analytic tools in Chapter 24.

NEXT STEPS

Designing a usable site means accounting for different user activities, actions, and operations, all built on a solid foundation of accessibility. In the next chapter, we look at sustainability, which concerns accessibility, usability, and other writing and design issues over time and as your site grows.

NOTES

1. Steven Krug, *Don't Make Me Think! A Common Sense Approach to Web Usability*, 2nd ed. (Berkeley, CA: New Riders/Peachpit Press, 2006), 134.

2. Jakob Nielsen, "Why You Only Need to Test with 5 Users" (March 19, 2000), http://www.useit.com/alertbox/20000319.html

3. Jakob Nielsen, "Usability 101: Introduction to Usability," http://www.useit.com/alertbox/20030825.html

4. Donald A. Norman, *Emotional Design: Why We Love (Or Hate) Everyday Things* (New York: Basic Books, 2004), 8.

5. Norman, *Emotional Design*, 17–18.

6. Victor Kaptelinin and Bonnie A. Nardi, *Acting with Technology: Activity Theory and Interaction Design* (Cambridge, MA: The MIT Press, 2006).

7. StumbleUpon, http://www.stumbleupon.com/

8. Peter Morville and Louis Rosenfeld, *Information Architecture for the World Wide Web*, 3rd ed. (Sebastopol, CA: O'Reilly Media, 2006), 35–38.

9. Krug, *Don't Make Me Think!*, 135.

CHAPTER 8

Sustainability

Accessibility requires designing for conditions. Usability requires designing for behaviors. Sustainability considers designing for conditions and behaviors in two dimensions: time and scale.

Unlike accessibility and usability, which are inherently user-focused in that your own ability to access and use your site is only one small part of a broader picture, sustainability determines how well and how easily you are able to develop and refine your site over time. However, a sustainable site also ultimately benefits users: the content, accessibility, and usability of a sustainable site are easier to revise and improve, ensuring the best content and experience for site users.

WHAT IS SUSTAINABILITY?

Sustainability is often referred to in the context of the natural environment. One of the more widely quoted definitions of sustainability comes from the 1987 meeting of the World Commission on Environment and Development, also known as the Brutland Commission. Their definition of sustainability reads:

> Development that meets the needs of the present without compromising the ability of future generations to meet their own needs.[1]

It is not a major effort to rework this statement with regard to Web design: sustainable Web design meets present needs of a site's creator and users, without compromising their future needs. Going a step further, one might say that sustainable Web design meets present needs while also planning for future needs.

Unfortunately, people who write and design for the Web (and other digital media) have tended to ignore sustainability at every turn, opting to follow fads and trends or the easy path of using a WYSIWYG editor to build pages. It is not enough for a page or site to be built (a present need); it should also conform to Web standards and be easy to revise and improve the page over time and as a site grows (future needs).

IS A SUSTAINABLE WEB SITE EVEN POSSIBLE?

That all might sound good in theory. And yet everyone has had experiences with the relentless change surrounding digital technologies. From file formats to computers themselves, there does not seem to be anything about digital technologies that approaches the kind of stability and permanence that "sustainable Web design" seems to imply.

However, sustainable Web design should not be misconstrued as a guarantee of indefinite stability and permanence. It's actually more of an attitude toward inevitable change: sustainable design involves making choices that will work now, and likely into the future—while also providing plenty of room for writers and designers to make adjustments to their sites in the future as the conditions on the Web continue to evolve.

More than anything, designing a sustainable site requires careful planning and organization. Thoughtful choices are essential, even for something as basic as carefully naming files and folders as described in Chapter 5. So are choices that help develop a sound site architecture, as described in Chapter 20. Writing XHTML that describes the structure of your content, and not its visual presentation, contributes to the long-term sustainability of your site: the structure of content is generally more stable than its visual design. A heading is always a heading; whether that heading appears big and purple or small and gray is another matter.

A sustainable Web site is possible, but it is not necessarily something that can be built intuitively. And a sustainable site certainly cannot be built without planning for the future. The advice in this chapter and the rest of this book is intended to help you to make your site sustainable by making it maximally useful over scale and time. Sustainable Web design does not resist change; rather, it prepares your site for change.

SUSTAINABLE DESIGN TECHNIQUES

The rest of this chapter consists of practical approaches to building a sustainable site: keeping records of your work, naming and organizing all of the elements of your site, favoring directly editable content, and reusing content as much as possible. It concludes by looking at the role of standards and open-source libraries in further pursuit of a more sustainable site.

Keep a Record of What You've Done

What was I thinking? That's the question that I often ask myself when preparing to redesign a Web site from a past course or project. Remembering what you've done on a site or a page is crucial to sustainable design. But of all of the things in life that are worth committing to memory, the details about Web sites that you have created are certainly not among them.

Some early Web logs, or what we now call blogs, were little more than a record of changes to a Web site. While that particular use for blogging does not seem to be as common anymore, any sustainable site should have a record of its development over time, regardless of whether the record appears on the site itself or in a notebook somewhere. In cases where you are collaborating with multiple people on a site, a record also serves the purpose of keeping everyone informed of everyone else's changes.

There are two basic things that you should do to help yourself remember what you've done on your site:

- Keep a wiki, a text or word processor file, or even a notebook where you make notes of your design activity and choices (also consider using a content versioning system; see the sidebar "Using a Content Versioning System (CVS)").
- Use the comment syntax in XHTML, CSS, and JavaScript to describe what you have written (see Chapters 9, 10, and 19).

Retracing your steps and being able to answer for why you made a particular design choice helps you to keep your site consistent, while preventing you from having to reinvent the wheel when an old challenge surfaces that you already figured out how to solve.

USING A CONTENT VERSIONING SYSTEM (CVS)

A type of software known as a content versioning system can extend your record-keeping of changes to your site over time. There are a number of systems available, although one of the more flexible of these is Git.* Essentially, a CVS such as Git establishes a repository of the files for a Web site or other digital project, and allows you to build a record of the changes you make. A CVS does not do this automatically, but rather requires you as the writer to periodically commit changes to the repository. If you make a mistake, or wish to return to an earlier version of your project, Git and other CVS software lets you do that in a few keystrokes. You can see the Git repository and history for this book's RPK at `http://github.com/karlstolley/rpk/`.

I have written a basic tutorial for using Git,** including instructions for installing Git on different types of computers. Some of my graduate students and I are also working on a more in-depth guide to Git, called "Git for Writers,"*** which is both an introduction to Git and an approach for using Git to collaborate with others on Web sites and other projects.

*Git: The Fast Version Control System, http://git-scm.com
**Karl Stolley, KarlWiki, "Git Tutorial" (October 16, 2009), http://wiki.karlstolley.com/GitTutorial
***Gewgaws Lab, "Git for Writers" (April 21, 2010), http://gewga.ws/git-for-writers/

In addition to keeping a log of your site's changes, it's very important to write comments in your XHTML, CSS, and JavaScript source. Not only does this help preserve your own sanity, but it can help to teach others who are impressed by your site and want to learn how to do something the way that you have. Chapter 12 describes some basic commenting practices, and the Web-available examples that support this book at `http://sustainablewebdesign.com/book/` are also filled with comments, in case you are looking for additional examples of commenting.

Call It Like It Is

Whether you are choosing a domain name, naming files and folders, or writing classes and IDs in your XHTML, the best thing that you can do is to name things to reflect what they are, and maintain a consistent naming style across all of your site's elements, including XHTML and CSS files, plus images and other media.

As the file-naming advice offered in Chapter 5 suggests, it's never good practice to use words like "new" in file names, as nothing remains new over time. But it's also not good practice to truncate or abbreviate file and folder names; little is gained by calling your resume page `res.htm`; call it `resume.htm`.

Both for you as the creator of a site and your visitors, file names in URLs provide additional clues to whether something should be clicked on, or where something is with respect to the rest of your site. If the URL reads `http://example.com/contact.htm`, it is reasonable to expect that the page will have information or the means (such as a form) for contacting the site's owner or organization. So be sure, too, that the content of a page matches what its file name suggests.

In terms of scale, any numbered, or serialized, file names should begin with leading zeros, such as `photo001.jpg`, `photo002.jpg`, `photo003.jpg`. This helps keep the listings of serialized files more readable when you are managing your site's files. Otherwise, `photo10.jpg` will be listed next to `photo1.jpg`, `photo20.jpg` near `photo2.jpg`, and so on.

When it comes to the structure of your XHTML pages, the "call it like it is" rule also applies. Even on a basic tag level, tag headings with heading tags, lists with list tags, and so on. Take extra care in naming classes and IDs, too. What in your current design is a big purple box may not be in a redesign. So rather than naming a class or ID something like `big-purple-box`, name it `promotional-content` or some other name that describes the content's structure and purpose, not its design (see Chapter 9).

A Place for Everything, and Everything in Its Place

Being able to quickly find a file that you need to edit helps you simplify your work toward a sustainable Web site. Take the time to develop a good site architecture (see Chapter 20), and discipline yourself in its maintenance by saving files in their designated places.

It is important that your URLs remain constant and functional over time; in basic Web sites, URLs are created based on folder structure and file names. You want your site to be found, and you want people to link to your site—but if pages move or disappear without warning when you move or rename files, it reflects poorly on the person doing the linking, not to mention it reflecting poorly on your own site.

For example, if you choose to post a vague folder or file name, like stuff/ or res.htm and later opt to rename it to something more meaningful, you risk making links to the older name obsolete, so be sure to both name things and place things in a thoughtful, sensible place the first time around.

There are some advanced techniques, such as using the Apache Web server's URL rewrite module,[2] to redirect old URLs to new and active ones. While those techniques are outside of the scope of this book, they do add a degree of flexibility for handling links to old URLs should you need to construct a new architecture for your site. See this book's companion site for additional information, http://sustainableweb design.com/book/.

Favor Content That You Can Edit Directly

There are certain types of files, such as Flash and PDF, that you cannot edit directly (at least not to a great extent); instead, you must do your editing in one software program or file, republish it as the .pdf or .swf, and post that published file to the Web. Again, this is a matter of scale: one or two PDFs may not be too much to manage, but dozens or hundreds pose a serious sustainability problem.

With XHTML, CSS, JavaScript, and all other plain-text-based files, you only need access to a text editor to do your edits before moving them to your Web server. If you use a content management system (CMS), such as WordPress (see Chapter 22), to maintain a dynamic site, you can edit your content using any good Web browser. However, if you rely on file uploads of PDFs or word processor documents, using a CMS will not make maintaining the content in those files much easier. The files will have to be changed on your computer and then uploaded through the CMS.

Don't Repeat Yourself

The idea behind CSS is that you can keep all of the design instructions for all of the pages on your site in one file (see Chapter 10). To maintain a consistent design across your site, you just connect all of your site's XHTML pages to one shared CSS file. Making a site-wide change to the design is then only a matter of editing that one CSS file;

publishing an entirely new design is accomplished by replacing your old CSS file with a new, redesigned one.

Like your design, any content that you repeat over pages—your heading, navigation, even brief "About Me" text—can also be kept in a single file, and then repeated over multiple pages using a server-side language like PHP (see Chapter 21).

But even the page-specific content you mark up in XHTML should also appear only in one place; using CSS and the `media` attribute, you can style one XHTML page to display differently on different devices or when the page is printed. There's no need, in other words, to have one XHTML file for print, one XHTML file for screen, and so on. As soon as you introduce multiple copies of the same content, you increase the labor involved in even the smallest changes. If you find a typo, you have to fix it in as many different files as you maintain copies.

Follow Web Standards

The Web design advice in this book adheres to standards for XHTML 1.0 Strict; Cascading Style Sheets 1, 2, and the stable parts of 3; the Document Object Model and other technologies whose specifications are maintained by the World Wide Web Consortium (W3C).

Following standards is an important practice that advances sustainability. Even when new versions of standardized languages appear, the older versions can continue to be used. You can, for example, still write in HTML 4.01—and even as HTML5 stabilizes, XHTML 1.0 Strict will still be going strong. The Web is unique in its standards' longevity; many software programs will stop reading previous versions of their own file types over time. (And here's a little trivia: by learning XHTML 1.0 Strict, as in this book, you're also actually learning parts of HTML5, too. See the book's companion Web site at `http://sustainable webdesign.com/book/` for more information on HTML5.)

The alternative to following standards (and it's not really an alternative, if a site is to be accessible and sustainable) is to follow the quirks of a particular browser or piece of Web-authoring software. But that introduces accessibility issues, both for users of other browsers and, in the future, for yourself, should you want to make a change or should the Web-authoring software company go out of business.

Build on Top of Open-Source Libraries

Another way to keep a site sustainable is to build on top of actively developed open-source frameworks and code. The Rapid Prototyping Kit (RPK) is one example of this. And even the RPK builds on other libraries: for handling DOM scripting, the RPK builds on the jQuery JavaScript library (see Chapter 19). Among other things, jQuery does things like make your JavaScript work uniformly across all modern browsers—while also protecting users whose old browsers might mangle advanced features of your pages. In other words, rather than you writing the JavaScript that does that kind of work, you entrust that work to the developers of jQuery.

And so long as you keep your copies of any libraries or software, such as WordPress, up-to-date, your site itself improves, thanks to the work of hundreds, even thousands, of people who are constantly working to improve the library or framework.

NEXT STEPS

Sustainable Web design isn't magic. It just requires thinking carefully about a lot of choices, such as naming things, that are easily overlooked and taken for granted. In the next section of the book, "Strategies for Success," we will see the issues of accessibility, usability, and sustainability in action as you get down to the work of building your site.

NOTES

1. Report of the World Commission on Environment and Development, "Towards Sustainable Development," *Our Common Future* (1987), http://www.un-documents.net/ocf-02.htm

2. Apache HTTP Server Version 2.2, "Apache Module mod_rewrite" (2009), http://httpd.apache.org/docs/2.2/mod/mod_rewrite.html

PART III

STRATEGIES FOR SUCCESS

This section of the book covers the construction and design of individual Web pages.

So far, we've looked at Web writing and design concerns at a fairly high level, in a somewhat abstract way. This section invites you to dive in and work on your own writing and design. And that will involve learning to write with the languages of the Web: XHTML, CSS, and JavaScript.

But it would be a mistake to think that writing with the Web's languages is a separate category, or even a separate activity, from what is more traditionally considered writing. XHTML and CSS are actually languages that describe writing. XHTML describes the structure of writing and allows writers to specify which pieces of text are headings, paragraphs, or items in a list. XHTML also enables writers to load an image or a piece of multimedia (often with the aid of JavaScript) and to provide supplementary textual content both for search engines and low-vision users. CSS complements the structural descriptions you write in XHTML by helping you describe the appearance of writing: the colors and sizes of headers, the line-spacing of paragraph text, and even the position of an item on the screen or the printed page.

Although the form of a book requires ordering chapters, know that Web writing and design is never a linear, step-by-step process. Changes in content may inspire you to change your design, and vice versa; changes to one part of your design, such as the navigation, may cause you to change another part, such as the content area. The key to creating your pages is flexibility; be ready to make changes.

CHAPTER 9

Structured Content: XHTML Overview

If a Web page were a house, then XHTML would be its foundation and structural walls. CSS would be the house's design and decorations. And JavaScript would be the house's appliances.

Content structured in XHTML is the most crucial part of any Web page: it is the framework that supports both the design and interactivity of a page. You might have a beautiful picture to hang on the wall where you live, but if the walls are so weak that they crumble when you try to hammer in a nail, hanging the picture will be impossible, regardless of its beauty.

This chapter introduces the basic concepts behind writing your content in XHTML and the global structure of the `<html>`, `<head>`, and `<body>` tags that all XHTML pages require. The chapter also looks at two attributes—`class` and `id`—that you can use to provide additional structure that describes content that's unique to your pages.

XHTML DESCRIBES THE STRUCTURE OF WRITING

XHTML is an acronym for Extensible Hypertext Markup Language. XHTML is a language that does nothing but describe the structure of writing and the location of media content. You can't use XHTML to calculate the answers to math problems or to instruct robots to attack your enemies. XHTML can only describe the structure of a Web page's content.

The key idea behind XHTML is that content should be described structurally, using a language that is separate from visual presentation and design. This allows your structured content to be interpreted and reused by Web browsers and other devices and, using multiple media-specific style sheets, presented in different ways for different devices and people. Structured content can, for example, refer to different CSS files so as to display on screen one way, and in print another. Screen readers and other adaptive technologies can use XHTML to provide a meaningful experience for low-vision users, without the interference that visual design might bring if design were blended in with the XHTML.

XHTML is challenging to write only because we are used to thinking about the structure of writing in visual ways. When you flip through a magazine, you recognize headings, paragraphs, bulleted lists, and other common structural features because of their visual design. Headings are often large, bold, and distinguishable from running paragraph text. Lists feature bullets, numbers, or even images next to short chunks of text, which might be indented differently from paragraphs.

That is a common way of thinking when we write, too. A word processor allows writers to highlight a piece of text and change its appearance: making it bold, changing its font and size, and adding color. The idea that a combination of design choices adds structure to the document may never enter a writer's mind.

But on the Web, structure is essential to making a Web page maximally accessible, even to nonvisual devices such as search engine spiders and screen readers. For that reason, structure on the Web is not indicated visually in XHTML. Yet as we will see, structured XHTML is essential to creating CSS-based design and adding page enhancements with JavaScript.

XHTML, like the XML rules it is based on (see Chapter 4), provides writers with tags to describe the structure of their writing. Headings are marked with heading tags (`<h1>` through `<h6>`); paragraphs are marked with paragraph tags (`<p>`); items in a list are marked with list item tags (`<li>`) and list items are grouped as either unordered (bulleted) lists (`<ul>`) or ordered (numbered) lists (`<ol>`).

TAGS ARE LIKE QUOTATION MARKS

An easy way to understand how XHTML tags structure writing is to compare tags to quotation marks.

Quotation marks do not make text especially beautiful; they function only to indicate structure. A quotation mark sets off text to indicate structural differences in writing: the speech or writing of another person, the title of a magazine article, or perhaps an unfamiliar word or phrase.

Quotation marks also appear in predictable ways, adjacent to the material they mark and without any spaces:

```
I said, "XHTML tags are a lot like quotation marks."
```

Not

```
I said, " XHTML tags are a lot like quotation marks. "
```

Once a quotation mark opens, it also must close, or the text becomes confusing:

```
"The Road Not Taken by Robert Frost is one of
America's most beloved poems.
```

And if single quotation marks appear within double quotation marks, there is another important rule: the single quotation marks must close before the doubles:

```
"Tonight I will read you a poem by Robert Frost,
'The Road Not Taken.'"
```

Quotation marks also look the same regardless of the content they mark:

```
"The Road Not Taken"
```

```
"Ask not what your country can do for you; ask what
you can do for your country."
```

Despite quotation marks looking the same, literate humans usually can distinguish whether the quotation marks are structuring a title ("The Road Not Taken") or a line from a famous speech ("Ask not…"). We rely on context and prior knowledge to make such distinctions.

Computers and Web browsers are not nearly as smart as humans. They must be told exactly what something is: the purpose of XHTML tags is to describe the structure of writing.

XHTML tags obey the same rules as quotation marks. XHTML, at least on its surface, can be seen as a set of fancy quotation marks that lets writers explicitly describe the structure of writing. If I write an article as a Web page and its title is "Simple Rules for Using XHTML," I might structure the title as a first-level heading (`<h1>`):

```
<h1>Simple Rules for Using XHTML</h1>
```

Structurally, this text is a first-level heading regardless of whether the CSS designs it to appear big and purple or little and green, in Times New Roman or Arial, or whether it even appears visibly on the page at all. Regardless of how the heading is visually designed, in other words, its structural meaning will always be the same.

THE SIX RULES OF XHTML

There are only 6 rules that you must follow when writing XHTML. All of these rules will become clearer over the course of this chapter and the rest of the book. It's also good practice to keep an XHTML reference handy, such as the one at HTML Dog[1] or SitePoint.[2] But briefly, the rules of XHTML are:

1. Every valid XHTML document's first line must be a DOC-TYPE declaration. This helps markup validators understand the type of XHTML that you write on your Web pages. The DOCTYPE declaration also prevents Web browsers from rendering a page in quirks mode, which is reserved for older, nonstandard Web pages. For XHTML 1.0 Strict, the DOCTYPE declaration is:

```
<!DOCTYPE html PUBLIC
  "-//W3C//DTD XHTML 1.0 Strict//EN"
  "http://www.w3.org/TR/xhtml1/DTD/xhtml1-
    strict.dtd">
```

It's not necessary to understand what all of that means; just be sure it appears as the first line of all of your XHTML documents. (The XHTML files in the Rapid Prototyping Kit, RPK, all use the XHTML 1.0 Strict DOCTYPE.)

2. Every tag that opens must close. If `<p>` opens, a closing tag, `</p>` must follow. (Just like quotation marks.) Some tags, such as the line break (`<br />`) and image (`<img />`) tags, do not surround text and are therefore self-closing: rather than having an opening and closing tag, they self-close with a space and a (forward) slash: `/>`.

3. Tags close in the opposite order that they open, just like single quotation marks inside of doubles:

```
<p>To structure text that will be bold, use the
<strong>strong tag</strong>.</p>
```

(`<p>` opens, then `<strong>`; `</strong>` closes, then `</p>`.)

4. All tag elements and attributes, and some attribute-values, must be lowercase letters. Here's an illustrative, nonsense bit of XHTML that illustrates the element, attribute, and value parts of the tag:

```
<element attribute="value">
```

So in this example,

```
<address class="office">
```

the **element,** or tag name, is `address`; it has one **attribute,** `class`, and that attribute's value is `office`. `office` can also be called an **attribute-value**. Not all attribute-values must be lowercase. For example, all `<img />` (image) tags require an `alt` attribute for alternative text that users will see or hear on devices that cannot display images. The attribute value for the `alt` attribute should actually be a descriptive phrase or a sentence:

```
<img src="apple-pie.jpg" alt="Photograph of the
 apple pie I baked." />
```

As that example also shows, tags sometimes have multiple attributes (in that case, `src` and `alt`), which are separated by a space.

5. All attribute-values must appear in quotation marks, immediately following the equals sign. There should also never be a space between the equals sign and the opening quotation mark; spaces are used to separate elements from attributes, and attributes from other attributes:

```
<h1 class="running-head">
```

6. All `class` and `id` values must begin with a letter, and must not contain spaces. Never begin a `class` or `id` value with a number or punctuation. Except for special values, such as microformats,[3] you must invent `class` and `id` values yourself, in ways that describe the content (not the visual design) of your pages:

```
<ul id="navigation" class="active">
```

Classes and IDs also should only contain lowercase letters and the hyphen. Other characters are allowed, including capital letters. But keeping everything lowercase will do good things for your sanity, particularly when you are writing CSS to design your XHTML: by consistently using only lowercase letters, you'll be certain that you've named your class `navigation`, not `Navigation`.

Also, some attributes allow writers to specify multiple values, each of which is separated by a space. For example, a paragraph tag could have the classes of "first" and "summary":

```
<p class="first summary">
```

For that reason, you cannot use spaces when creating class names (or IDs).

Keeping those six rules in mind (refer back to them if you need a refresher later), let's examine the global structure of all standard XHTML pages.

THE GLOBAL STRUCTURE OF WEB PAGES

The chapters that follow look more closely at the function and structure of the different components of XHTML page structures. But stripping away everything else, including the `<!DOCTYPE>` declaration, XHTML source looks like this:

```
<html>
        <head></head>
        <body></body>
</html>
```

Each of those tags can appear only once per page. Let's walk through these so that you can begin to build a mental model of the structural blocks required for all XHTML pages.

The Root Tag: `<html>`

Except for the DOCTYPE declaration, XHTML pages are entirely contained by the `<html>` tag. While there are some important attributes that should appear in the `<html>` tag, its primary structural function is to serve as the tag that groups both the `<head>` and `<body>` tags. Because of this, the `<html>` tag is sometimes referred to as the **root element** of all Web pages. It is the tag that contains all others.

But page content does not appear immediately inside the `<html>` tag. Instead, `<html>` is divided into two parts: `<head>` and `<body>`.

Metadata in the `<head>` Tag

Appearing before the `<body>` tag of every XHTML Web page is a `<head>` tag. At minimum, the `<head>` must contain two basic but important tags (both of which appear in the RPK's XHTML files).

The first tag is `<title>`; this is the tag that contains the title for the Web page. Whatever you write there appears in the title bar or tabs of most Web browsers, and as the label for pages that people bookmark, either in their browser or in a service like Diigo. It is also the clickable, hyperlinked text for your page that will appear in a list of search results. Note that it's not uncommon to see sloppily constructed Web pages whose title reads Untitled Document. Be sure to always include a meaningful title (see Chapter 13).

The second tag that must appear in the `<head>` is a `<meta>` tag with a particular set of attribute-values:

```
<meta http-equiv="Content-Type"
 content="text/html; charset=utf-8" />
```

The first attribute-value pair of `http-equiv` describes the page's content type to search engines and browsers. This helps browsers to accurately render the type of content that your XHTML page contains. In this case, the `content` attribute tells search engines and Web browsers that the page content that follows is of a particular type, `text/html`, and that it uses the character set `utf-8`. We will look at these and other `<meta>` tags in subsequent chapters on metadata (Chapter 13) and sharing (Chapter 24).

Page Content in the `<body>` Tag

All of the content of a page that you expect to be visible in a browser's **viewport** must appear inside the `<body>` tag. Most of the work of writing and building the content of your pages happens inside the

<body> tag. Subsequent chapters break down the typical contents of Web pages to help you better organize and design your page content inside of <body>.

ADDING ADDITIONAL STRUCTURE THROUGH ID AND CLASS

The basic XHTML tag set goes a long way to establishing meaningful structure for your page content (see Chapter 16). But sometimes, you need to describe your content's structure more specifically than just as headers, paragraphs, and lists. XHTML includes two structural attributes for additional structural description: id and class. class and id both serve the same basic purpose of providing additional structural information, but they are used in different contexts and follow different rules.

Uniquely Identifying Pieces of Structure with id

A particular id value, or unique ID, can only be used once per page. IDs are often used for describing a page's major structural features: navigation, header, footer, content, often in conjunction with the division tag, <div>. Consider this XHTML fragment:

```
<body>
 <h1>John Smith's Home Page</h1>
 <h2>Portfolio Overview</h2>
 <p>Read all about <a href="portfolio.htm">my
  portfolio</a>...</p>
 <h2>Latest Projects</h2>
 <p>Read all about my <a href="latest-projects.htm">
  latest projects</a>...</p>

 <ul>
  <li><a href="index.htm">Home</a></li>
  <li><a href="resume.htm">Resume</a></li>
  <li><a href="contact.htm">Contact</a></li>
 </ul>

 <p>All site content is licensed for use under a
  <a rel="license" href=
  "http://creativecommons.org/licenses/by/3.0/us/">
```

```
Creative Commons Attribution 3.0 United States
License</a>.
</p>
</body>
```

In that basic, structural form, there is nothing indicating the different content areas of the page, such as a page header, a main content area, a site navigation (the unordered list), or a footer (the Creative Commons license). With the addition of some <div> tags, whose purpose is to group page content into divisions, and structurally named id attributes to distinguish the different sections, the page's source might look like:

```
<body>
 <div id="header">
  <h1>John Smith's Home Page</h1>
 </div>
 <div id="content">
  <h2>Portfolio Overview</h2>
  <p>Read all about <a href="portfolio.htm">my
  portfolio</a>...</p>
  <h2>Latest Projects</h2>
  <p>Read all about my <a
  href="latestprojects.htm">latest projects</a>
  ...</p>
 </div>

 <ul id="navigation">
  <li><a href="index.htm">Home</a></li>
  <li><a href="resume.htm">Resume</a></li>
  <li><a href="contact.htm">Contact</a></li>
 </ul>

 <div id="footer">
  <p>All site content is licensed for use
  under a <a rel="license"
  href="http://creativecommons.org/licenses/by
  /3.0/us/">Creative Commons Attribution 3.0
  United States License</a>.</p>
 </div>
</body>
```

Note that in some cases, `<div>` tags have to be added to structurally group areas of your page; however, because the `<ul>` tag on the site navigation already groups the list item tags, I put the `id` attribute directly on the `<ul>` tag. The lesson here, which will be made clearer in Chapter 16's treatment of XHTML tags for page content, is never to use or add a `<div>` tag if there is a more suitable structural tag available. The less XHTML you write, the easier your pages will be to maintain.

Also note that you can use add the hash (#) followed by a unique ID in your URL to point a visitor to a particular part of your page. For example, to point someone's browser to the site navigation in the example above, we could write a URL like `http://example.com/#navigation`. Most browsers will scroll to the hash-referenced area of the page automatically.

Associating Similar, Repeated Structures with `class`

Once an `id` value has been used on an XHTML page, regardless of the tag it has been used with, it cannot be used again. For structural elements that might appear more than once, use the `class` attribute to add additional structure. For example, it has become conventional to use the `<cite>` tag to structure titles of materials that you refer to or quote from. Suppose you cite different types of materials in your page and want to structurally identify the types of material (perhaps so that you can style them differently in CSS). You might invent a class called `film` and another called `book`, adding the relevant class to the `<cite>` tag:

```
<p>
 I enjoyed Peter Jackson's
 <cite class="film">Lord of the Rings</cite>
 films, especially
 <cite class="film">The Two Towers</cite>, but I do
 not think that they were as good as the original
 <cite class="book">Lord of the Rings</cite>
 books by J. R. R. Tolkien.
</p>
```

Like unique IDs, you can add classes to any tag requiring more specific structure. Note that the class and ID names do not appear in a browser view of your Web page, but as we will see in the coming chapters, they can be very useful when applying additional CSS styles and advanced DOM Scripting.

Naming Classes and IDs

When naming classes and IDs, always opt for structurally descriptive names: e.g., `supporting-content` instead of `sidebar` or `blue-box`. The content's presentation as a sidebar, or as a blue box, may change if the CSS and design changes; but its structural function as supporting the page's main content will not change.

Classes and IDs always begin with a letter, and are best limited to lowercase letters a-z and the hyphen. Your XHTML will not validate if you begin a class or ID name with a number.

Div-itis and Class-itis

It's all too easy to get carried away and start adding `<div>` tags and classes all over a page. It's best to use `<div>` tags sparingly, and only to group more structurally descriptive block tags (headings, paragraphs, and lists; see Chapter 16). Some sites are made up almost entirely of `<div>` tags—even for marking up headings, paragraphs, and lists—a practice that completely misses the point of using structural XHTML. `<div>` has no structural value other than to group related pieces of XHTML content into divisions. If you catch yourself writing something like `<div class="heading-one">`, stop, think, and use the `<h1>` tag instead.

Class-itis, too, results in too much meaningless or redundant markup. For example, writers sometimes write markup like:

```
<ul>
    <li class="favorite-foods">Pizza</li>
    <li class="favorite-foods">Cheeseburgers</li>
    <li class="favorite-foods">Cake</li>
</ul>
```

In that case, rather than adding the class to every single list item, it would be better to add it on the `<ul>` tag that groups all of the list items:

```
<ul class="favorite-foods">
    <li>Pizza</li>
```

```
    <li>Cheeseburgers</li>
    <li>Cake</li>
</ul>
```

That will keep the page's markup lighter, easier to read, and easier to revise. I'll say it again: the less XHTML you write, while still being descriptive of your content, the better.

NEXT STEPS

This chapter has covered the basic rules of XHTML, and the major structural features of every XHTML page. The next chapter will introduce CSS, which you can begin to write while you develop your skills with XHTML. See also the chapters in the "Issues and Challenges" section to review XHTML's importance to the accessibility, usability, and sustainability of Web sites.

NOTES

1. HTML Dog, "HTML Tags," http://htmldog.com/reference/htmltags/
2. SitePoint, "HTML Reference," http://reference.sitepoint.com/html
3. Microformats.org, http://microformats.org

Presentation and Design: CSS Overview

Cascading Style Sheets (CSS) enable the visual presentation and design of Web pages. From typography to color, page layout to textural and other design images, CSS controls the look of content structured in XHTML. While you can look at an XHTML file directly in a Web browser, which will provide default styling (Figure 10.1), CSS cannot be viewed directly (all you'll see is the CSS source itself); a browser has to layer CSS over an XHTML file. That means you must have your structural XHTML in place before you can test your design work in CSS.

A primary capability of CSS is inheritance, which refers to the abilities of certain style properties to transfer from parent elements (e.g., the <body> tag) to their children (e.g., <p> inside of <body>; familial relationships are covered later in this chapter). A good CSS reference will let you know whether a given property is inherited or not, although the majority of inherited properties are text- and font-related. If, for example, you want all of your text on a page to be in Arial font, you do not need to specify Arial for each and every tag; because the CSS font-family property is inherited, you can just specify it on the <body> tag, which is the parent (or ancestor) element of all content on an XHTML page. The "cascade" in CSS refers to the ability of styles to come from multiple sources (files, selectors, plus the default browser styling—which should be removed using a reset CSS file; see Chapter 11), with the more specific style being applied. Figure 10.2 shows the default browser styling, with the exception

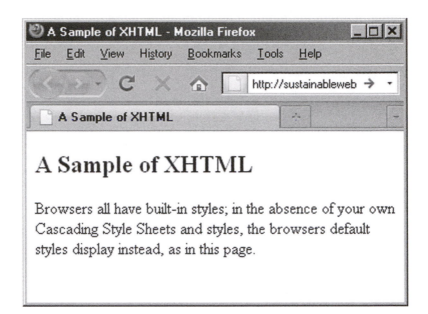

Figure 10.1. A sample of XHTML, with the browser's default styling.

Figure 10.2. The same sample as Figure 10.1, but with Arial font on the body selector in CSS.

of this style declaration for the <body> tag—which is inherited by all text on the page:

```
body { font-family: Arial, sans-serif; }
```

CSS STYLE DECLARATIONS

A CSS file is nothing more than a list of styles, or **style declarations.** A Web browser then attempts to match those styles to the structures in your XHTML document. CSS styles comprise three parts: **selectors,** which determine what structural parts of the XHTML document will be styled, and **properties** and **values,** which determine what style property (e.g., text color, font) will be set and what value it will be set to (e.g., blue, Verdana). Some properties take a single value, while others can take multiple values. Properties and values are all grouped with a selector using curly braces, { }, and each property-value combination ends with a semicolon, ;.

The basic form of a CSS style declaration, then, is something similar to this pseudo-code (using selector, property, and value to show their positions in the style declaration):

```
selector {
 property: value;
 /*For styles that take a single value, e.g.,
   color: blue;
 */

 property: value, value, value;
 /*Commas separate values ordered by
   preference, e.g.,
   font-family: Verdana, Arial, sans-serif;
 */

 property: value value value;
 /*For styles that take multiple values, e.g.,
   border: 10px solid red;
 */
}
```

Style declarations, as above, can contain many different property-value combinations.

BASIC SELECTORS

Selectors in CSS describe the XHTML structure that will be styled. Using the house metaphor from the XHTML chapter, CSS selectors are like instructions to interior decorators for what they should decorate: "the fireplace," "the upstairs bathroom," "the closets in the master bedroom." Except instead of referring to rooms in a house, CSS selectors refer to tags and tag relationships in your XHTML source.

Element Selectors

The most basic CSS selectors are XHTML tag elements (sometimes called type selectors). The only thing to remember is that while XHTML puts the element in angle brackets, like <body> or <p>, in CSS the element appears by itself: body or p. Any XHTML tag can be a selector in CSS, and the selector will style that particular tag the way you specify, wherever it appears on your page.

For example, to set all paragraph text to appear in blue, you'd write in CSS:

```
p { color: blue; }
```

ID and Class Selectors

IDs and classes can also be selectors. Class selectors begin with a . (dot) and ID selectors begin with a # (hash). For example, to set the background color of your footer to gray (and assuming your document has <div id="footer">), your CSS would be either:

```
#footer { background: gray; }
```

or

```
div#footer { background: gray; }
```

Either method works; I prefer to put the element with the ID, just to help myself remember more about what I'm styling.

If you had a class called "warning" (e.g., <p class="warning">), perhaps on a site with instructions for doing something that might be potentially dangerous (such as operating a power saw), you could style that class as either

```
.warning { color: red; }
```

or

```
p.warning { color: red; }
```

Adding the tag element to the class selector can give you finer-grained control over the look of your page, particularly if you use the same class on different XHTML tags, but want to style the class differently, depending on the tag the class appears on.

RELATIONSHIP SELECTORS

CSS selectors can also be formed based on the relationships between elements in XHTML pages. CSS (like the DOM, see Chapter 19) relies on relationships in terms you already know from your family tree: parents, children, siblings; as well as ancestors and descendants.

Descendant Selectors

Descendant selectors are formed by a list of at least two elements or classes/IDs, each separated by a space. The selector styles the last element listed. For example, to style all of the anchor tags (links) in the navigation so that they are not underlined (Figure 10.3), you could write a descendant selector:

```
ul#navigation a { text-decoration: none; }
```

All anchor tags (<a>) inside of <ul id="navigation"> will appear without the default underlining of hyperlinks. Other links on the page will still have an underline. To remove underlining from all links, you could just refer to the a element selector:

```
a { text-decoration: none; }
```

Child Selectors

Child selectors are a more specific form of descendant selector intended to style an element only if it is a child, or direct descendant, of the parent element. The child selector is most useful for noninherited CSS properties, such as list-style-type. Child selectors are written by putting an angle bracket between two elements. The following selector will style all child <li> tags of <ul id="navigation">,

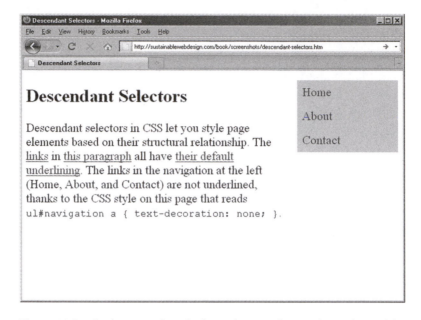

Figure 10.3. In this example, only the anchor tags that are descendants of the navigation list have their default underlining removed.

but not the `<li>` tags of any more deeply nested lists (which would be descendants, but not children; see Chapter 16):

```
ul.colors > li { list-style-type: none; }
```

You can see in Figure 10.4 that the immediate children of `<ul class="colors">` have no bullet points, but the grandchildren still do.

Sibling Selectors

Sibling selectors target adjacent XHTML elements that share a parent. For example, if someone wanted a paragraph appearing immediately following a heading two (`<h2>`) tag to run in bold, the sibling selector, +, accomplishes this:

```
h2 + p { font-weight: bold; }
```

One limitation of the sibling selectors is that you can only target the sibling appearing after the first. That is, if this were the XHTML:

```
<div id="content">
      <h2>My Header Two Tag</h2>
      <p>My paragraph text.</p>
</div>
```

SELECTORS AND SPECIFICITY

The "cascade" in Cascading Style Sheets refers to the method by which a browser applies one of a competing set of styles. Multiple selectors can refer to the same elements; for example,

```
a { color: blue; }
a.external { color: red; }
ul#navigation a { color: green; }
```

The first selector styles all link text blue; the second styles links with an `external` class as red, while the third styles links in the navigation green. But given that all three styles ultimately refer to `<a>` in the XHTML, how does a Web browser know to style the external links red and all other links blue—given that the selector in the first style is supposed to style *all* of the links on the page?

Selectors have different levels of specificity in CSS. Andy Clarke has a fascinating blog post that uses Star Wars characters to illustrate selector specificity visually.* Along with that, Clarke's post refers to a point system for calculating specificity; essentially, elements in a selector get one point, classes in selectors get 10 points, and IDs in a selector get 100 points. When multiple selectors match the same element, the selector with the most points determines how the element is styled. So in the examples above, the first selector gets one point, the second gets 11 points (element plus class), and the third gets 102 points (an element plus an ID plus another element).

The more specific style—that is, the style with the most points in this system—is the one that gets applied to the matching XHTML structure. That's why the navigation items in the list of styles above will appear green, not blue—even if there were an `<a class="external">` match within `<ul id="navigation">`; to style that would require a selector like

```
ul#navigation a.external { /*Styles here*/ }
```

whose point value would be 112 (two elements, one class, and one ID) and therefore more specific.

*Andy Clarke, "CSS: Specifity Wars," *Stuff and Nonsense*, http://www.stuffandnonsense.co.uk/archives/css_specificity_wars.html

the sibling selector would allow us to style the paragraph element, but not the heading-two element. That is, we can say in CSS "style paragraphs appearing immediately after heading-two" but *not* "style heading-twos appearing before a paragraph." That's just a limitation of

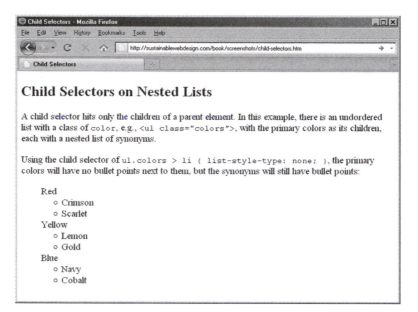

Figure 10.4. Using the child selector, only the first children of this list appear without bullets; more deeply nested lists still have their bullets.

CSS; but there are always other solutions. To style that heading two, it might just be better to add a class to it in your XHTML when it appears before paragraphs (if there is something structurally special about the heading two in that situation).

Universal Selector

One final selector worth mentioning is the universal selector, *, sometimes called the wildcard selector. Used by itself, it will style all elements on the page; for example,

```
* { color: green; }
```

will style all text on the page to make it appear green. (However, because color is inherited, it is generally better to set it using the body element selector.) For both class and ID selectors, the wildcard selector is implied. That is, there is no difference between

```
.warning { color: red; }
```

and

```
*.warning { color: red; }
```

The wildcard selector is at its most useful in relationship selectors. For example, if a page contained the following XHTML:

```
<p>
 This is <strong>an example</strong> of
 <a href="example.htm">styling the text in
 <strong>this strong tag</strong></a> <em>as well
 as <strong>this strong tag</strong></em>.
</p>
```

only the first `<strong>` tag (marking "an example") is a child of `<p>`. The other two are children of other tags (`<a>` and `<em>`). To style the strong tags that *aren't* children of `<p>`, use the wildcard selector:

```
p * strong { /*Style information*/ }
```

That would style all strong tags that are grandchildren of paragraphs: meaning, there must be one or more descendant elements between p and strong for this style to be applied. We could also use the child selector, rather than the descendant selector, for more specific parent-child relationships (e.g., that only one element appears between p and strong):

```
p > * > strong { /*Style information*/ }
```

However, in those two cases, both selectors would apply the same styles to the XHTML above.

Combining Selectors

You can write selectors as descriptively and specifically as you like, so long as they match actual familial relationships and structural components in your XHTML. A match is what triggers a Web browser to apply the style. For example, to style a paragraph that is an adjacent sibling of a heading-two tag that is a child of `<div id="content">`, provided that `div#content` is not a child of the body tag, the CSS selector would look like:

```
body * div#content > h2 + p { /*Style information*/ }
```

However, you'll probably be relieved to know that it's rare to have to write such complicated selectors. Rare, but possible. (See the "Selectors and Specificity" sidebar above, which will be useful knowledge if you have to write complex selectors.)

Grouping Selectors

There are times when you might want multiple structural features in your XHTML to be styled the same way; for example, both the <b> (bold) and <strong> tag might be styled as bold by your CSS. The long way to do that would be to write two separate style declarations:

```
b { font-weight: bold; }
strong { font-weight: bold; }
```

But by using the comma, both selectors can be styled together. The comma enables designers to style many additional elements to appear in bold, such as all of the headings:

```
b, strong, h1, h2, h3, h4, h5, h6 {
 font-weight: bold;
}
```

Then, any distinct styles for a given selector could be handled by additional selectors in the same style sheet; for example, h1 has already been styled bold, but to make it purple (as well as bold) requires only another style declaration that contains only the color property:

```
h1 { color: purple; } /*Already made bold above.*/
```

Pseudo-Class Selectors

CSS provides five special pseudo-class selectors, which are most often used for styling link text appearing inside the <a> tag:

- :link styles a link in its unvisited state
- :visited styles a link that has been visited
- :hover styles a link that is being moused over, and should usually be combined with
- :focus, which styles a link that has been, for example, tabbed to by a keyboard
- :active styles a link during the brief moment that it has been activated by a mouse click or pressing the Return key on the keyboard

So to make links green and no underline, hovered/active links underlined and green, and visited links red, a style sheet might have a cluster of styles like:

```
a,a:link { color: green; text-decoration: none; }
a:visited { color: red; }
a:hover,a:active { text-decoration: underline; }
```

`:hover` and `:focus` also work on XHTML elements in forms for entering user information.

COMMON CSS PROPERTIES AND VALUES

There are hundreds of properties in CSS for designing the look of XHTML pages. References at HTML Dog[1] or Sitepoint[2] are essential to have on hand as you write CSS; but here are some of the more common properties to get you started, once you've begun to design your site.

Fonts and Text

A basic capability of CSS is styling text. CSS properties enable you to change fonts and font sizes, as well as setting styles such as bold, italic, and color. You can also set the amount of space between lines of text.

- `font-family`: The font-family property takes a list of fonts; the Web browser will keep moving through the list until it finds a match on the user's system. If no match is found, it will use whatever it has to match the generic font style mentioned at the end of the list. For example, if the style is

  ```
  font-family: "Times New Roman", Times, serif;
  ```

  the Web browser will display Times New Roman (which is placed in quotation marks because of the spaces in the font's name, but place the comma *outside* the quotation marks); if the computer the browser is running on does not have Times New Roman but does have Times, it will use Times; if it doesn't have Times either, it will display whatever serif font is available on the system. For accessibility purposes, always be sure to specify a generic font alternative at the end of all lists of fonts: `serif`, `sans-serif`, or `monospace`. You can find a current list of commonly available fonts at this book's companion Web site, `http://sustainablewebdesign.com/book/`.

- `font-size`: Font sizes can be set in a number of different units; points (`pt`) are used for print style sheets. Screen style sheets can use keywords, such as `small`, `medium`, and `large`; pixels (`px`); percentages (`%`); or ems (`em`).

- `font-weight`: Font weight can be specified as a number in multiples of 100, but is more often specified as `bold`, which makes the font appear bold, or `normal`, which makes the font appear normal (not bold). Normal is often used to reset a bold style inherited from another selector; if the strong tag, by itself, is set to bold, `strong { font-weight: bold; }`, but you don't want bold on strong inside of an anchor tag, you'd write:

```
a strong { font-weight: normal; }
```

- `font-style`: Font style is usually either set to `italic`, for italics, or `normal` for nonitalic text.

- `color`: The color property specifies text color. You can write color keywords like those found in small boxes of crayons (e.g., `red`, `blue`, or `green`). To gain better control over color, write the hexadecimal number for a color (e.g., `#FFFFFF` for white) or the RGB value using `rgb(255,255,255)`, which would also produce white.

- `line-height`: Line height can be expressed as numbers without a unit; for example, `line-height: 1.5;` makes text one-and-a-half-spaced, `line-height: 2;` makes text double-spaced. You can also use pixel units, although that may cause problems if a user tries to resize the text on your site.

- `text-indent`: To indent the first line of text, use the text-indent property and a value in pixels or ems. To mimic a hanging indent (see Figure 10.5), run a negative number for `text-indent` and then the same but positive value for `padding-left`. For example,

```
ul.citation li {
        text-indent: -50px;
        padding-left: 50px;
}
```

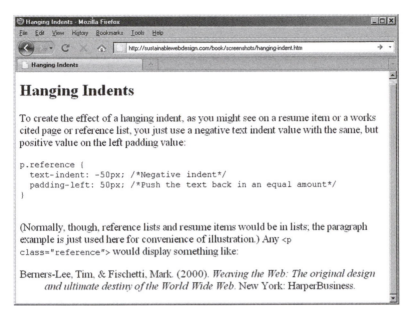

Figure 10.5. Example of a hanging indent on a paragraph at the bottom of the screen; ordinarily, references or works cited should be in list items in ordered or unordered lists.

Boxes: Borders, Padding, and Margin

Block level elements—such as headings, paragraphs, lists, list items, and divisions—are by default displayed as boxes; that is, they are as tall as the content they contain, but block-level elements always take up the entire width of the screen regardless of their content. Although we will look more closely at the CSS box model in Chapter 17, for now it's important to know that `border` and `padding` will add to the size of a box whose width or height you specify, while `margin` will move the box away from other elements on the page, or from the edge of the browser window.

- `border`: Border is a shorthand property for specifying the width, style, and color of a border. To set only the borders of one edge, use `border-top`, `border-right`, `border-bottom`, or `border-left`.
- `padding`: Padding increases the distance between the content in an element and the edge of the element. Padding can take a single value to add the same amount of padding to all sides of

COLOR AND CSS

There are three common methods to specify colors in CSS, whether you are coloring text, a background, or a border.

The first method is to use color keywords, which give you very limited control of color; they are like small boxes of crayons, allowing you to specify `red`, `blue`, `yellow`, `green`, and other basic colors in your CSS.

The second method is to use hexadecimal numbers for red, green, and blue (RGB) color values. This method works very well across operating systems and Web browsers; a hexadecimal value is made up of six hexadecimal, or hex, numbers. (Hex numbers run 0–9 and continue A–F.) The first two numbers are the red value, the second two the green value, and the third two are the blue value. So to set a color to the brightest purple (red and blue), a hex value of `#FF00FF` would be required. A Google search for *hexadecimal color palette* will turn up dozens of pages that show the hex values for colors; you will also see a 216-color "Web-safe" palette. Designers used to be restricted to those 216 colors, but can now use any of the millions of color combinations enabled by hex colors.

The third method, which is supported in all contemporary browsers, is to specify RGB color in decimal numbers (0 to 255); instead of using the hash (#) as on hex numbers, RGB requires this form: `rgb(255,0,255);`

the content, or it can take four values in "trouble" order: Top Right Bottom Left (TRBL).

- `margin`: Margin increases the distance between the element and other elements on your page, or from the edge of the browser viewport. Without a background color or background image, margin and padding appear to do the same thing (increased space), but margins are transparent.

- `height`: It is possible to set the height on an element. This is usually done in image replacement situations (see Chapters 14 and 17). The problem with `height` is that some browsers will maintain the height you specify, even if the content is longer/taller, whereas other browsers will expand the height to fit the content.

- `width`: By contrast, width is specified quite often, especially to help build page layouts. It is usually best practice to set widths on a containing division or ordered or unordered list, rather than individual elements. As with height, elements that have their width specified will add any padding to the total width. So for example,

```
ul#navigation {
      width: 200px;
      padding: 20px;
}
```

will result in the navigation appearing 240 pixels wide (200 width + 20 left padding + 20 right padding = 240).

Layout and Positioning

The most advanced use of CSS is to create entire page layouts, which were once created with HTML tables. CSS layouts are much more flexible than tables, because they are layered over a page's structure—not part of it, as tables were. Chapter 17 looks at building CSS layouts using these properties:

- position: There are three common values for positioning elements: static, which is the default position of elements as they appear in source order and therefore the document flow; absolute, which removes an item from the document flow; and relative, which is usually specified for setting a **positioning context** other than the whole browser window for absolutely positioned items.
- top, right, bottom, left: Each of these four values can place an absolute- or relative-positioned element a certain distance from the top, right, bottom, or left of either the browser window or its positioning context. Negative values can also be used, sometimes to the effect of moving things off screen (such as a navigation intended for users of screen readers).
- float: Some Web sites use floats to create their layouts; however, positioning is a much better alternative. But floats do come in handy for some forms of horizontal navigation bars, or when you have images or other media that you want other content to flow around.

- `display`: Display is a versatile property for setting how and whether an item displays. `display: none;` causes the item to disappear from view (potentially also to assistive technologies, which may be an accessibility issue). `display: block;` causes an item to appear as a block element, while `display: inline;` will make an item appear like an inline element, such as `<strong>` or `<em>` usually appear.

Design Images and Textures

Background colors help you to add visual interest to your pages. Design images let you put the finishing touches on a design. But unlike images loaded in the XHTML `<img />` tag, CSS background images keep design images independent of your page content; redesigning your site, even its design images, is just a matter of changing your CSS.

- `background-color`: Like `color`, `background-color` can be specified using color keywords, hexadecimal numbers, or the RGB numbers. You can specify a background color on any element, as well as `<body>` and even `<html>` to set a background color for your entire page. Just be sure you have high enough contrast between your text and background to keep your pages readable (see Chapter 6).
- `background-image`: You can also specify a background image on any element; for background images that are textures suitable for appearing behind text, it's also a good idea to specify a similar background color to the image, so as to keep text readable in the absence of images, or while the image loads.
- `background-repeat`: By default, background images tile horizontally and vertically to fill an entire element. However, you can set `background-repeat: no-repeat;` for an image to appear only once, or to `background-repeat: repeat-x;` to tile horizontally, or `background-repeat: repeat-y;` to tile only vertically.
- `background`: You can also use the shorthand background property; to set only a color, specify the color: `background: green;`. To specify a background image (and a color for imageless devices), the shorthand is `background: green url`

(`'tiled-leaves.jpg'`)`;`. Again, be sure to have a CSS reference nearby, especially for shorthand properties like `background` and `border`.

NEXT STEPS

Now that you've had an introduction to CSS and have a list of some (but certainly not all) of CSS's properties, it will be easier to see how both XHTML and CSS can be used to build different parts of your pages: the branding, navigation, content, and so on. To get started, we will get to work with the Rapid Prototyping Kit (RPK) and, in Chapter 12, explore writing with source in a text editor.

NOTES

1. HTML Dog, "CSS Properties," http://htmldog.com/reference/cssproperties/

2. SitePoint, "SitePoint CSS Reference," http://reference.sitepoint.com/css

CHAPTER 11

Rapid Prototyping

One of the better ways to stay motivated to complete your Web site is to make visible progress on it quickly. The Rapid Prototyping Kit (RPK), available as a free download at `http://sustainablewebdesign .com/book/`, will aid you in building a site with solid, standards-compliant pages.

This chapter looks at the benefits of rapid prototyping and the basic steps of building a Web page using the RPK: gathering content, sketching out a rough layout, structuring content in XHTML, and adding design features in CSS. Those steps will be explored further in subsequent chapters. But consider this chapter part road map, part crash course.

BENEFITS OF RAPID PROTOTYPING

Some books advise you to spend long stretches of time developing wireframes, sketches, mockups, and other kinds of throwaway prototypes that aren't part of the final project. While those types of development tools have their place and their benefits, my preference is to get to the work of actually building a site as quickly as possible. It's better to avoid throwing away work, and better still to be doing things that directly reveal the possibilities (and limitations) of Web design with XHTML and CSS.

Keep in mind that a Web site is never really finished; there are just periods of time when it may not change as much. Rather than trying to draft the perfect site before going live with it, it's better to get something together that works basically the way you want it to. Then you can devote yourself to the site's ongoing improvement and expansion over time.

As Chapter 3 urged, have some content on hand and ideas in mind as you begin to rapidly prototype your Web site. The best preparation for building a Web site is to gather and create as much of the site's content as possible (knowing, of course, that content will change over time and based on your design). It is actual content that drives the design of your site.

THE COMPONENTS OF RAPID PROTOTYPING

One of the reasons that WYSIWYG Web editors are so popular is that they enable people to build pages quickly, and serve as all-in-one development environments. The pages that WYSIWYGs spit out may not be standards-compliant, lightweight, or easily revised, but they are pages.

But handwritten, standards-compliant pages can be written quickly, too, and edited and revised even more quickly, which is why I have created the RPK: a collection of files and folders to help you build rapid prototypes for your Web site. These files and folders will help you transition from the sketching and planning aspects of your site development to full-on site creation. I call it *prototyping*, but this activity builds more than a throwaway prototype like you would get from wireframing or mockups. This is the real work of building your site. What makes it prototype-like is your attitude: if something doesn't work, modify it. Otherwise, throw it away and start anew.

Put another way, when I am building a new site, I often keep in mind the words of Eric Raymond: "You often don't really understand the problem until after the first time you implement a solution." For this reason, "be ready to start over at least once."[1]

Rapid prototyping requires three things:

- **The RPK,** which is a flexible, skeletal shell for putting together almost any type of Web site; I have released the RPK under a permissive open-source license, so you are free to use it for any kind of site, including commercial sites.

EATING MY OWN DOG FOOD

Many open-source projects try to live by a phrase that I have come to love: "Eat your own dog food." The idea behind this phrase is that people who create digital materials (software, templates, plugins, etc.) for others should use the materials themselves.

That is actually how the RPK came to be: instead of reinventing the wheel for each of my Web projects, I started working to build a kit that would put a lot of things in place that I would otherwise be writing from scratch.

So in all of my XHTML sites, including the site that supports this book, I have eaten my own dog food: they are all based on the RPK, with modifications as necessary (which is exactly the point of the RPK: it's a start, but you will still have to modify it to suit your own needs).

- **A development environment,** which should be comfortable for you to use but experimented with as part of learning (see Chapter 5).
- **A long-term attitude toward writing and designing for the Web,** which expects only steady progress and learning (and lots of mistakes), not perfection or instant mastery.

THE RAPID PROTOTYPING KIT

The Rapid Prototyping Kit is nothing but a small collection of files and folders for quickly building a Web site (see Figure 11.1). You can open, manipulate, and customize the kit on any operating system (Windows, Mac OS, Linux) using any good text editor. You can download it from the Web site as a ZIP file (`.zip`); most operating systems have a built-in utility for unzipping files. But if you're looking for an open-source program for creating and extracting ZIPs and other compressed/archived files, you might consider 7-Zip.[2] Although 7-Zip is a Windows program in origin, there are versions available for Linux and Mac, too.

(Because I use the RPK in my own Web design work, I frequently make subtle improvements to it. The companion site at `http://sustainablewebdesign.com/book/` notes any changes, although the

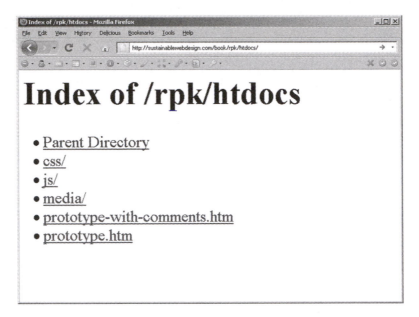

Figure 11.1. You can browse the RPK's files on the Web; this is a view of the contents of the htdocs/ folder.

version of the RPK used in this book will always be available. Below is a rough outline of the RPK as of the writing of this book.)

The Rapid Prototyping Kit Folders

Once you extract the RPK's ZIP file, you will find a folder called htdocs/ (named for easy use with the XAMPP Web server, which is discussed in Chapter 20).

The htdocs/ folder is a **root Web folder**, which contains all of the files and folders that make up a Web site. Depending on your Web host, you might need to transfer the contents of this folder to www/, httpdocs/, or even html/ once you get to the point of uploading your site (see Chapter 23). But for development and experimenting purposes, htdocs/ will be fine, especially if you build and test your site using the XAMPP Web server (see Chapter 20).

In addition to two XHTML files, which are described below, htdocs/ contains several folders as listed in the "Essential Folders" sidebar in Chapter 5. In short, the Rapid Prototyping Kit includes folders for every kind of site content that you might wish to post.

(Chapter 20 provides guidance for adding your own folders to structure and organize your site architecture.) The RPK's folder structure can be changed as needed; but if you are new to Web design, it provides workable solutions to keep the contents of your site organized.

The Rapid Prototyping XHTML Files

In addition to a folder structure intended to help you organize your site's content, the RPK includes an XHTML file containing a global structure for all site pages. This file is named `prototype.htm`. (There is also a file, `prototype-with-comments.htm`, that has the same structure but that explains in detail all of the prototyping features.) Composed mostly of `<div>` tags and some accessibility features, `prototype.htm` is what will help you begin to structure your site's page content immediately, and enable you to build CSS over the top of that structure for a standards-compliant page design.

Most Web pages, regardless of their purpose, share a few common areas:

- A header with the site name and branding
- A content area that may consist of one or more subdivisions of content
- A navigation bar or menu to help users find their way to other pages on the site
- A footer area with copyright and licensing information and other information about the page or site

The next several chapters are devoted to breaking down and considering the purpose and potential design approaches to those structures, which are shared across all pages in your site.

The `prototype.htm` file also reflects a sensible **source order**, meaning its ordering of content divisions—header, content, navigation, footer—would make sense and be useful even if there were no design elements on the page, or if the page were being read aloud to a low-vision user (see Figure 11.2).

For example, it may surprise you that the navigation appears so far down in the source order of the page. After all, most Web sites feature their navigation areas near the top of the page. With CSS positioning,

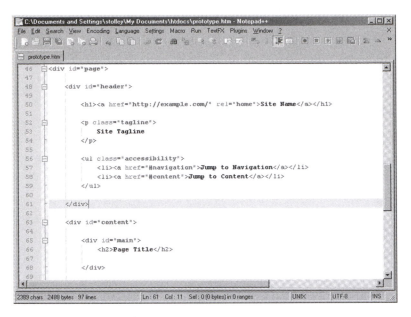

Figure 11.2. A part of `prototype.htm` visible in the Notepad++ editor, revealing the file's source order.

however, it is possible to place the navigation wherever you would like it to appear on the page—while keeping the source order friendly to search engines and low-vision, text-only users (who can jump down the page to the navigation using special accessibility links discussed in Chapter 14).

The Rapid Prototyping CSS Files

One of the reasons I've found that beginners struggle with CSS design is that it's often a toxic mix of designing for a page, but against the browser. When you view a plain XHTML file, without any of your own CSS styles, the Web browser itself is actually styling the page with its own built-in set of CSS styles (see Figure 11.3). And as luck would have it, every browser is a little different in its default styles. And that makes cross-browser CSS design unnecessarily frustrating, even for simple things like styling text.

That is why the RPK contains the Yahoo! Reset Min CSS file (`reset.css`),[3] which has the effect of removing any styles that might be added by a Web browser (Figure 11.4). It gets rid of all the margin

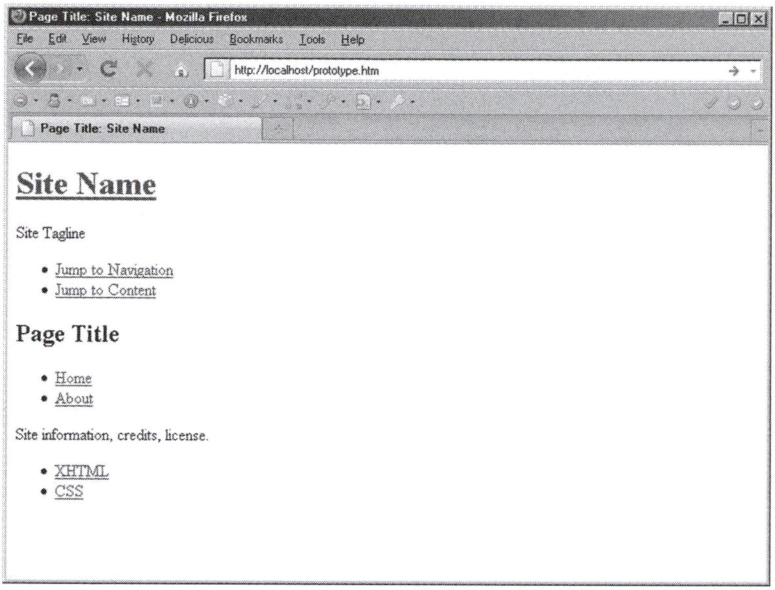

Figure 11.3. This is what prototype.htm looks like without any styles of its own, and therefore styled by the Firefox's default CSS styles.

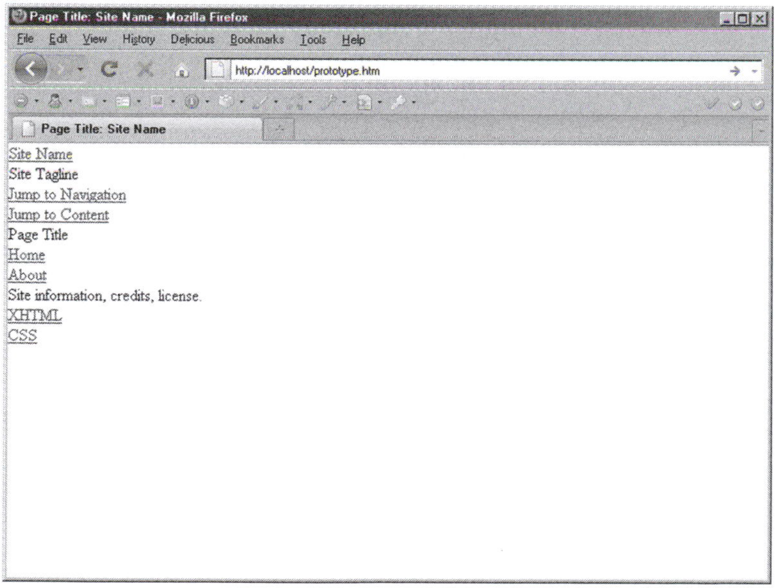

Figure 11.4. The same page as Figure 11.3, but with the Reset CSS in place.

and padding around elements, removes all of the font sizes on the different headings, and even removes bold and italic styling from tags that would otherwise be bold and italic in most browsers.

To account for that, the RPK also includes CSS at the top of `screen.css` that adds back some of the common styles that the Reset CSS removes (see Figure 11.5). Specifically, it puts bold back on the headings and the bold and strong tags; italics back on the italic, emphasis, and cite tags; and puts a dotted border back on the acronym and abbreviation tags. If you do not wish to use the base styles, remove or adjust them. The basic lesson from the Reset CSS is that you have to specify *everything* about your design—even things like bold on tags where you would expect bold.

Everything else is completely unstyled: there is no space around any of the headings, paragraphs, or lists, which also lack even bullets. The idea behind this is that you are now free to style your page exactly as you want it to appear. If you need bullets next to your unordered lists, for example, you have to specify them in your CSS. It's potentially

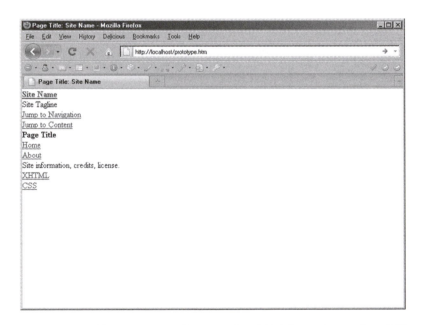

Figure 11.5. The same page as Figures 11.3 and 11.4, but with some base CSS styles added back in after applying the Reset CSS. This is how `prototype.htm` will look when you first open your own copy.

extra work to add bullets, yes, but only if you want those and other design features to appear. If, for example, you want no bullets next to your navigation list, no problem. They're not there anyway. But if you do want bullets, you can be more confident that they will appear as you intend across standards-compliant Web browsers.

For adding those and other custom styles, there is a `screen.css` file that is empty except for the base styles mentioned above and some useful selectors (see Chapter 10) for styling particular content areas and structural features found in `prototype.htm`.

Rapid Prototyping JavaScript Files

There are two JavaScript files in the RPK: the jQuery JavaScript library,[4] which has its own folder, `jquery/`, inside of the `js/` folder and a JavaScript file, `site.js`, where you can write the JavaScript for your own site. I have included some functions in `site.js` that are useful for all kinds of sites and that are explained in Chapter 19.

WRITING AND DESIGNING WITH THE RPK

Chapters 12 through 18 cover the specifics of working with different parts of your pages, but here is a rough outline of how to proceed in your Web writing and design using the RPK. Note that this is rarely a linear process; for example, your content may force you to rethink your page design, and vice versa. Still, every writer should address each of these tasks as part of Web writing and design, with or without the RPK:

- **Generate and gather your text and image content.** You will need to have structured XHTML available before you can test your design work in CSS; so drafting your page content, and preparing some images and media (see Chapter 3), will allow you to accurately describe the structure of your page content as discussed in Chapters 16 and 18.
- **Set up your basic metadata, branding and rough navigation.** Edit the `prototype.htm` file according to the guidance in the metadata, branding, and navigation chapters (Chapters 13, 14, and 15) and save it as `my-prototype.htm` so that you can

create pages based on your own starter page that has most of your shared page features in place. (See Chapter 21 for building a more dynamic, reusable set of shared content features.)

- **Develop a representative page from your site.** The urge that most designers have is to start with the home page, but it is often very different from the content pages of a site. I recommend starting with an "About Me"–type page; not only will that likely be representative of your site's other pages, but its contents will also help you to figure out what other pages to include in your site.

- **Mark up your text and image content in XHTML.** Once you have a rough draft of your content, start tagging it with XHTML, particularly its headings, paragraphs, and lists (see Chapter 16).

- **Begin to develop site typography.** Choosing fonts and font sizes, as well as line heights, will help you to get your page into a shape that makes it readable and lead you to creating a site style guide for text (see Chapter 16). A current list of fonts that are safe to use on the Web is available at `http://sus tainablewebdesign.com/book/`; just because a font is on your computer does not mean it will be available on others. Be prepared to adjust your typography later on to maximize readability according to your page layout.

- **Sketch out a rough layout for your site.** This is mostly about geography, not the site's actual look: Where will the header and footer appear? The navigation? Your content and subcontent areas? Your rough sketch will guide your work in Chapter 17 on page layout.

- **Use CSS to position your page elements.** As Chapter 17 demonstrates, CSS layouts are basically illusions, sort of like the little slider puzzles you may have had as a child, where there were nine spots for eight pieces of an image to go, and you had to slide things around in order to get the picture to look the way it's supposed to.

- **Use an image editor to build in textures and background images,** and finalize dimensions, particularly widths, for the different elements on your page. This is where you work to really build the look and feel of your pages. Once you know you are able to get your page elements to roughly where you want them, you can use your image editor to create a striking design.

Cultivating a Long-Term Attitude toward Site Development

A Web site is, to some extent, always in draft form. You will want to make changes to your content as your career progresses, or as your business or organization develops over time. Your design might start to look dated, and you will want to update it, too. Here are some basic habits to cultivating a long-term attitude toward site development (see also Chapter 8 on sustainability):

- **Write as little source as possible.** Beginners in my Web design classes tend to write way more XHTML markup and CSS styles than are necessary. I think this happens because they are nervous about working in these new languages, and expect that interesting pages will have lots of markup and CSS styles. That is not true. The guidance in the chapters that follow will show you how to write lean source, which makes a site much easier to revise and maintain.

- **Think about relationships between your page elements.** One of the strengths of both CSS and JavaScript is their leverage of relationships between page elements. For example, perhaps there is a paragraph you want to display entirely in bold, so you write something like this:

```
<p><strong>This paragraph's text is all in
  bold.</strong></p>
```

But when you see that kind of markup, where two or more tags mark the same content, it's time to rethink your strategy. One alternative to that use of the `<strong>` tag is to add a class to the paragraph, like `<p class="important">` and then in the CSS specify `p.important { font-weight: bold; }`. Don't forget to remove the unnecessary `<strong>` tags from your markup, though.

- **Think about the general, then move to the specific.** The advice above suggests to begin site design by working with a representative content page from your site; this helps you think about what *most* pages will include structurally and how they will be designed. From that, you can design pages that are slightly different, such as the home page. Chapter 13 suggests using a class on the body tag to give you a hook to style different types of pages, while maintaining lean source and a single CSS file.

- **Devote a little time every week or so to improve something on your site.** Like any other skills, your Web writing and design skills depend on your exercising them every so often. Coming back to your site regularly, as your schedule allows, will keep your current skills fresh—and help you to learn new ones (see the "Resources for the Future" section for material that will advance your abilities beyond this book and keep you current on the latest and best approaches to Web design).

NEXT STEPS

To build and edit your pages with the RPK requires only a simple text editor, which the next chapter discusses. If you're comfortable working with a text editor, you may want to skip ahead to Chapter 13.

NOTES

1. Eric S. Raymond, *The Cathedral and the Bazaar: Musings on Linux and Open Source by an Accidental Revolutionary*, revised and expanded ed. (Sebastopol, CA: O'Reilly Media, 2001), 25.

2. 7-Zip, "Download," http://www.7-zip.org/download.html

3. Yahoo! Developer Network, "YUI 2: Reset CSS," http://developer.yahoo.com/yui/reset/

4. jQuery.com, *jQuery: The Write Less, Do More JavaScript Library*, http://jquery.com/

CHAPTER 12

Writing with Source in a Text Editor

If you're used to writing in a word processor or a WYSIWYG Web editor, one of the first things that may strike you about writing in a simple text editor like TextWrangler or Notepad++ is the relative lack of buttons and other screen clutter (see Figure 12.1). At first, this lack of buttons can be disorienting, even alarming: word processors and even email programs have conditioned us to write with a lot of machine assistance, particularly for formatting.

But the text editor's simplicity is actually a good thing. In a text editor, what matters most is what you write yourself. And that's what you do in an editor: you write.

The important thing about a text editor, like the Web pages that you create with it, is that there are no hidden mysteries. The WYSIWYG acronym's popular usage aside, in an editor, what you see really *is* what you get—at least in terms of the sets of instructions that browsers turn into Web pages.

If you've ever used a word processor, you know that sometimes, weird things happen. For no apparent reason. A paragraph gets a bullet point next to it, and nothing you do to appease and reassure the software seems to remove the bullet point. A paragraph changes font right in the middle, but again with no apparent or apparently fixable reason. Most people confronted with such a situation will just start a new document from scratch—or live with the weirdness.

In the text editor, nothing you write and nothing about your Web pages is hidden from view. And that means that, with even a little bit

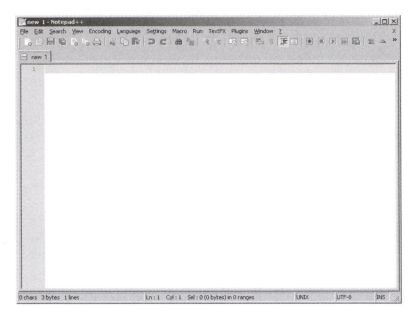

Figure 12.1.   The Notepad++ editor, open and empty.

of source literacy, you have maximum control over your pages. More important, when something is wrong with one of your pages, you can be certain that it's something you can fix.

ONE PAGE, MANY VIEWS

To understand why someone would want to roll back to a piece of software as primitive as a text editor, it's important to understand that there are many different views of the same Web page. The text editor is very good at managing its particular view of the page's source. But there are three views to monitor as you write your pages and build your site:

- **File View:** The listing of files and folders provided by your computer's operating system, or on your Web server via an FTP program, is the file view; that is, the list of files that make up your Web page or Web site (see Figure 12.2). It is best practice, in most situations, to separate the languages that make up your pages into individual files: CSS in `.css`

Figure 12.2.   The file components of a simple page, as displayed by the operating system: in this case, an XHTML file, a CSS file, and a PNG image file.

files, JavaScript in .js files, and so on (be sure that you have configured your operating system to show all file extensions; see Chapter 5). The file view also guides you in how to write URLs so that when you write a reference from one file, like an XHTML page, to another file, like an image, the link between the two actually works (see the discussion of links and paths in Chapter 20).

- **Source View:** When you use your editor to open up an XHTML or CSS file, you are looking at the file's source view (see Figure 12.3). You can also access the source view of any page on the Web by choosing something like View > Source from within a Web browser. Looking at the source of other pages on the Web is a great way to learn how other people build pages.
- **Browser View:** This is how we usually experience Web pages; the browser view is how pages display or render in a browser itself (see Figure 12.4). However, each browser or mobile or adaptive device provides a different, unique view of a given Web page, as discussed in Chapter 2.

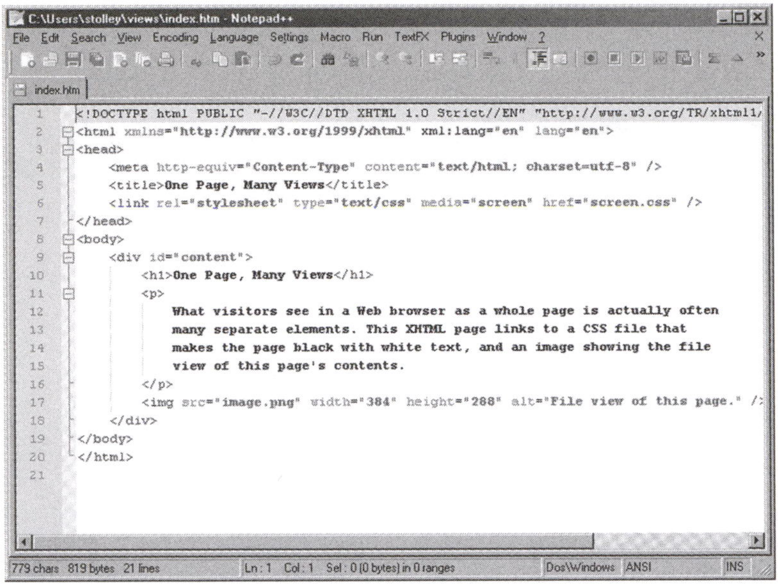

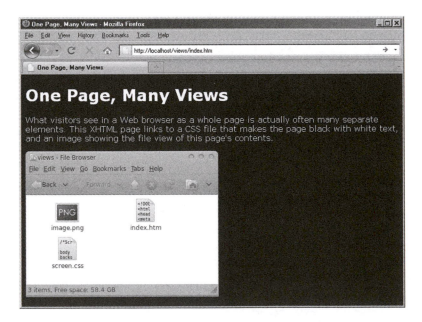

Figure 12.3. The source view of an XHTML file, which links to the CSS file on Line 6 and the image file on Line 17.

Figure 12.4. The browser pulls all the files together, thanks to the instructions in the XHTML file, which references the CSS and image files. The image file is actually a screen shot of the file view in the Ubuntu Linux operating system.

Each view—file, source, and browser—will be slightly different, depending on details such as your operating system (Mac OS, Windows, Linux), your editor (TextWrangler, Notepad++), and your browser (Firefox, Chrome, Safari). Available fonts, screen resolutions, and even display types (LCD panels or older CRT displays) all affect views. But regardless of those details, what each view represents in terms of your site's files, source, page rendering is the same.

SYNTAX HIGHLIGHTING

Good text editors can provide more than views of source in simple black and white text, though. Colorized text, better known as **syntax highlighting,** makes writing XHTML, CSS, JavaScript, and your content more comfortable and efficient.

Despite their general lack of features, one feature that any good text editor will have is syntax highlighting. Syntax highlighting provides a set of visual cues about the contents of your files. Good editors will

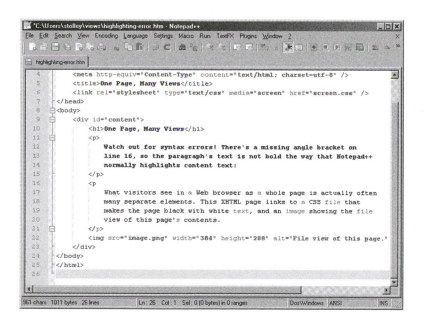

Figure 12.5. A missing angle bracket on line 16 causes Notepad++'s syntax highlighting to colorize all of the following text as though it were a tag. To fix these kinds of errors, watch for the line at which they start, then study your source more closely.

display XHTML files, for example, with tags colored differently from the text content that the tags structure. Attributes and attribute-values may be colored differently from the tag element, and so on.

The colors for syntax highlighting vary from editor to editor (e.g., coloring tags blue, green, or purple); the individual colors do not matter. What does matter is the differences in color from one feature of your source (e.g., tags, attributes) and another (e.g., text content). For example, if you forget to put a closing angle bracket on a tag, or a closing quotation mark on an attribute-value, the colors for tags or attribute-values will colorize everything that follows as a tag or attribute-value (see Figure 12.5).

This is an important way to track down the simplest and most common errors that most of us create when we write Web pages. If the syntax highlighting of a page suddenly stops changing over a large stretch—or otherwise looks different from other, similar areas of the page—look for the spot at which the change begins. It's more than likely that you will find the source of the problem nearby.

SOURCE FORMATTING

Unlike word processors, which format text to a particular printed page size, text editors have no associated page or screen size. If you begin typing a paragraph or long sentence in an editor, it will often continue on the same line for as long as you keep typing, without breaking the text onto the next line.

Source formatting, or the style of line breaks and indentation you use to keep your source readable, is a necessary skill that you will develop over time as you work with your editor.

Line Breaks

There are a couple of different options for handling line breaks. Some editors will create so-called soft breaks, which visually wrap text onto new lines in your text editor's particular view of the file. But soft breaks are not saved with the file itself. If you view the file's source in a browser, it will appear as one 10-mile-long line.

The other option is to create hard breaks by hitting the Enter/Return key on your keyboard. Hard breaks are special characters that are stored in a file; these break the lines of your source for anyone viewing it (including people who choose the View > Source option in their Web browser).

It is tradition to put hard breaks in source files after 80 characters, but running out to 100 characters is fine, too. Line length is, in source formatting as in page design, a matter of reading comfort. Your editor can probably set up a visual onscreen guide to show you where the 80- or 100-character mark is, so you know when to hit Return.

LF, CR+LF, AND CR: THE MOST BORING SIDEBAR IN THE BOOK

So I have been telling a little bit of a lie so far. There is one thing that you cannot see in a text editor—or that you usually don't see, unless something has gone very wrong: the special character that different operating systems put in text editors when you hit the Enter key for a line break.

This is primarily a Windows issue; the details are below, but suffice it to say that the preferred break for files destined for the Web is the linefeed character, **LF**. It is preferable because it works well across all operating systems, including and especially the Linux or Unix-like operating system that will probably be run by your Web host, as Chapter 5 suggested.

Most Windows editors, including Notepad++, allow you to specify what character should be used for new lines. In Notepad++, go to Settings > Preferences and then find the New Document/Default Directory tab. Make sure you choose Unix as the default format. If you open up older files, you can always choose Edit > EOL Conversion, and change the current file to Unix. (EOL means "end of line.") Doing so will make work easier for you and your collaborators if you move, or might move, between Windows, Mac OS, and Linux.

If you're struggling to stay awake, you can skip back to the main text. But if you're interested in a little history/trivia, here goes: Carriage Return and Line Feed, or CR+LF, is the double character inserted by Windows editors; what it results in most often is text files appearing double-spaced on LF systems, such as OS X and Linux. (CR by itself is basically ancient, although if you want to fire up your old Apple II or even a Mac OS 9 machine, you'll find a piece of living history.)

For those troubled few who find this discussion fascinating, consult the Wikipedia page for Newline: `http://en.wikipedia.org/wiki/Newline`

You can also put in breaks whenever it helps make your source more readable. Except in a very specific instance (the `<pre>` tag), white space (spaces, tabs, hard breaks) in XHTML source (Figure 12.6) is not reflected in the browser's rendering of your page (Figure 12.7). (This means that inserting a tab or five spaces at the beginning of a paragraph will *not* indent your paragraph; to indent paragraphs, use the CSS `text-indent` property.) Format your source in the source view of your editor however you'd like, it will render the same in a browser view.

Indentation

Another means for making source more readable is to use indentation. Some text editors will insert multiple spaces for each strike to the Tab key, while others will insert actual tab characters. Look through your editor's preferences, as you can change this to whatever you wish. Tab characters are easier to delete and reformat than a whole bunch of spaces—plus it's usually possible to tell the text editor how wide to

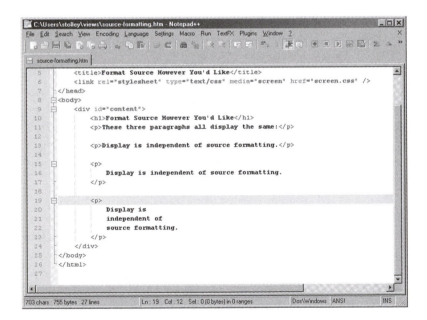

Figure 12.6. The same paragraph, formatted three different ways using tabs, spaces, and line breaks in the source.

Figure 12.7.   Despite the differences in source formatting shown in Figure 12.6, all three paragraphs display exactly the same in the browser view.

CHARACTER ENCODING: UTF-8 WITHOUT THE BYTE ORDER MARK (BOM)

Another invisible matter your text editor will handle is your text file's encoding; while you should specify UTF-8 as the encoding in the metadata for your XHTML pages (see Chapter 13), you must make sure that your text editor is actually encoding UTF-8 (not ANSI or ASCII, which are common default encodings), and without a pesky little creature called the Byte Order Mark (BOM). Most editors, such as Notepad++, have an Encoding menu. Watch carefully, though; Notepad++ has an option for "Encode in UTF-8," which *sounds* right, except you should actually choose "Encode in UTF-8 without BOM." Check also for setting up the default encoding of your files in some kind of Preferences menu in your editor; if you accidentally save a file with the wrong encoding, most editors provide some way to convert encoding to UTF-8 without the BOM.

display a tab. But you can find passionate, almost religious discussions across the Web where people debate indents-as-spaces versus indents-as-tabs. (The RPK is indented using spaces, by the way.)

Whether by tab characters or spaces, indentation makes XHTML more readable by making nested tags even more clear; here is a heading two and paragraph tag nested inside of a division tag:

```
<div class="tip">
     <h2>Indentation Makes Source Readable</h2>
     <p>
          However, some text editors require you to
          do your indentation manually.
     </p>
</div>
```

Likewise, indentations and line breaks can help make CSS source more readable:

```
body {
     font-family: Helvetica, Arial, sans-serif;
     font-size: small;
}
```

Some Web designers even like to indent selectors to visually track which styles appear within other styles:

```
div#content { width: 500px; }
     div#content h2 { font-size: 26px; }
     div#content p { font-size: 14px; }
          div#content p a { color: green; }
```

How your format the source for your XHTML, CSS, and JavaScript is up to you, because in most cases, it has no impact on how your pages display. But it will have a major impact on your ability to collaborate with others, and even how easily you are able to read and understand your own source later.

COMMENTING ON YOUR SOURCE

Another feature that has no effect on page display, but that makes source more readable and understandable over time, is comments.

Every computer language has some sort of syntax for writing comments that is meant for humans, not computers. To help make your pages more sustainable, it's wise to get into the habit of commenting on your source. Not only will comments make it easier for you to edit your pages in the future, but it will also help you to think through what you are doing. If you describe, in the comments, what your source means and what you intend it to do, you will deepen your understanding of how Web languages work.

So in addition to formatting your source for readability using line breaks and indentation, you can also write comments to your source. In XHTML, comments begin with `<!--` and end with `-->`. For example:

```
<!--Here is a comment in XHTML.-->
```

XHTML comments are not rendered on your page in the browser, nor is the browser affected by their contents. (However, it is actually the two hyphens, `--`, that close the comment, so do not use a double-hyphen in your comment text itself. This is a hard habit to break for those of us who use two hyphens in email to mimic an em dash.)

CSS and JavaScript both use a slash-star (`/*`), star-slash (`*/`) pattern to start and end comments:

```
/*Here is a comment in CSS*/
/*Here is a comment in JavaScript*/
```

Writing Useful Comments

Writing useful comments is an art of writing all its own. When written well, comments can explain aspects of your source (you can also throw in line breaks and tabs on your comments, too):

```
a.skip { display: none; }        /*For fully graphical
                                  screen displays, hide
                                  links that are used
                                  to skip to different
                                  page sections*/
```

Here are some general tips for writing useful comments:

- **Write comments as though you were trying to teach or explain what you're doing to someone else.** Many teachers will tell you that they never really learn a subject until they've taught it to others. Writing comments that attempt to teach and explain will help others who might look at the source of your pages—and it will help your future self, who will probably have forgotten why some feature of the page was written to begin with.

- **Provide human-readable information to accompany information for the computer.** In CSS, for example, you usually specify colors by numbers—either hexadecimal or RGB (see Chapter 10). But few of us can remember that #FF3399 is hot pink. Some designers even write color references at the top of their CSS so they know which numbers to write:

```
/*
Colors in this Design:
#339900 - Deep Green
#FFCC33 - Sandy Orange
#993300 - Deep Red
*/
```

- **Be careful about referring to line numbers in your comments.** Consider a comment like:

```
<!--This closes the <div> tag from line
15:-->
</div>
```

It will only be true so long as no lines are added or removed before line 15. A better approach is to refer to actual structural features that can be found using a text editor's search function:

```
<!--This closes the <div id="gallery">
tag from above:-->
</div>
```

- **Ask questions or set to-do lists for yourself or others you are working with.** Having a question or to-do item in with your source is just more convenient than having it stashed away in a notebook or an email.

```
<!--
Can someone please check the XHTML
```

```
below? It's not validating for some
reason, but I don't understand the
error output from the validator.
-->
```

- **When you update the source, update the comments.** Like all commenting practice, it can be time-consuming to update the explanation that goes with each change you make. But the long-term benefits to your sanity outweigh the inconvenience. Trust me.

Commenting Out Problem Code

Comments can also be used if you have some sort of problem with your pages, and you're trying to isolate the problem. Comments can contain source code just as easily as human-readable messages; their effect is the same: to hide the content from the browser, the validator, or any other machine reading the source:

```
p { width: 100px; /*padding: 50px;*/ }
     /*The padding is changing the width,
     so I've commented it out for
     testing purposes.*/
```

Yes, you could just delete the problem source. But by just commenting it out, you prepare for testing and possibly further revision, while keeping the Web browser from reading problem source as you test. (Although eventually, if you determine that the source you've commented out will never be revised, it's probably better if you delete it.)

NEXT STEPS

Working with your text editor is, like all aspects of Web writing and design, an ongoing process of learning. As you work on your pages and read through the remainder of this book, keep in mind the practices suggested in this chapter—particularly indenting and formatting your source, and using comments to explain to yourself what it is that you have written.

The remaining chapters in this section of the book get into the specifics of individual components of page writing and design. We will set up and inspect some basic page metadata before delving into page content and text styles. The chapter on branding will look at the headers and footers that appear on all of your pages and some interesting CSS techniques for image replacement and hiding elements. In the navigation chapter, we look at how to build a usable site navigation (you will also want to revise it as you work through the site architecture chapter, Chapter 20). The chapter on page layout brings the content, branding, and navigation elements together, and the chapters on multimedia and performance and interaction will look at ways to enhance your pages for cutting-edge devices—while still meeting the accessibility needs of all users.

CHAPTER 13

Page Metadata

Well-written XHTML pages include a variety of metadata, which is information about the contents of each of your pages. Search engine spiders, Web browsers, and even sites like Facebook and Diigo can make use of your pages' metadata, which in turn improves your site visitors' experience.

This chapter looks at essential metadata for describing the contents and construction of your site's pages; there are some additional, advanced metadata topics for sharing your content in Chapter 24.

DESCRIBING THE CONTENTS OF YOUR PAGES

As we saw in the basic rules of XHTML in Chapter 9, every page should begin with a DOCTYPE declaration; those that don't trigger what is known as quirks mode rendering in browsers. This book advocates the XHTML 1.0 Strict DOCTYPE, which is used in the RPK's XHTML files and appears at the very top of each XHTML page. (It does not, however, appear in CSS or JavaScript files; that should be obvious—but I've seen more than a few beginners put DOCTYPE declarations in their first CSS files.)

The `<html>` tag in XHTML strict should have three attributes; one, `xmlns` which specifies the XHTML namespace using the XHTML specification's URL as its value; and two tags that specify the language of the page: `xml:lang`, which newer browsers understand, and `lang`, which all browsers understand. For English-language Web pages, both of these attributes take the value of `en`. (The Library of Congress has a page that lists all of the language codes according to the two-letter ISO 639-1 and three-letter ISO 639-2 standard, if you are writing a page in a language other than English.[1] If both two-letter and three-letter codes are listed for the language you are writing in, the W3C specifies that you must use the two-letter code.[2])

So, a metadata-rich `<html>` tag opening a Web page written in English will look like:

```
<html xmlns="http://www.w3.org/1999/xhtml"
 xml:lang="en" lang="en">
```

The RPK contains one additional attribute-value pair on the `<html>` tag: a unique ID whose value should be the domain name of your Web site. For example, my Web site's domain is `karlstolley.com`; on all of my site's pages, I add a unique ID of `karlstolley-com`, replacing the dot with a hyphen, as dots are not allowed in ID or class names. So, my completed `<html>` tag looks like:

```
<html xmlns="http://www.w3.org/1999/xhtml"
 xml:lang="en" lang="en" id="karlstolley-com">
```

Adding that unique ID, known as a CSS signature,[3] on each of your pages will allow visitors to write custom CSS to change how they view your site, often by using a browser plugin such as Stylish for Firefox.[4]

THE HEAD AREA: PAGE METADATA

Although none of the content in the `<head>` area of a page is displayed in the browser viewport, the head affects the display of page content in the `<body>` area. The most important metadata to include in the `<head>` specifies the character set of your text content, the title of your pages, and the links to your site's CSS and JavaScript files.

Specifying the Content Type

Almost every kind of file, from Word documents to JPEG images, has a particular Multipurpose Internet Mail Extension, or more simply, MIME type. (Search the Web for lists of MIME types; the Web site *Webmaster Toolkit* maintains a very good list.[5]) Web servers share

MIME type information with other computers and software, such as Web browsers, so that content can be displayed correctly and by the appropriate software application.

The basic HTML MIME type is `text/html` and can be used with XHTML. (Note that in XHTML, the content type should actually be `application/xml+xhtml`; however, because certain browsers do not understand that content type, the content type must remain `text/html` for the time being.)

Your Web pages should all have a `<meta>` tag that reads:

```
<meta http-equiv="Content-Type"
 content="text/html; charset=utf-8" />
```

The other crucial value in that tag, in addition to the `text/html` MIME type, is the UTF-8, or Unicode, character set, or `charset`. Older Web editors often set a default character set of ISO-8859-1, which is a limited set of characters used by older computers (see Figure 13.1). UTF-8 is a much larger character set and lets you use fancy

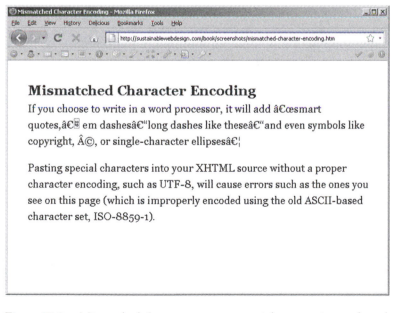

Figure 13.1. Mismatched character sets cause special punctuation marks and symbols to display as clusters of garbage characters.

typographer's quotes (instead of straight quotes), em dashes, and other character enhancements that word processors often add to text (see Figure 13.2). UTF-8 also makes it possible to write special characters from languages other than English.

MISMATCHED CHARACTER SETS

If you've ever gone to a Web site where most of the punctuation appears as question marks or empty boxes, like

```
Welcome to Jim?s Web site
```

the root of the problem is usually a mismatched character set. Specify `utf-8` as described in this chapter, and your site should not have any problems like that. See Chapter 12 for a discussion of setting your text editor to encode your text files as UTF-8 *without* the Byte Order Mark (BOM), which must be done in addition to specifying `utf-8` in your XHTML documents.

Figure 13.2. By specifying the UTF-8 character set and setting your editor to properly encode the XHTML file (UTF-8 without the Byte Order Mark, BOM), you can include text with special characters without having to use XHTML entities.

Character Entities

The XHTML specification allows for particular character entities, which a browser will display as a special character. To display a copyright symbol in the browser, for example, you could write the XHTML entity `&copy;`.

However, XHTML entities are worth avoiding for a few reasons: first, they are not easy to remember. With a good entity reference,[6] that may not be a problem. But entities may make your content less portable, particularly if you are reposting your content as an RSS feed. RSS is limited to a much smaller collection of entities; any XHTML entities beyond that collection will probably cause your feed to malfunction.

With the UTF-8 character set, you do not need to use XHTML entities except the three listed below. You can just use the character directly in your source; most word processing programs will create these characters automatically (such as typographer's quotes, or even the copyright symbol if you type `(c)`). For other characters, you can go to the character map or other listing of characters on your computer.

The only case where you must use entities is for angle brackets, which would be interpreted as part of XHTML tags, and the ampersand, because it is used to indicate the start of an entity (using the ampersand by itself with throw an error in the XHTML validator, too). These, then, are the three characters for which you must use entities:

```
&lt; to display <
&gt; to display >
&amp; to display &
```

There are also entities for straight double quotation marks, `&quot;`, and the straight apostrophe, `&apos;`. You rarely need to use those, although they are essential for use in JavaScript or in your `<meta>` tags for sharing (see Chapter 24) unless you use the typographer's (sometimes called "smart") quotation marks—along with the UTF-8 character set.

SPECIFYING A PAGE TITLE

The first piece of human-readable content on your pages is written in the `<title>` tag. The text you write there appears in the title bar on most browsers, on browser tabs (on browsers that support

tabbed browsing), and in browser bookmarks. The content of the
`<title>` tag is also the clickable link in the results list of most search
engines.

The title tag should contain both the specific title of each Web
page plus the name of your site. Which order you put them in (page
title then site, or site title then page) is a matter of personal preference. I prefer to put the unique page title first, followed by the site
name:

```
<title>Title Bar Example - Sustainable Web Design
 </title>
```

The reason for the page-before-site order is that the contents of
`<title>` tags may be shortened in browser tabs, and I prefer to
have the unique part of the page title visible, particularly if someone
were to have more than one tab opened to a page on my site. Not
that that happens with my site, but it's important to dream. (See
Figure 13.3.)

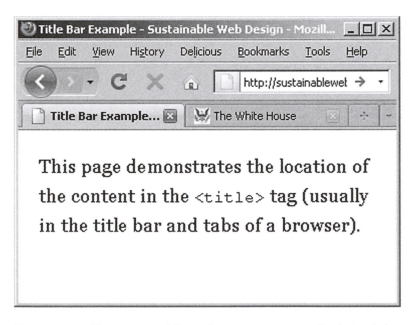

Figure 13.3.   The contents of the `<title>` tag appear in Firefox's title bar
and on the tab.

DON'T DESIGN TITLES WITH PUNCTUATION

Web writers sometimes use punctuation to visually separate the title of the page from the site name. Some symbols, such as the pipe (|), the double-angle quote (»), or sets of colons (::) can be trouble for users of screen readers, which may pronounce or describe the symbols. Writing titles with a single colon or a hyphen is a more accessible way to subdivide the portions of the content you put in the `<title>` tag.

See `http://www.webaim.org/techniques/screenreader/` for other tips on designing pages that will work with screen readers.

LINKING TO A SHORTCUT ICON OR "FAVICON"

If you find that you prefer to put a unique page title before your site name in your `<title>` tag, you run into the problem of identifying your site uniquely to someone with multiple tabs open in her browser, or with your page listed in a series of browser bookmarks. In addition to branding your pages with your site's name in the `<title>` tag, you can also specify a shortcut icon, or what's more commonly referred to as a favicon (pron. "fave icon"). A favicon is a small image that provides a branded icon for your site. These often appear in browser address bars and, more recently, on the tabs of some tabbed browsers.

It is possible to specify a favicon that is in any number of formats: the original ICO format or common image formats including GIF, JPEG, and more recently, PNG. However, Internet Explorer—even as of version 8—only displays the ICO format. (If you wish to use ICO, you may have to use some kind of conversion utility if your graphics editor will not save as `.ico`.)

When creating your favicon, it is important to save the file at 16px by 16px. However, it is difficult to design a good favicon at that size, so most Web designers will create the icon at 32px by 32px, or even 64px by 64px, and reduce the image dimensions down to 16px by 16px. Both 32px and 64px work well because they are multiples of 16, which means that their reduction down to 16px will be clear and crisp.

While it is possible to store favicons in a default location and in a default format that will be picked up by some Web browsers, my preference is to specify the location explicitly in the link tag. Favicons are important enough to site branding that I prefer not to leave their appearance to default browser behaviors and therefore to chance. So to explicitly state the location and type of your favicon, your `<head>` should include the full URL to your icon in a `<link>` tag:

```
<link rel=" icon" href="http://example.com/
  favicon.png" type="image/png" />
<!--For Internet Explorer; no type must be specified-->
<link rel="shortcut icon" href="http://example.com/
  favicon.ico" />
```

If you opt to use PNG or another format, it must have the proper MIME type associated with it, e.g., `image/gif` for GIF files.

LINKING TO CSS AND JAVASCRIPT FILES

XHTML pages are only the structured content of your site. To design and enhance XHTML pages with CSS and JavaScript, you must use XHTML to refer to your CSS and JavaScript. The `<head>` area of your XHTML pages provides two different methods for enhancing your site with CSS and JavaScript.

One method is to use the `<script>` tag for JavaScript and the `<style>` tag for CSS in the `<head>` area of your Web pages. Those allow you to write JavaScript or CSS code directly in your XHTML file. Although that method can be helpful for quick drafts and tests, it traps the CSS and JavaScript in individual XHTML files. That method therefore fails to scale with your site—and makes revisions to design and scripting more time-consuming and repetitive.

A better method (and the one advised in this book) is to keep your JavaScript and CSS in separate files, and link to them from the `<head>` area of each of your XHTML pages. There are two important advantages to linking to JavaScript and CSS files:

- Changes to a shared `.js` or `.css` file will be reflected across your entire site; this keeps pages uniform and revisions to your design a simpler activity than if you write the same JavaScript or CSS in each XHTML page.
- By sharing the same set of `.js` and `.css` files across your pages, your site visitors' Web browsers only have to download each

file once, no matter how many pages on your site they view. Once the `.js` or `.css` file has been downloaded, the browser caches the file—meaning it makes a copy on the visitor's computer. That speeds up the performance of your site, because only the XHTML and content of subsequent pages have to be downloaded. On slow Internet connections or mobile devices, shared design and scripting files dramatically improve your site's performance.

However, even though the concept behind linking to CSS and JavaScript files is the same, they each use different XHTML.

Linking to CSS

Links to CSS are created using the self-closing `<link />` tag with some special attributes: `rel="stylesheet"` tells the browser the link is to a style sheet and `type="text/css"` specifies that the style sheet contains CSS instructions (and yes, `text/css` is the MIME type for CSS). The `href` attribute points to the style sheet's location, while the `media` attribute allows you to specify whether the style sheet is for the screen, for printing, or other formats. A complete link to a style sheet for screen design looks something like:

```
<link rel="stylesheet" type="text/css"
 href="/css/style.css" media="screen" />
```

Note that you can load multiple style sheets on a single XHTML page just by adding additional link tags in the `<head>`; for example, the Rapid Prototyping Kit (RPK) loads three different style sheets for the screen using this method (see Chapter 11).

Linking to JavaScript

Linking to JavaScript files is done using the `<script>` tag (as with the on-page method of writing JavaScript described above). However, when linking to external scripts, the `<script>` tag opens and closes but remains empty. Like the `<link />` tag for CSS, it is essential to tell browsers what type of script you're linking to. In one of the little idiosyncrasies of XHTML, however, to link to the script, you must use the `src` (source) attribute instead of `href`:

```
<script type="text/javascript" src="/js/site.js">
</script>
```

Again, note that there are opening and closing tags for `<script>`, even though they surround no content.

THE BODY TAG

One last piece of valuable metadata is a class on the `<body>` tag, which holds all of the visible content of your page. A class on the body tag gives you an extra structural hook to design pages in major parts of your site differently.

For example, on the home page of a site, you could add a class of home or overview: `<body class="home">`. Then, if there were something special that you wanted to do stylistically, such as present a larger branding header on the home page, your CSS can use the home class as a hook (see Chapter 14):

```
div#header { /*Styles for header on all pages*/ }
body.home div#header { /*Styles for header on the
  home page*/ }
```

You can also use the different elements from the navigation as classes for other site pages. For example, a resume page would probably be linked from a Resume item in the site navigation; that page could take `<body class="resume">`; if your site has a portfolio area, all of those pages could take `<body class="portfolio">`. Chapter 15 notes that you can even use body classes as part of wayfinding (see Chapter 7) by styling the navigation according to which area of your site a user is viewing.

Chapter 19 will also show how JavaScript can automatically add additional classes on the `<body>` tag; the RPK adds a hasjs class to `<body>` if a user has JavaScript enabled:

```
body { /*Body styles for all CSS-enabled users*/ }
body.hasjs { /*Body styles for CSS- and JavaScript-
  enabled users*/ }
```

You can also use JavaScript to add other classes for users viewing sites on wide screens; that class can be yet another selector in CSS that enables you to style your page to take advantage of wide screens or other viewing conditions. Remember, though, that it's always best practice to design your pages to be accessible and usable without JavaScript. Once you have done that, you can go back and progressively enhance your pages, so long as they degrade gracefully (see Chapter 6).

NEXT STEPS

This chapter has covered some of the basic metadata that should appear in your XHTML's <head> area, as well as a class on the <body> tag.; Chapter 24 looks at a few additional things to place in the <head> to make your content easier to share. In the next chapter, though, we will get to writing something more interesting: the visible content of your pages, beginning with the branding shared across all of your pages.

NOTES

1. Library of Congress, "Codes for the Representation of Names of Languages," http://www.loc.gov/standards/iso639-2/php/English_list.php

2. W3C, "Language Tags in HTML and XML," http://www.w3.org/International/articles/language-tags/RFC3066.html

3. Eric A. Meyer, "CSS Signatures" (September 28, 2002), http://archivist.incutio.com/viewlist/css-discuss/13291

4. Jason Barnabe, "Stylish," *Add-ons for Firefox*, https://addons.mozilla.org/en-US/firefox/addon/2108

5. Webmaster Toolkit, "MIME Types," http://www.webmaster-toolkit.com/mime-types.shtml

6. Elizabeth Castro, "Character Entity References in HTML 4 and XHTML 1.0," *HTML, XHTML, and CSS*, 6th ed. (2002), http://www.elizabethcastro.com/html/extras/entities.html

CHAPTER 14

Page Branding

Branding identifies a page as belonging to your site. Although branding is usually associated with logos and color schemes, the branding of Web pages also depends on the structure and design of the whole page, including headers and footers that are consistent from page to page. Navigation (covered in the next chapter) also plays a role in branding, both visually and by representing your site as having a sensible, usable architecture.

The terms "header" and "footer" come from print design, where they typically refer to the very top (header) and bottom (footer) of a page. However, while structurally your header appears at the beginning of your XHTML source and the footer at the end, CSS enables you to create page designs that display the header and footer in other places.

Regardless of their location on a designed page, the header and footer serve important and unique branding functions:

- **The header** is the place to provide a consistent label for your pages, usually by writing your site name in an <h1> tag. The header is also a place to offer a logo or logotype (your site's name presented in a unique font, perhaps as an image) and to have that logo link back to the home page of your site. Most sites also clarify their purpose to visitors by including a short description of the site, also known as a tagline. Finally, to aid accessibility, the header should provide a list of links for visitors using devices with limited or no visual display to skip to the navigation and perhaps other areas of your pages. These links make the page more accessible on mobile and assistive devices, but might be hidden from view on fully graphical browsers.

- **The footer** often features site credits and perhaps a link to a Creative Commons license, which makes it easier (and legal) for people to share and reuse your content, and therefore build your reputation and identity across the Web (see Chapter 24). The footer may also be used to provide links to validate your XTHML and CSS and perhaps to promote any libraries or software you use to create and maintain your site.

For strong branding, your header and footer should be structurally and perhaps visually identical across all of your pages. Some Web pages may have CSS that presents a more prominent header area, such as on the home page of a site. But it's generally a good practice to design most, if not all, pages' headers and footers the same.

THE HEADER

The most basic page header will include the title of the site, a description or tagline, and accessibility links for jumping to different areas on the page.

```
<div id="header">
 <h1>
  <a href="http://example.com/" rel="home">Site
   Title</a>
 </h1>
 <p class="tagline">Site Description</p>
 <ul class="accessibility">
  <li><a href="#navigation">Jump to Navigation</a>
  </li>
  <li><a href="#content">Jump to Content</a></li>
 </ul>
</div>
```

In the Rapid Prototyping Kit, the header appears in `<div id="header">`, which is the first major structural unit of the XHTML source inside the `<body>` and `<div id="page">` tags.

Site Title

The site title belongs in an `<h1>` tag and should probably be the only use of the `<h1>` tag on your site. For all other headings, use `<h2>`, and `<h3>` for subheadings (see Chapter 16). If you are building a site to promote yourself, your name is a great choice for a site title.

However, if you are primarily running a blog on your site, you might use the title you've given to your blog (see Chapter 22). If you're creating a page for a business, club, or other organization, then use that name for the site title. It's unnecessary to add obvious phrases like "Home Page of . . ." or "Web site for . . ." to the site title.

Placing your name or that of your organization or business in a heading-one tag may also help your rankings on Google searches for your name or organization. The site title in the header area complements the `<title>` tags in your pages' `<head>` area, while adding a visible title on your page, too.

In addition to the `<h1>` tag, it's an established convention on the Web to also link the text of the site title to the home page of your site. Usually, this link will include the full URL to your home page. Anyone who wants to return to your home page can simply click on your site title in the branding area. So for example, on my Web site, I have:

```
<h1><a href="http://karlstolley.com/">Karl Stolley
  </a></h1>
```

This is one of the only cases where writing a link with your full site URL is necessary, as it lets you do some unique things with your site title, such as add additional information about its home page. For example, you can use the rel-home microformat to indicate that the link on your site title points to your home page:[1]

MICROFORMATS

XHTML describes the structure of content, but XHTML on its own has no capacity for expressing the *meaning* of content. For example, a link to a Creative Commons license is indistinguishable from any other kind of link that appears in `<a href=" ">`.

Microformats change that. A link to a Creative Commons license can include `rel="license"` in the `<a>` tag, indicating to search engines and computers that understand the rel-license microformat that the link not only takes someone to another destination, but that it actually means that the page where the link appears is licensed under a specific Creative Commons license.

You can learn about many other types of microformats at Microformats.org.

```
<h1><a href="http://karlstolley.com/" rel="home">
Karl Stolley</a></h1>
```

Site Description or Tagline

A tagline briefly conveys your site's content or purpose to visitors. Whether you're building a personal or professional site for yourself or a site to promote your club, a tagline is useful to include. It may even help you clarify your own sense of purpose and guide how you select and organize appropriate content for your site.

The RPK suggests writing the tagline inside of a paragraph tag with a class of `tagline`, `<p class="tagline">`, in the header area of your XHTML document.

On personal sites, the tagline should be a description of you: "Professional photographer in Seattle, Washington"; "Engineering student at State University"; "Salt water aquarium enthusiast and consultant." A professional site may instead use your job title as the tagline: "Associate Mechanical Engineer at High Tech, Inc."; "Assistant to the regional manager for Dunder-Mifflin, Inc." Be wary, though, about including your company name: some companies have restrictive policies about employee Web sites, not to mention that a search on the company name may return your site. If those are concerns, or if you are using your site to support your job search, consider describing your line of work or expertise, rather than your job title and company.

For blog sites, a tagline can clarify the purpose and content of the blog: "Tracking news and views of interest to greater Chicagoland area residents"; "Fishing tips and tricks for the weekend warrior"; "A blog about knitting for fun and profit."

Business and organizational Web sites might describe their business/organization and clientèle or membership: "Serving the insurance needs of Northern Wisconsin"; "An online community for sharing the best barbecue recipes"; "The official computer club for students at Big Brain University."

Accessibility Links

Because the RPK places the site navigation in the list `<ul id="navigation">` (see Chapter 15) and page content in `<div id="content">` (see Chapter 16), the accessibility links in the RPK header point to #navigation and #content. Those links, known as fragment identifiers, allow mouseless users (such as people on mobile phones) as well as users relying on screen readers to quickly jump to different areas of your page—without having to scroll through or to listen to unnecessary information.

One of the features of unique IDs is that you can reference them in URLs that instruct Web browsers to automatically scroll to a specific part of the page. So, for example, if you have your navigation marked with id="navigation", the URL http://example.com/home .htm#navigation will instruct a Web browser to scroll to that portion of the page (see Figures 14.1 and 14.2).

STYLING THE HEADER

Even with the simple contents of a site title and tagline, you can design your page header to spark visual interest in your page and visually establish strong branding. As Chapter 17 will show, page elements are usually best designed together, echoing and reflecting one another, but here are some simple styling techniques that you can try

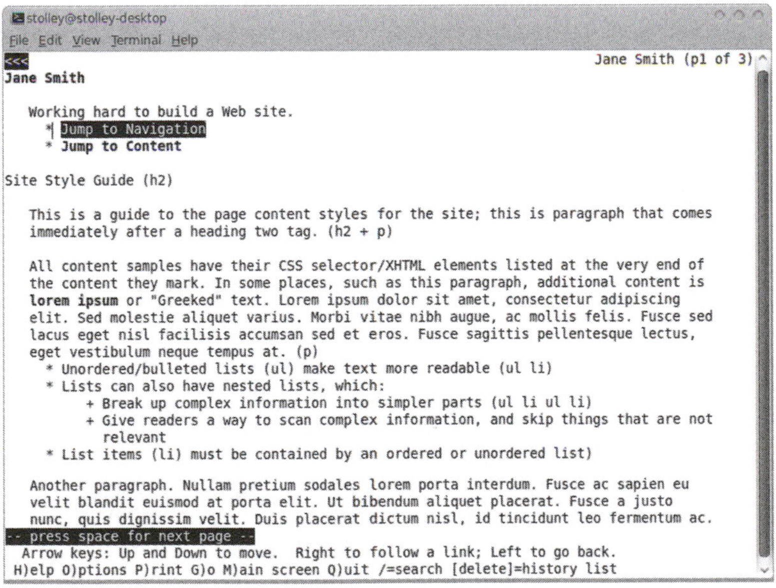

Figure 14.1. Accessibility links are important in mouseless, text-only environments, as in this view of a page as displayed in Lynx.

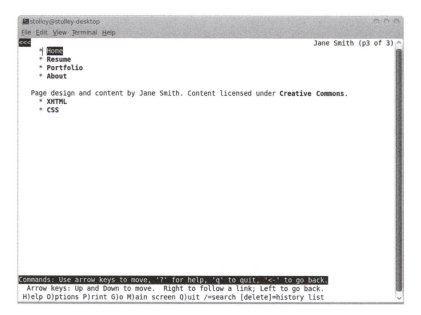

Figure 14.2. Activating the "Jump to Navigation" link takes Lynx users straight to the navigation.

out as you learn to design with CSS while you craft the branding for your site.

Styling the Accessibility Links

The first thing to do in styling any part of your pages is to hide anything you don't wish to appear for users of graphical browsers, such as accessibility links (see Figure 14.3), which you can hide from view with a little CSS in your `screen.css` file.

One method to hide the links is to use `display: none;`:

```
ul.accessibility { display: none; }
```

The trouble with that method is that `display: none;` may also hide the links from screen readers. An alternative method to hide the accessibility links from screen view (while keeping them accessible to screen readers) is to position the accessibility links absolutely, which removes them from the document flow (see Figure 14.4; Chapter 17 provides additional discussion of document flow). Then, setting the `left:` property to an extremely large negative pixel value basically

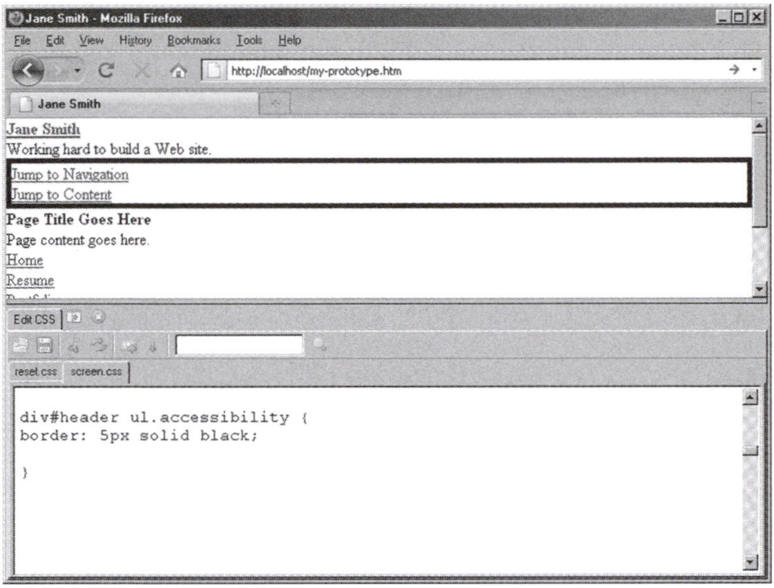

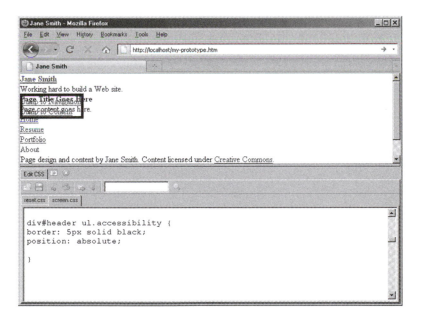

Figure 14.3. The accessibility navigation is outlined here in black, just to show the space that it fills by default.

Figure 14.4. Positioned absolutely, the accessibility link area shrinks to fit the text of the links, and the rest of the page jumps up to where the accessibility links were.

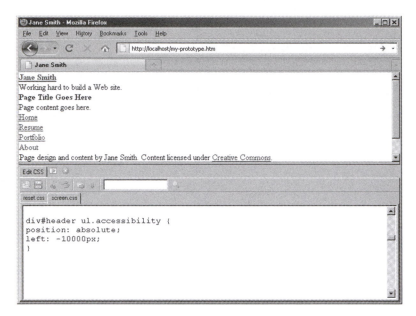

Figure 14.5. A large negative left value effectively hides the accessibility navigation from view and does not affect the remaining visible page elements.

moves the accessibility links way off to the left of the screen, hiding them from view (see Figure 14.5):

```
ul.accessibility {
  position: absolute;     /*Remove from document flow
                          and prepare for positioning*/

  left: -10000px;         /*Move way off to left;
                          browser will not create a
                          horizontal scroll bar*/

}
```

Styling the Whole Header Area

The `<div id="header">` tag that contains your site title and tagline provides a block for styling the overall look of your header. Adding a border on the bottom of `div#header`, for example,

```
div#header { border-bottom: 5px solid black; }
```

is a very basic way to add the smallest bit of visual interest, while distinguishing the header from the rest of your page (see Figure 14.6).

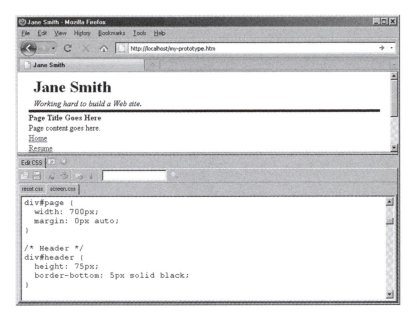

Figure 14.6. Adding a border to the header adds a bit of visual interest and distinguishes the header from the rest of the page.

You might echo this simple design choice by adding a border to the top of the footer area, as described below.

Another simple design choice is to specify a background color on `div#header` and, if needed, a contrasting color on the text:

```
div#header {
 background-color: #000; /*Set the background to
  black*/
 color: #FFF; /*Set the text to white*/
}
```

As you can see in Figure 14.7, because no specific background color has been set on the site title or tagline, they appear as transparent—sharing the black background set on `div#header`.

There is nothing wrong with using borders and background colors to design a basic header; but sites that want to establish an even more unique design often employ background images, which behave very similarly to background colors in that descendant elements (like the site title and tagline in the header) appear to have transparent backgrounds. Figure 14.8 shows the header with a simple background image

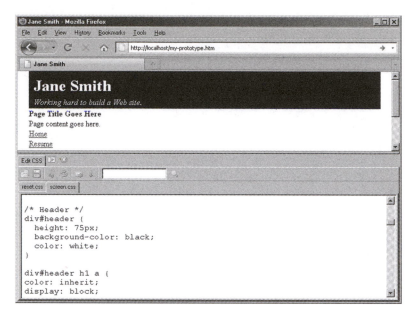

Figure 14.7. A background color on the header appears to be shared by the site title and tagline, which are transparent (unless assigned their own background color).

that is only a few pixels wide, but that is tiled horizontally to fill the entire width of the header, e.g.,

```
div#header {
 background-image: url('gfx/header-tiled-
  background.png'); /*Load the image*/
 background-repeat: repeat-x; /*Tile the image
  horizontally only*/
 background-position: bottom left; /*Always show the
  image at the very bottom*/
 background-color: black; /*Background color in case
  image is ever broken*/
 color: white; /*Text color set to white;*/
}
```

Even more complex effects can be achieved by designing background images that anticipate other content areas; as of CSS 2.1, only one background image can be attached per XHTML element, so to have, for

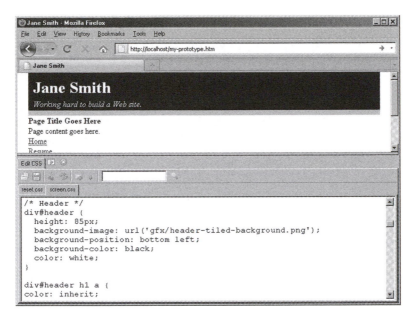

Figure 14.8. The border at the bottom of this version of the header is achieved by tiling a background image horizontally. In Chapter 17, it will be clear why this is done with an image, rather than a CSS border property.

example, a unique top and bottom image on the content area, use other elements and some of the CSS positioning tricks discussed in Chapter 17.

Styling the Site Title

Because the site title is usually a link, it will appear the same as all other links on the page. This is usually not desirable, particularly if your links are just blue and underlined. Using its structure as a child of h1 inside of #header, you might write:

```
div#header h1 a {
 color: inherit; /*Share the color set to the rest
  of #header*/
 text-decoration: none; /*No underline*/
}
```

Then, to size the text to appear larger, just work with the h1 descendant selector of div#header:

```
div#header h1 { font-size: 200%; }
```

Figures 14.6 and 14.7 show those styles as they appear on the site title.

Of course, with something as unique and important as the site title, simple styles like this are often not enough to uniquely and memorably brand your pages. To add a logo or logotype, you can use one of a number of CSS image replacement techniques.

What image replacement does is use CSS to set a background image on an XHTML element together with some method of hiding the XHTML text from view. One way to do this is to load the image in CSS, set height and width of the XHTML element it's loaded on to match the image (in the RPK's case, using the `div#header h1 a` selector, so that the image is clickable), and then set the CSS `text-indent` property to a large negative number to effectively pull the text off the screen (see Figure 14.9). That approach should keep the text accessible to screen readers. For example,

```
div#header h1 a {
  background-image: url('gfx/logotype.png');
  background-repeat: no-repeat; /*Don't tile*/
  display: block; /*Show anchor as a block*/
  text-indent: -10000px; /*Pull text off of screen*/
}
```

CSS IMAGE REPLACEMENT

CSS provides an alternative to loading images with the XHTML `<img />` tag. When an image is part of your content, that is, if you use it in the sense of "Have a look at this picture of something" and would have it appear in all cases—including when your page is printed—the `<img />` tag is your best choice.

But when an image is a part of your design, it's generally better to use `background-image:` or the shorthand `background:` property to have CSS load your image as the background of one of your XHTML elements.

Dave Shea, of CSS Zen Garden fame, maintains an exhaustive list of image replacement techniques at `http://www.mezzoblue.com/tests/revised-image-replacement/` that show the many ways you can replace XHTML text with images.

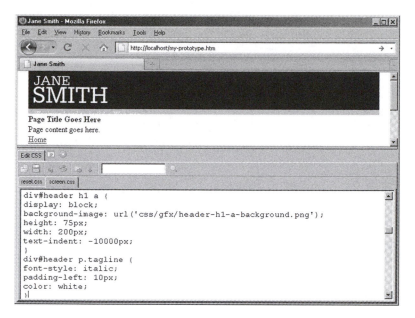

Figure 14.9. Image replacement on the site title; a large negative text indent pulls the XHTML text off of the screen, leaving the background image unobstructed. Note the tagline text running along the bottom; it will be fixed in the next section.

Styling the Tagline

In the RPK, the tagline is the only paragraph inside of div#header, although it also includes a tagline class. You can style it as you would any other paragraph text (see Chapter 16); in Figure 14.10, it has been run in italics. Figure 14.10 also shows the tagline styled using a left margin to suggest a second column adjacent to the image-replaced header.

You might also hide the paragraph from view, using the method for the accessibility links above, and include the tagline text as part of your header image.

THE FOOTER

Closing out the RPK's branding XHTML is <div id="footer">.

```
<div id="footer">
 <p class="credits">
 Site information, credits, license.
 </p>
```

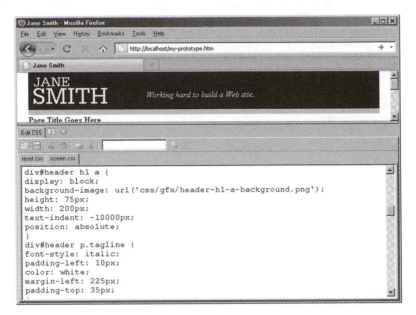

Figure 14.10.   Adjusting the left margin and top padding on the site tagline gives it a more prominent place in the header.

```
<!--These links only work on live,
web-available sites:-->
<ul class="validators">
 <li><a href="http://validator.w3.org/check?
   uri=referer" title="Validate this page's
   XHTML">XHTML</a></li>
 <li><a href="http://jigsaw.w3.org/css-validator/
   check/referer" title="Validate this page's CSS">
   CSS</a></li>
 </ul>
</div>
```

It's useful to include information in your footer about the design and content of your pages. A line such as "Page design and content by Jane Smith." may be added. If you wish to allow others to use your content or design, you can also add a link to a particular Creative Commons license (see Chapter 24). For information about copyright statements, you should read Chapter 4 of Title 17 of the *United States Code*[2] and

VALIDATE WHILE YOU WORK

The RPK includes validation links for XHTML and CSS, although note that these only work when your pages are posted to a live URL on the Web (they will not work in a localhost environment, in other words). Before you post your site and as you revise, use the Validate By File Upload feature at `http://validator.w3.org/` for XHTML and `http://jigsaw.w3.org/css-validator/` for CSS.

Alternatively, Pederick's Web Developer Add-on for Firefox will upload your files for you; choose to Validate Local CSS or Validate Local HTML in the Tools menu.

For information about handling validator errors that you encounter, see Chapter 16 and this book's companion site, `http://sustainablewebdesign.com/book/`.

Chapter 37 of the *Code of Federal Regulations*[3] and consult with a lawyer for additional details.

STYLING THE FOOTER

A simple way to style the footer is to make it the inverse of your header: in the border-only example from above, you might just put a `border-top: 1px solid black` style on your `div#footer`. You can even reuse your header image and flip it upside down in your image editor, and reuse it on the footer (see Figure 14.11).

Styling the Site Credits

You can style your site credits however you would like, of course; one suggestion is to style it as a kind of fine print, which might echo the tagline styling of your site.

If you choose to license your content under Creative Commons, you can choose from a number of images that Creative Commons provides for showing that your content is licensed. These images can be loaded either in your CSS or in an XHTML image tag; the benefit

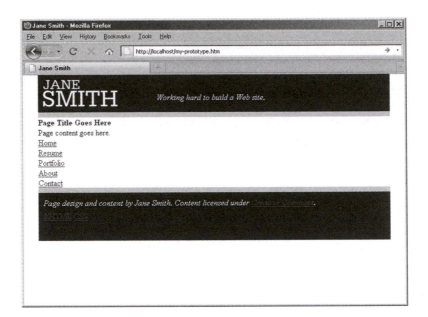

Figure 14.11. Reusing the border image from the header ties the page together nicely.

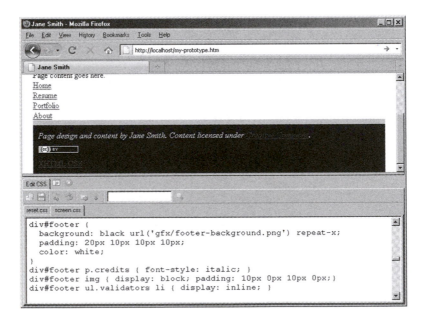

Figure 14.12. The Creative Commons license image is loaded in XHTML's image tag, but CSS controls its presentation by displaying it as a block on its own line.

of opting for an image tag is that the image will print along with your content (by default, background images will not print—and some browsers do not allow background image printing at all). A printed license icon would help clarify how your content is licensed, even in paper form.

Even when images are loaded in XHTML, CSS allows you to control their position with respect to other elements. In Figure 14.12, the comparatively large CC license icon is offset from the rest of the footer content using a little bit of CSS (see Chapter 17).

NEXT STEPS

Once you have written your header and footer, save your `my-proto type.htm` file and `screen.css` if you've also written styles for your work so far. The content and structure of your header and footer should remain more or less the same across all of your pages, although you can use a class on the `<body>` tag, as Chapter 13 suggested, as a hook to style any differences on particular pages. The next chapter will cover another piece of content that should be consistent from page to page across your site: the navigation.

NOTES

1. Microformats.org, "rel-home," http://microformats.org/wiki/rel-home
2. *Copyrights, U.S. Code* 28, §§ 401 et seq.
3. "Patents, Trademarks, and Copyrights," *Code of Federal Regulations*, title 37, § 202.2.

CHAPTER 15

Navigation

Navigation is a key feature found on almost every Web site. Although structurally it is nothing more than a list of links, site navigation can be designed many ways so long as it simplifies how users move around the different areas of your site. And even if users do not click on every item in your navigation, it should still give them a sense of what your site contains and how its contents are organized. It can also contribute to wayfinding, by highlighting the navigation element that represents the section of the site a user is currently viewing. While it may be tempting to build a navigation that includes a link to every single page on your site, if you have too many items in your navigation, it may become less usable for your users.

One way to begin thinking about the design of your navigation area is to compare a Web site's navigation to the signs over the aisles at your local supermarket. Supermarkets don't list every single item for sale in the aisle, but rather general types of items (soup, pasta) or categories of items (cleaning supplies, baking). If the signs *did* list every single item, it would probably take shoppers longer to read all of the signs in the store than it would to walk the aisles, one by one.

But there is another important lesson about navigation that can be learned from supermarkets: signage on their aisles probably does not do much to entice shoppers to buy things. Neither do navigation areas encourage visitors to explore your Web site. To get people to shop beyond their lists or habits, supermarkets often feature sale displays at the end of aisles and even place staple groceries, such as milk, at the very back of the store. It's important to complement your site's navigation area with features like promotional sidebars to encourage exploration; even a well-designed navigation area may not be enough to interest all visitors to look around.

STRUCTURING AND NAMING YOUR NAVIGATION ITEMS

As Chapter 20 urges, sites should strive for a shallow architecture, which can be complemented by a corresponding simple navigation area that suggests how your site is organized and what kinds of content the site includes (rather than a massive navigation area with links to every single page).

There are two basic challenges to writing and designing your site navigation. The first challenge is to come up with brief labels for each item, considering how the navigation as a whole represents the content on your site. The second challenge is to develop a visual design that is easy for users to scan with their eyes and that does not take a lot of fine-grained effort to click on.

In XHTML, site navigation is nothing more than a list of links. That is exactly how you would write your navigation in XHTML, regardless of how you want it to appear. Yes, by default, lists display vertically, but with CSS, you can design the lists to display horizontally, too, as we'll see below.

The XHTML for a very basic navigation area for a personal site might look something like this:

```
<ul id="navigation">
 <li><a id="nav-home" href="/">Home</a></li>
 <li><a id="nav-resume"
  href="/resume.htm">Resume</a></li>
 <li><a id="nav-portfolio"
  href="/portfolio.htm">Portfolio</a></li>
 <li><a id="nav-about"
  href="/about.htm">About</a></li>
 <li><a id="nav-contact"
  href="/contact.htm">Contact</a></li>
</ul>
```

Note that in that example, with the exception of Home, the navigation labels match the file names in the links. Navigation item labels that match your file names will help keep your navigation manageable as you build your site. But they will also inspire your visitors' confidence that the label in the navigation is reflective of the page it links to. The anchor tags in the navigation also have unique IDs that match the labels but are prefixed with `nav-`. Those will be used with the CSS to enhance wayfinding in conjunction with classes on the `<body>`, which Chapter 14 suggested including.

Whenever I design Web sites, I make it a personal challenge to try and develop single-word navigation labels. Single words are easier to style, particularly in horizontal navigation areas, because you can pack navigation items closer together. Navigation labels with multiple words necessarily have spaces between the words, so the space between individual navigation items must be noticeably larger.

Sometimes multiple words are unavoidable. But it's always possible to avoid pronouns that often appear in navigation items, such as

ONE NAVIGATION AREA IS ENOUGH

I've sometimes seen my Web design students replicate their navigation at the top and the bottom of every page. They seem to do this especially if their pages get really long.

One navigation area is enough, though. One could even argue that two navigation areas, particularly if they contain a lot of items, may confuse users, who may not immediately understand that both navigation areas contain the same items.

If you are concerned that scrolling up to your navigation will be a problem for your visitors, add an anchor link to the end of your content that scrolls to the navigation of your page (e.g., if your navigation is at the top, `<a href="#navigation">Back to Top</a>`, or `<a href="#page">` to take people to the very top of the page, if you use `<div id="page">`, as in the RPK). However, if your pages are getting so long that you feel it necessary to include a link that scrolls back to the top, it might be time to revise your page for length—or split its content up over multiple pages.

"my," "us," "our," and so on. "My Resume" is redundant, if it's your resume on your site; "Resume" will suffice. For groups and businesses, "About" and "Contact" will imply an "us," making "Contact Us" similarly redundant.

For a personal Web site, navigation might include links to key pages, such as a resume, a portfolio of work, an about/biography page, and perhaps a page of contact information. And in addition to a home page link on your logo or branding (see the previous chapter), it's never a bad idea to include a navigation link to the main page of your site. Whether you label this "Home," "Overview," or "Main" is up to you, but "Home" is short and sweet and something of a convention on the Web.

Business Web sites will want to include their core products or services in the navigation, as well as an About and Contact page. Contact pages on business sites are not just for new or potential customers, but also for current customers who may have some sort of issue that needs to be resolved. Make it easy for all customers to contact you by placing a link right in the navigation—rather than off of a page deeper in the site.

DESIGNING THE LOOK AND FEEL OF YOUR NAVIGATION

Another challenge is designing the visual look and feel of your navigation, including whether you will design a vertical menu or a tabbed/horizontal navigation bar. Even though an unordered list displays vertically by default, with a little CSS, you can design your navigation to appear horizontally, perhaps mimicking a set of tabs.

Maximizing the Clickable Area

Regardless of whether your navigation will be designed horizontally or vertically, it's always important to maximize the clickable area of your individual navigation items.

By default, the anchor tag only makes clickable the actual text in the link. If you stick with single-word navigation items, that reduces the total area that is clickable and makes clicking on a link an unnecessarily delicate action. It's not uncommon to see Web sites that have navigation like that in Figure 15.1, where there is a large box with a comparatively small clickable area for each item.

POP-UP NAVIGATION: JUST SAY NO

It's far easier for users to browse with their eyes than their mice. Pop-up navigation—that is, navigation that reveals additional items on a mouse over—may seem to be a great choice on the surface: present basic categories of navigation, and when those categories are clicked on or hovered over, show more options. The problem is, that makes the work of browsing a page more labor-intensive; people generally don't mind scanning with their eyes, but requiring a mouse is probably a bit much to ask—and may make your navigation inaccessible to mouseless users. That includes users of the Apple iPad and other touch screens.

Furthermore, you have entire pages to engage people's attention; an overly complex navigation may keep users focused on only one small (and uninteresting) part of your pages.

By increasing the padding on anchor tags (and by displaying anchor tags as blocks rather than their default inline display), it is possible to create much larger clickable areas:

```
ul#navigation li a {
     display: block; /*Treat links as blocks*/
     padding: 20px; /*Padding is also clickable*/
     background-color: gray;
}
```

Larger clickable areas make using your site navigation less labor-intensive for visitors, because they can be much sloppier with their clicking. In Figure 15.2, you can see that hovering the mouse changes the entire box's color.

That change in background color is achieved with the :hover pseudo-class; by adding the :focus pseudo-class to your selector, the hover effect should be visible for keyboard users tabbing from link to link, too:

```
ul#navigation li a:hover,
ul#navigation li a:focus {
     background-color: white;
}
```

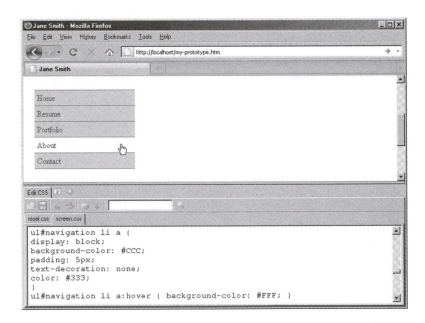

Figure 15.1. Even though there is a generous box for each navigation item, only the text is clickable.

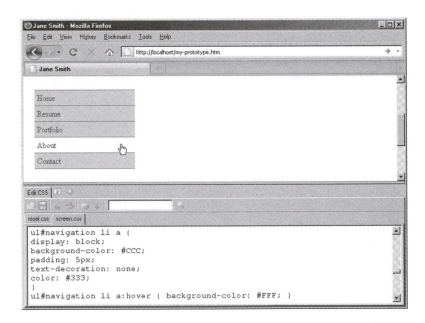

Figure 15.2. Using CSS, each navigation item has a much larger clickable area, and is therefore much more permissive in terms of where users can click.

EASY ON THE :HOVER STYLES

Don't go crazy adding a lot of styles to the `:hover` selector. Mouse pointers already change over links, so there is already some indication that an element is clickable.

At the same time, hover properties are helpful in two situations. The first is when clickable elements are very close to one another, such as in a navigation bar; a hover effect can clarify which navigation item will actually be activated upon clicking. The second is when someone is using a keyboard to navigate links, and therefore does not benefit from a pointer that changes to indicate whether an item is clickable. (Some browsers will provide a dotted border to indicate clickable items for keyboard users, but the border is sometimes difficult to see.)

Hover properties that change text or background colors generally work well, as do hovers that change background images by altering the `background-position:` property (see the book's companion Web site, `http://sustainablewebdesign.com/book/`).

What you should avoid at all costs are hover properties that change the size or width of contextual link text or navigation elements; this includes not just font sizes, but bold and italics as well as border widths, padding, and margins. Those shifts may cause all of your page content to jump around, particularly for contextual links in your site's content.

Wayfinding Made Simple

If you include a class on the <body> tag for different pages or areas of your site, such as home, about, and resume, and if you put a unique ID on each link in your navigation, you can use descendent selectors to style the link in the navigation that matches that area of the site. You will often see Web sites that duplicate the hover/focus state of their navigation as the normal link state for the link on a given page. In other words, the "About" link in the navigation appears styled on the "About" page the way it appears when hovered over on other pages.

Adding to the hover/focus styles above, your CSS can include a style declaration like this:

```
ul#navigation li a:hover,
ul#navigation li a:focus,
```

```
body.home ul#navigation li a#nav-home,
body.about ul#navigation li a#nav-about,
body.resume ul#navigation li a#nav-resume {
      background-color: white;
}
```

The links in that navigation will still have a white background when moused over or focused via the keyboard. But on the home page, the link to home in the navigation will always have a white background; on the about page, the about link's background will be white, and on the resume page, the resume link's background will be white. In each case, the design simply tells users "You are here" through a tiny visual enhancement, using bits of XHTML structure that are already in place.

You can see this technique in action on the navigation at this book's companion site, `http://sustainablewebdesign.com/book/`.

Designing Vertical Navigation

Vertical navigation can easily accommodate an expanding navigation area—whether the navigation expands by the addition of more items or if a visitor wants to increase the size of the text on your site.

Because the RPK suggests that you structure your navigation as an unordered list, items display vertically by default; your design tasks—other than maximizing the clickable area as described above—are mostly about integrating the navigation with the rest of your design, a topic that is covered in Chapter 17.

Designing Horizontal Navigation

It is not uncommon to encounter Web sites that present navigation as a horizontal bar or set of tabs. For sites with only a few navigation items, a horizontal navigation can be ideal—particularly on designs that need to have content areas as wide as possible (such as photography portfolios) and therefore can't spare the horizontal space that a vertical navigation would occupy.

The limitation to horizontal navigation is that it can only contain a few items before it becomes confusing: it's generally easier to scan a vertical list of items than a horizontal one. And running horizontal navigation onto a second line is usually disastrous: readers don't know whether to move their eyes horizontally or vertically, and they may wonder whether the items in the second line of navigation are less important.

If you only have a few navigation elements, say three or four, and they all use very short words, they will display nicely horizontally, on a single line. But if you wish to add many more navigation elements, a second line may becomes necessary—and will take a visitor even longer to scan.

There are a number of methods for displaying list items in a horizontal line; the simplest and most flexible is to use floats. When an element floats in CSS, it remains part of the document flow, but allows other elements to appear next to it horizontally. By floating all of the items in a navigation list and maximizing the clickable area, a simple horizontal navigation can be built in CSS like this:

```
/*Horizontal Navigation, Float Method, Automatic
Width*/
ul#navigation {
      overflow: hidden; /*Necessary style for best
       handling floats*/
}

ul#navigation li {
      float: left; /*Float items to the left*/
      display: inline; /*Fix a float issue in older
       IE browsers*/
      margin-right: 5px; /*Put some space between
       items*/
}

ul#navigation li a {
      display: block; /*Maximize clickable area*/
      padding: 5px 10px 5px 10px; /*Generous padding
       on top and bottom, less on right and left*/
      background-color: #CCC; /*Background color for
       the items*/
}
```

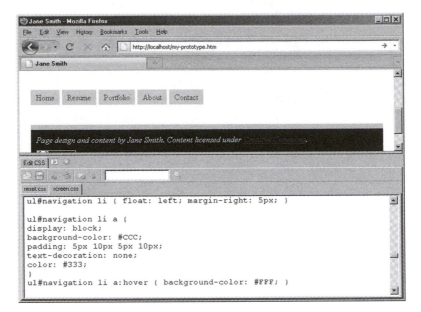

Figure 15.3. A horizontal navigation bar with buttons of different widths, depending on the length of the label text.

That particular method will create items or buttons (as they appear) of varying width, depending on how long the name of the label is (Figure 15.3). For uniformly sized clickable areas, one can adjust the example above by adding a fixed width to the `ul#navigation li` selector (see the rendering in Figure 15.4):

```
/*Horizontal Navigation, Float Method, Fixed With*/
ul#navigation li {
        width: 100px; /*All buttons 100px wide*/
        float: left;
        display: inline;
        margin-right: 5px;
}
```

By adding `text-align: center;` to the style declaration for `ul#navigation li`, you can regain the centered-text appearance of the variable-width buttons from Figure 15.3, as in Figure 15.5

One word of caution regarding floated, horizontal lists, though: if your layout is flexible, or if someone increases the text size on a page,

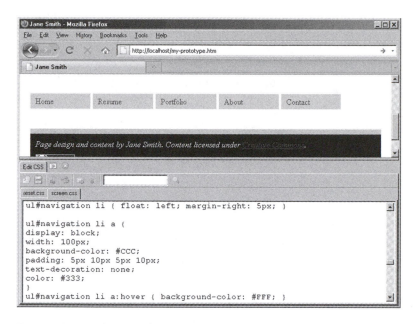

Figure 15.4. A horizontal navigation bar with buttons of the same width, and the text aligned left by default.

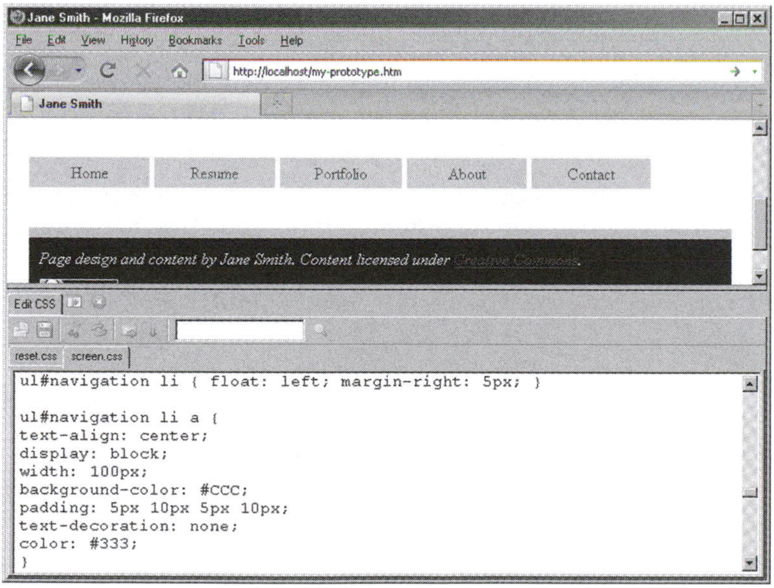

Figure 15.5. A horizontal navigation bar with buttons of the same width and centered text.

your navigation links may be broken onto a second line, making your navigation less usable by reducing how quickly someone can scan it with their eyes. Be sure to test your navigation under a variety of conditions, including multiple screen and font sizes, and on different operating systems.

NEXT STEPS

Navigation is a simple list of links—and styling that list is itself not too difficult. By maximizing the clickable area of a short list of items that reflect your site's content and organization, you will have the foundation for visitors to move quickly through your site.

With your branding and navigation drafted, you should now have the essential, repeated parts of your page in your `my-prototype.htm` file. Rather than starting from scratch, you can now start writing each new page of your site with your branding and navigation ready to go; just open `my-prototype.htm` and choose Save As. . . and immediately name it `about.htm` or `index.htm` or whatever page it is that you're about to build. (See Chapter 21 for ways to repeat your branding and navigation dynamically across all of your pages, in case you need to make changes to them.)

The next chapter turns to writing the text content of your pages, including how you can develop your own style guide for writing markup to make writing with XHTML simple and even fun. Unlike branding and navigation, of course, content differs from page to page, and so it requires a writing approach that is more flexible, but that a style guide can make more consistent.

CHAPTER 16

Text Content

Once you have established the XHTML structures for your page branding and navigation, you can reuse them across all of the pages of your site, perhaps changing the class on the <body> tag (Chapter 21 shows how to dynamically repeat the branding and navigation across all of your pages, to simplify site-wide changes to them).

Where you spend most of your time creating new markup for your pages is in the content portion of your page. Branding and navigation can be structurally and visually constant across pages, but the structure of text content is almost always unique (unless you're writing a Web site full of five-paragraph essays—and please don't). This chapter walks through approaches to marking up your content in XHTML. It also suggests developing some basic site typography for your pages using CSS to create a site style guide to simplify your markup and design.

DEVELOPING A SITE STYLE GUIDE

XHTML is meant to be flexible enough to allow you to mark up most common structural elements of Web content, particularly headings, paragraphs, and lists. You can mark up in XHTML as you write, or mark up your existing writing with XHTML. But it is useful to create a style guide for your site, especially when you begin to add classes and other special pieces of structure to your page content. A style guide is even more important when you are collaborating with others on a site, so that pieces of content are marked up consistently and uniformly.

The simplest way to write your style guide is to put together a page that includes all of the structural elements you use to mark up your page content, and provide a sample rendering using the site's actual CSS by linking to the site's CSS file. Then, any changes to your CSS will also change the style guide's appearance. Save your style guide's XHTML file as `style-guide.htm` for easy reference.

While you can use *Lorem ipsum* text to show off the examples, it's good practice to use the sample text to convey what kind of content should be marked up as paragraphs, lists, or any other structural pages for your site. That will help it serve as a refresher for your memory—and as guidance for any collaborators. The example style guide in Figure 16.1 also shows the XHTML markup required for each site style. Different pieces of this example style guide will be shown in figures throughout the chapter.

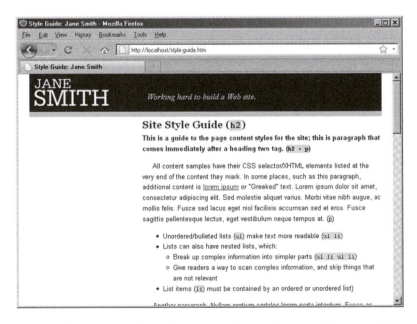

Figure 16.1. A site style guide can remind you and your collaborators of the available content styles, and even what the XHTML is to achieve them.

MARKING UP CONTENT: HEADINGS, PARAGRAPHS, AND LISTS (OH MY!)

You can build a really solid Web page using only headings, paragraphs, and lists. Why? Well, most writing is made up of headings, paragraphs, and lists.

Conveniently enough, there are three basic types of structural blocks in XHTML for marking up written content: headings, paragraphs, and lists. Blocks are nothing more than text that, in the absence of any fancy formatting (such as a plain text email), would probably be separated by empty lines:

```
Primary Colors

There are three primary colors that occur in nature.
They are:

Red
Yellow
Blue
```

Marked up in XHTML, that little chunk of text could be described accurately with the heading, paragraph, and list tags:

```
<h1>Primary Colors</h1>

<p>There are three primary colors that occur in
nature. They are:</p>

<ul>
     <li>Red</li>
     <li>Yellow</li>
     <li>Blue</li>
</ul>
```

Let's look at each type of block piece by piece.

Headings

There are six levels of headings in XHTML. <h1> is a top-level heading; <h2> a subheading; <h3> a sub-subheading, and so on. Stylistically, it's usually better to limit your use of <h1> to once or twice a page; <h2> can be used often, as can <h3>, provided that <h3> is used for subheadings that separate content under an <h2>.

When using headings, though, remember that their purpose is to break up long stretches of text with meaningful labels. <h1> might provide the site title (as in the RPK). <h2> can mark up the titles of individual pages, whose major sections are subdivided by <h3> tags; the sections labeled by <h3> tags could then be broken up further by <h4> tags.

Consider a concrete example. Imagine that John Smith used headings to mark up his resume; if we took away all of the content and left only the headings in his resume, we might see something like:

```
<h2>Resume for John Smith</h2>
 <h3>Objective</h3>
 <h3>Work Experience</h3>
      <h4>Industry</h4>
      <h4>Government</h4>
 <h3>Software Skills</h3>
```

Now it's important to note that the indentations are only to enhance readability of the XHTML source code (see Chapter 12). Particularly for the two <h4> tags, indents also illustrate that the heading tags are used for further subdividing content, not for enumeration. (I once had an undergraduate student who kept adding more and more numbers to his headings each time he used one. When I told him there was no such thing as an <h27> tag, he took the news pretty hard. The most minor subheading in XHTML is <h6>.) Figure 16.2 shows a sample style guide's styling of <h3>.

Paragraphs

There is only one paragraph tag in XHTML: <p>. You should use the paragraph tag to describe actual paragraphs of text—and nothing else. If something is structurally a heading, do not use the paragraph tag. I also often see beginners misuse the paragraph tag like this:

```
<p><h2>This is So Wrong</h2></p>
```

I'm not quite sure why beginners tend to do that. I suspect it may be due to word processors displaying the paragraph mark, ¶, after every

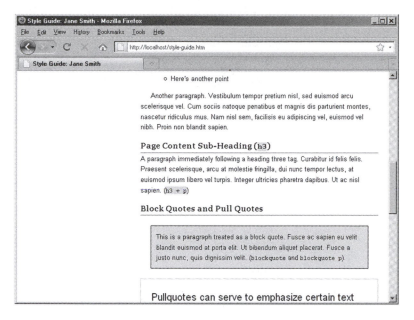

Figure 16.2. This sample style guide runs <h3> tags in Georgia font (the rest of the body text is Arial) with a bottom border for visual interest.

break (including headings and lists). But reason it out, XHTML-style: if something is a heading, it's a heading—not a paragraph. Paragraph tags should appear only when you have a need to describe content whose structure is an actual paragraph, not a heading or a list.

Lists

Lists are an extremely useful structural element in XHTML. In addition to helping readers quickly read through content, lists are also useful for marking up site features such as navigation and menus, and even for postal addresses and contact information.

There are three types of lists in XHTML: ordered (<ol>), unordered (<ul>), and definition (<dl>) lists. Individual items in ordered and unordered lists are marked up with list item tags (<li>):

```
<li>Red</li>
<li>Yellow</li>
<li>Blue</li>
```

A good approach to marking up lists is to begin with the list items first. Then, determine whether there is any specific order to the items: for example, if they are steps in a process, or an enumerated list of things, they should be grouped using the <ol> (ordered list) tag. If the items are more or less in random order or if their order does not matter, as with the primary colors, group the list items with the <ul> (unordered list) tag:

```
<ul>
 <li>Red</li>
 <li>Yellow</li>
 <li>Blue</li>
</ul>
```

Because the RPK loads the reset.css file in the XHTML, unordered and ordered lists appear without bullets or numbers, so you must specify them directly using the list-style-type: property on the individual items within the list, as shown in Figure 16.3. Consult

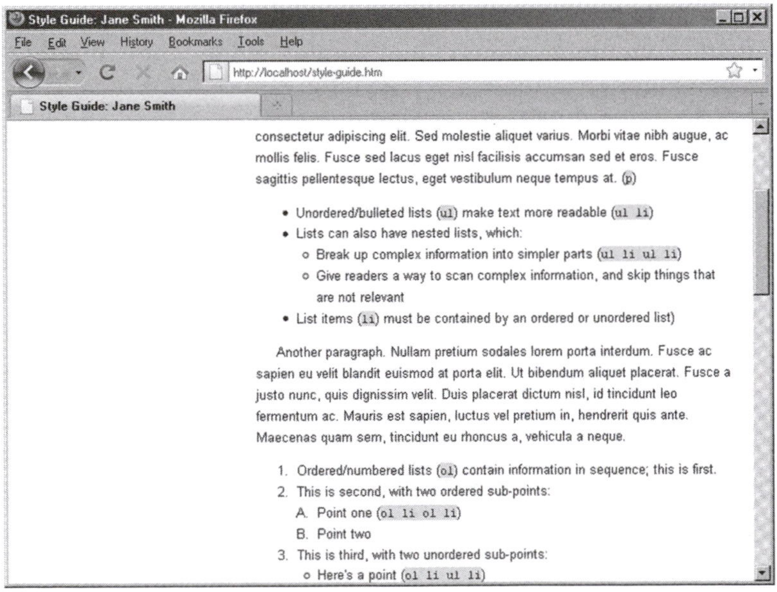

Figure 16.3. This sample style guide shows bullets on unordered lists and decimal numbers and uppercase letters on ordered lists.

your favorite CSS reference to learn about the many different types of bullets and numbers that can be applied to lists.

Nested Lists

Lists can also be nested in XHTML, meaning that individual list items can contain their own sublists (not unlike an outline for a term paper). But nested lists must be structured in a particular way. Nested lists are, in XHTML, considered structurally to be a part of a parent list item. Taking the primary color example, we could nest lists with synonyms for each color:

```
<ul>
 <li>Red
      <ul>
            <li>Crimson</li>
            <li>Scarlet</li>
      </ul>
 </li>
 <li>Yellow
      <ul>
            <li>Lemon</li>
            <li>Gold</li>
      </ul>
 </li>
 <li>Blue
      <ul>
            <li>Navy</li>
            <li>Cobalt</li>
      </ul>
 </li>
</ul>
```

Notice that on Red, the list item opens, the word Red appears and then a nested unordered list opens, with two list items of its own: Crimson and Scarlet. Then, that unordered list closes, and finally the list item tag that opened before Red closes. As Figure 16.4 shows, you can create additional styles for nested lists, including when ordered lists are nested inside of unordered lists and vice versa.

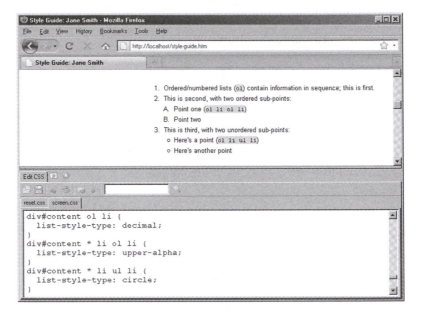

Figure 16.4. This sample style guide shows a few different styles for nested lists, particularly ordered and unordered lists nested inside ordered lists.

VALIDATION ERRORS, AND HOW TO FIX THEM

As you are writing your XHTML pages, it is important to regularly upload your files and check them against the W3C Markup Validator at `http://validator.w3.org/`. Don't wait until your pages are completely finished; errors are easier to catch if you get into the habit of validating after small sets of changes to your XHTML.

And don't be surprised if you get errors. The important thing about validator output, particularly when there is an error on your page, is to worry only about the first error that's listed. Early errors (like forgetting to close a tag near the top of the page) have a snowball effect on the validator, causing it to report dozens, sometimes hundreds, of errors—even if there's only a single one on the page.

The validator is just a machine, after all. So do not assume that the number of errors the validator reports reflects the reality of your page. Look for the first error it reports, try and fix it, and then revalidate. Five times out of seven, you'll find that your page only had an error or two, particularly if you were cautious as you were writing the page to begin with—and checked them often in the validator.

See the companion site for this book for additional help with validators, `http://sustainablewebdesign.com/book/`.

STRUCTURED PHRASES: ANCHOR, STRONG, EMPHASIS, AND CITE

Of course, not all writing is structured in blocks: some structure is limited to words and phrases. XHTML has a number of tags for structuring phrases within blocks.

Anchor Tags

The anchor tag, <a>, is behind the Web's signature feature: the hyperlink. The anchor tag is used to turn phrases of text into links that can be activated to take a user to another page on your Web site or any other place on the Web.

The anchor tag has one required—and very important—attribute: href, or "hypertext reference." The value of href is the address of the Web site or Web page that you want your text to link to. For example,

```
<p>
    Read the news at
    <a href="http://news.google.com">the Google
    News portal</a>.
</p>
```

will create a hyperlink out of "the Google News portal" that can be clicked on or otherwise activated by a user. Whenever you are linking to a Web site other than your own, you must include the http:// prefix to the full URL.

However, when you link to pages in your own site, you need not include the full URL, but merely the path to the file. The path is everything that comes after the domain name; so, for example, if your domain is http://example.com/, the path is everything that comes after .com. If you have a home page at http://example.com/index.htm and your resume is at http://example.com/resume.htm, you can link to your resume from the home page in one of two ways. The first is to use a relative link:

```
<p>View my <a href="resume.htm">resume</a>.</p>
```

The second way is to use a root-relative link:

```
<p>View my <a href="/resume.htm">resume</a>.</p>
```

The difference? A relative link uses the linking document as its starting point; a root-relative link uses the site root as its starting point; Chapter 20 will examine different kinds of links in greater depth. But other than on your site title (see Chapter 14), avoid using the full URL (also known as an absolute link, e.g., `http://example.com/resume.htm`) when linking to Web pages that are part of your own site.

Strong, Emphasis, and Cite

By default, Web browsers use the `<strong>` tag to display text as bold text, and the `<em>` (emphasis) tag to display text as italic. However, their structural names will also allows screen readers to read text in a strong voice or an emphatic voice (what, exactly, the difference is between those two remains a matter of some dispute in the Web design community).

For titles of works, use the `<cite>` tag, e.g.,

```
<p>Read the online Web magazine <cite>A List Apart
</cite> for the latest developments in Web design.</p>
```

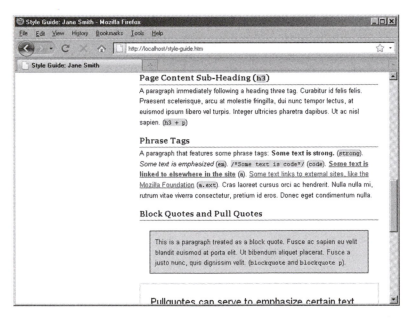

Figure 16.5. This sample style guide uses fairly common styles for phrase elements.

By default, the `<cite>` tag will appear in italic text; but as with `<strong>`, `<em>`, and any other tag, its display is ultimately dictated by CSS, not XHTML. The `screen.css` file in the RPK establishes the typical styles for strong, emphasis, and cite, but you can change them to appear however you wish. Figure 16.5 shows a sample style guide's visual design of phrase tags.

INHERITED STYLES

Cascading Style Sheets enable certain styles to be inherited. One basic example of this is using the `<body>` tag as a selector to set the base fonts and font sizes for your entire page, for example:

```
body {
  font-family: Arial, sans-serif;
  font-size: small;
}
```

Figure 16.6 shows all of the text rendering in Arial, except in the header (which was styled more specifically in Chapter 14). Inheritance

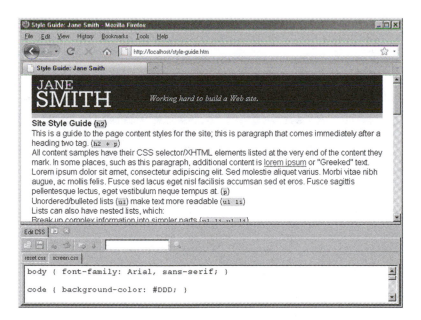

Figure 16.6. Setting the Arial font on the body tag causes all of the text on the page to appear in Arial—except the tagline in the header, which has its own style elsewhere in the style sheet.

works on other selectors besides the body and can help you keep your styles short and lean. Remember that it's always better to write as little source as possible.

For example, if you wish to have a shared line height on all of the text in the content area on your page (see Figure 16.7), you can set that on div#content:

```
div#content { line-height: 1.6; }
```

Not only will that keep all of your text looking uniform across the content area, but it also makes changing the line height a matter of fixing that one line of CSS (as opposed to having to change the line height on every style).

If you find that you want to alter styles that are inherited, perhaps by setting a shorter line height on your supporting content text, the browser rendering your CSS will replace the inherited style with the new, more specific style.

```
div#supporting-content { line-height: 1.2; }
```

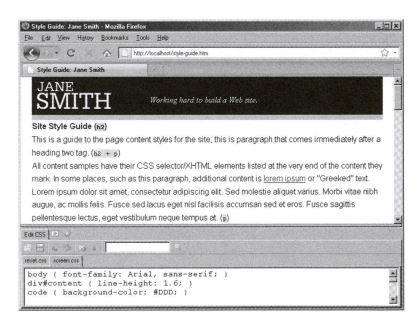

Figure 16.7. The line height is inherited by all text in the content division.

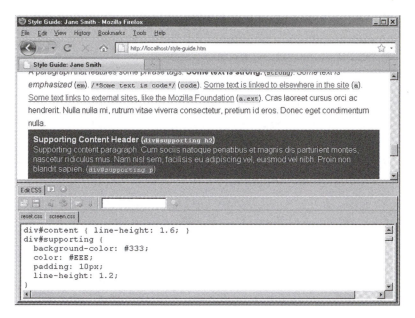

Figure 16.8. The line height on the supporting content (in the darker area) has been set to be tighter than in the rest of the content division, whose line height would otherwise have been inherited.

With that style applied, all of your supporting content will have 1.2 for its line height, rather than 1.6 (see Figure 16.8).

Descendant Selectors and Inheritance

Descendant selectors provide better control over inheritance, so that you set the styles for only specific areas of your page content. Think about the paragraph tag; while you will probably use it in your content area, it may also be in your header and footer, too (as it is in the RPK). So rather than styling the paragraphs for your page content area using the p selector, write a more specific selector, such as

```
div#content p { text-indent: 20px; }
```

Figure 16.9 shows that the descendant selector applies (in that case) the text indent only to paragraphs inside of div#content. (Odds are you wouldn't want to indent paragraphs in your header and footer; you'd move them with margin or padding instead.) The screen.css file in the RPK has many descendant selectors for the content area already written for you to use.

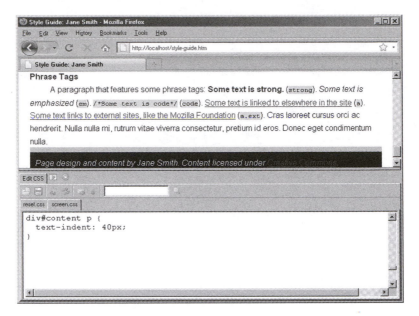

Figure 16.9. Using the descendant selector, paragraphs in the content area are indented—in this case, a paragraph showcasing phrase tags as we saw in Figure 16.4—but the paragraph marking site credits in the footer is not indented.

SPECIAL STYLES

You can go a long way marking up blocks of content with headings, paragraphs, and lists. But sometimes, you will have unique pieces of content that should be treated differently from an ordinary heading, paragraph, or list.

Block Quotes

The `<blockquote>` tag is an example of adding a bit of structure to paragraphs or long stretches of material quoted from another source. For example,

```
<p>The United States Constitution opens with:</p>
<blockquote>
        <p>We the People of the United States, in
        Order to form a more perfect Union, establish
        Justice, insure domestic Tranquility, provide
        for the common defence, promote the general
```

```
    Welfare, and secure the Blessings of Liberty
    to ourselves and our Posterity, do ordain and
    establish this Constitution for the United
    States of America.</p>
</blockquote>
```

The `<blockquote>` tag requires that some other block-level tag appear inside of it (headings, paragraphs, or lists). Using CSS, you can style blocks of quoted material:

```
blockquote {
    border: 1px dotted black; /*Dotted border*/
    padding: 20px; /*Padding adds space between
      the text and border*/
}
```

If you have reason to style a paragraph within a block quote differently from your other paragraphs, the descendant selector again comes in handy; simply refer to `blockquote p` in your CSS.

Classes

As we have seen in earlier chapters, XHTML allows you to write a class (or even multiple classes) on any tag. This structural flexibility is useful for marking up page content, because it allows you to specify additional, unique structural features for your content that can be styled using CSS.

A class can be called anything you like (though review the naming rules covered in Chapter 9), but the more structurally you name a class, the better. Suppose you wanted pull quotes, which are usually bits of text pulled from your own writing, to appear on text-heavy pages to add visual interest. You might want to style those paragraphs as a big box, but `<p class="big-box">` may not accurately describe future designs (or the page as it appears when printed). Opting for `<p class="pullquote">` is the better, more sustainable choice. CSS can make it as big and boxy as you'd like (see the rendering of both block quotes and pull quotes in Figure 16.10):

```
p.pullquote {
    font-size: x-large;
```

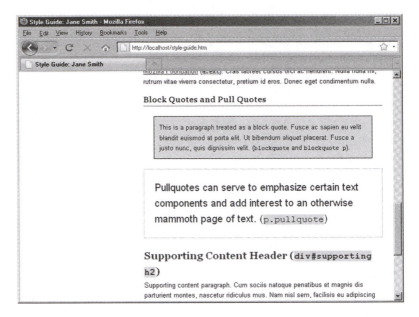

Figure 16.10. The sample style guide's treatment of block quotes and pull quotes.

```
border: 1px dotted black;
padding: 20px;
}
```

NEXT STEPS

Marking up text content is just a matter of being honest: if something is a paragraph, mark it as a paragraph; if it's a list, mark it as a list. Thinking about the general types of content on your site will help you to develop your own style guide, which can help you keep your markup consistent—even when you collaborate with others.

Once you have some content together and your branding and navigation drafted, you can start to position all of the elements of your site to create the layout for the whole page, which is what the next chapter will cover.

CHAPTER 17

Page Layout

Put together your page's branding, navigation, and content and you have your whole page. And while so far those elements have been discussed mostly in isolation, an appealing page layout must arrange all of the page elements in harmony. This chapter looks at building page layouts in CSS over well-structured XHTML.

PREPARING FOR PAGE LAYOUT IN CSS

In the past, Web designers relied on HTML tables for page design, because that was the only reliable cross-browser technique to create page layouts. That is no longer good practice, as tables for layout can introduce accessibility problems in addition to adding more markup to a page. Tables also lock page content into a particular design, and make creating alternate designs—such as for mobile phones—difficult or impossible.

Web designers now use CSS positioning to create flexible layouts over well-structured XHTML, such as you have been writing in the previous chapters with the RPK. By default, all block-level elements (such as the various `<div>` and `<ul id="navigation">` tags that form the major page areas in the Rapid Prototyping Kit) are displayed in the same order as they appear in the XHTML source, and take up the entire width of the screen (see Figure 17.1).

The first step to page layout in CSS, then, is to determine which page elements must move far away from where they appear

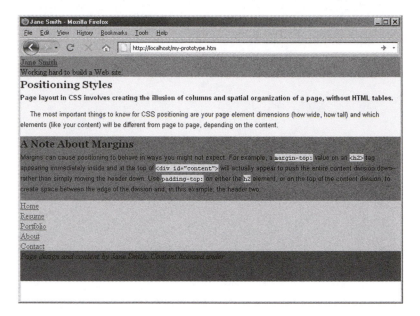

Figure 17.1.   Adding illustrative background colors to each major division of the document reveals that browsers display blocks to the full width of the screen and in source order.

by default. The second step is to move those elements into place, using CSS positioning, before finally moving other elements out of the way of positioned ones in order to create the illusion of a page layout. And that is really what CSS page layout is: an *illusion* of columns created by moving some things, and moving other things out of their way.

ROUGH SKETCHES AND MOCKUPS

Rough sketches done on scrap paper are more than enough to start you thinking about page design. They do not have to be works of art; sketches only have to provide a rough representation of the content where you would like it to appear your page. Once you have done some sketching on paper, it may be helpful to create a mockup of your page in an image editor, so that you can get a better sense of how big things will appear on screen in actual pixel dimensions (see Figure 17.2).

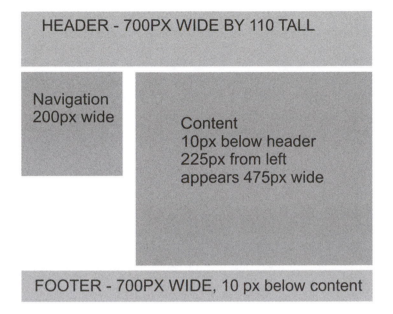

Figure 17.2. A rough mockup of a page, created using an image editor.

Start with a Typical, Representative Content Page

Although designers might begin page designs by starting with the home page, the home page is often different from the other pages in a site. Designing by thinking first about a more typical content page will help you develop a design that works for most of your pages. From that general idea, you can work to build a home page that is different from (but complementary to) the typical pages of your site (see the sidebar "Modifying Designs for Special Pages").

As has been mentioned throughout this section of the book, you can almost never go wrong following this rule of Web design: begin by building things that represent a typical page or feature on your site. Whether that's sizing images, determining a text content area's width, or deciding to include JavaScript for an audio player in the `<head>` area of your pages, design to the general first—and to the specific later.

With a representative content page sketched, you can turn the focus of your work to the home page and any overview pages that your site has. For example, you might have a portfolio as

MODIFYING DESIGNS FOR SPECIAL PAGES

Chapter 13 suggested placing a class on the body tag to distinguish different pages. If your home page's body opens with `<body class="home">`, you can use that class as a **hook** in your CSS to create special home page styles. For example, if your header is 150 pixels tall on most of your pages, but you want it 300 pixels tall on home, your CSS might read:

```
div#header { height: 85px; } /*85px tall on all pages*/
body.home div#header { height: 300px; } /*300 tall
  on home page*/
```

There's no need, in other words, to modify the structure of an individual page element (e.g., by writing a special header ID for the home page XHTML) or to create a separate style sheet for the home page; all the styles can live in one CSS file, using the body class as a hook to target the appropriate pages automatically.

one part of your site that comprises an overview of your portfolio, which links to individual projects. You can even add unique classes such as `class="home"` or `class="overview"`, or even `class="portfolio-overview"` on the `<body>` tag to help you make specific home- and overview-page adjustments in your CSS later. (See Chapter 20 for help making these kinds of architectural choices for your own site.)

DESIGNING WITH A GRID

Grids can provide a solid foundation for any design, even if elements violate the rigid columns on the grid to add visual interest. I often urge Web design students to focus on the rough, geographic areas of a page first, placing elements like the header, footer, navigation, and content and subcontent areas in relationship to each other. From there, thinking more carefully about the design of content in the different areas through sketching, image editor mockups, and prototyping will help you with additional details for your design.

GRID SYSTEMS

Do a Google search for *Web design grid system* and you will find links to the work of many different Web designers who have released their own grid system that others may use.

One of my favorite grid systems is Nathan Smith's 960 Grid System, which includes templates for 12- and 16-column grids in the formats of a number of different image editors. It also includes a PDF file for printing out ready-made grid pages to sketch on. As Smith, the 960 Grid System creator, notes:

"All modern monitors support at least 1024 × 768 pixel resolution. 960 is divisible by 2, 3, 4, 5, 6, 8, 10, 12, 15, 16, 20, 24, 30, 32, 40, 48, 60, 64, 80, 96, 120, 160, 192, 240, 320 and 480. This makes it a highly flexible base number to work with."*

Although the 960 Grid System and others like it include XHTML and CSS, they are usually not structurally meaningful the way the RPK is. So try working with some of the sketch sheets and column layouts, but stick to writing your own XHTML and CSS.

*Nathan Smith, *960 Grid System,* http://960.gs

Even if you decide to try a simple two-column layout consisting of a 475-pixel-wide area for your content, and a 200-pixel-wide area for your navigation, separated by 25 pixels of space (as in this chapter's example), a column structure will help guide you in your image editor mockup—particularly if you opt to enhance your pages with background images to give it a unique look and feel. Figure 17.3 shows an image-editor mockup of the page for this chapter; different areas were sliced from it and saved as separate image files to create the background images in the actual page.

Note that the 700-pixel width of the design for this chapter was chosen only because it would work well for images in this book; as in Smith's 960 Grid System (see "Grid Systems" sidebar), it's common to build fixed-width pages that are closer to 1000 pixels across.

Figure 17.3.   Another image-editor mockup, with images that can be used for the actual design.

CSS POSITIONING

CSS includes the `position` property, which is often used in conjunction with properties for dimensions (especially widths) and left-, right-, top-, and bottom-offsets to produce all kinds of page layouts from the same XHTML structure.

By default, block elements are positioned by the browser statically (`position: static;`). Two other position values, `relative` and `absolute`, are what provide designers the ability to create compelling page designs.

When you need to position something far away from where it appears by default, such as the navigation in this chapter's examples, position it absolutely. Absolute positioning removes the element from the document flow—meaning that the rest of the page's content behaves as though, for example, the navigation is simply gone (see Figure 17.4).

To determine what needs to be positioned absolutely, compare where it appears in the normal flow of things (as in Figure 17.1) with where it

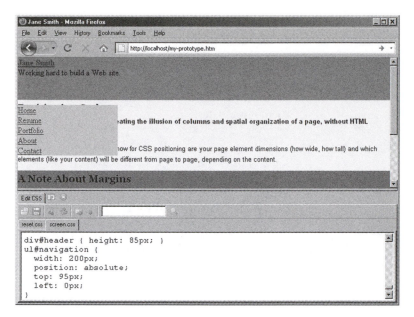

Figure 17.4. The navigation positioned absolutely, and over the content, which must be moved out of the way.

needs to appear (as in the sketches in Figures 17.2 and 17.3). Because this chapter's example header is 85 pixels tall, and the design specifies a space of 10 pixels between the header and the navigation (and content), we write a style like:

```
ul#navigation {
        width: 200px; /*200px wide navigation area*/
        position: absolute; /*Pull from flow to
         position*/
        left: 0px; /*Keep with left edge of design*/
        top: 95px; /*Appear 10px below 85px-high
         header*/
}
```

At this point, though, the page is a mess; the navigation and the content appear layered over the top of one another. So the next task is to move other elements out of the navigation's way. In Figure 17.5, some left margin on the content area is all that it takes. This margin will also be the only sizing on the content area (that is, no width will

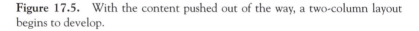

Figure 17.5. With the content pushed out of the way, a two-column layout begins to develop.

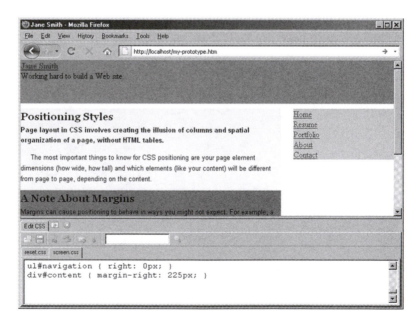

Figure 17.6. To create a layout with right-hand navigation is just a matter of a few CSS adjustments.

need to be specified for `div#content`; it will become clear why in a moment):

```
div#content {
    margin-left: 225px; /*200px nav + 25px between
    nav and content*/
}
```

The great thing about CSS-based layouts is that they are easily revised. Figure 17.6 shows roughly the same layout as Figure 17.5, but with the navigation on the right rather than the left (and with the content moved off to the right).

Refining the Whole Page Design

With the navigation and content areas looking roughly as they should, it's possible to move on to the less drastic CSS to make the page design work.

The rough sketch called for a 700-pixel-wide design; to achieve that, the CSS just needs `div#page { width: 700px; }`. With everything appearing inside the page division, the whole page is now 700 pixels wide. The content area, which is offset from the left by 225 pixels, automatically fills the remaining space (575 pixels wide, if you are keeping count); that's why there is no need to specify a width on `div#content`.

Because 700 pixels is a rather narrow design, it might appear better on larger screens if the page were centered horizontally, an effect achieved by adding `margin: 0 auto;` to the `div#page` style. But Figure 17.7 reveals a problem with that style: everything is centered *except* the navigation, which is still at `left: 0px` and therefore hugging the edge of the browser window.

Here is where relative positioning becomes useful. The reason the navigation appears all the way to the left despite the centered page division is that, lacking a **positioning context**, the navigation is positioned with regard to the browser window. By adding `position: relative;` to the `div#page` style declaration, navigation will then be positioned with regard to the page division—not the window. That is, because the page division is now positioned, it becomes the positioning context for the navigation, meaning that the navigation's `left: 0px` property will be the `0px` position *relative to* the relatively positioned container (Figure 17.8).

Jane Smith - Mozilla Firefox
File Edit View History Bookmarks Tools Help
http://localhost/my-prototype.htm
Jane Smith
Working hard to build a Web site.
Home
Resume
Portfolio
About
Contact
Positioning Styles
Page layout in CSS involves creating the illusion of columns and spatial organization of a page, without HTML tables.
The most important things to know for CSS positioning are your page element dimensions (how wide, how tall) and which elements (like your content) will be different from page to page, depending on the content.
Edit CSS
reset.css
screen.css
div#container {
width: 700px;
margin: 0 auto;
}

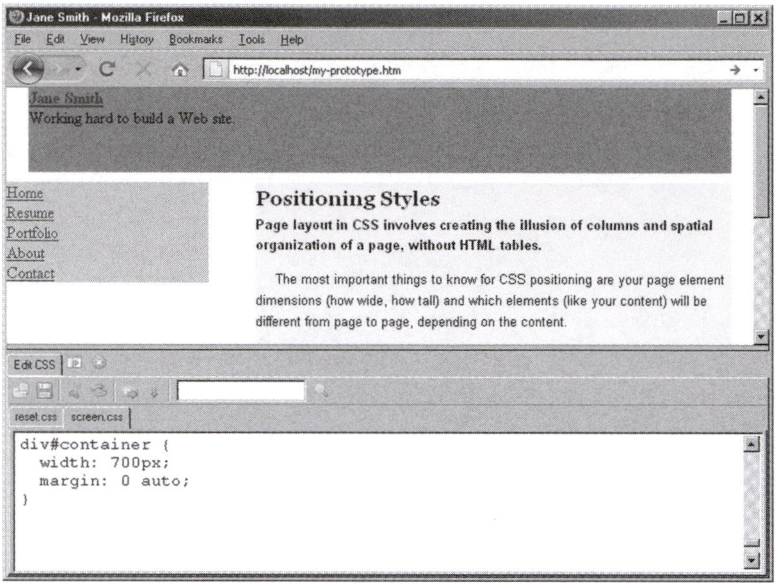

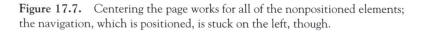

Figure 17.7. Centering the page works for all of the nonpositioned elements; the navigation, which is positioned, is stuck on the left, though.

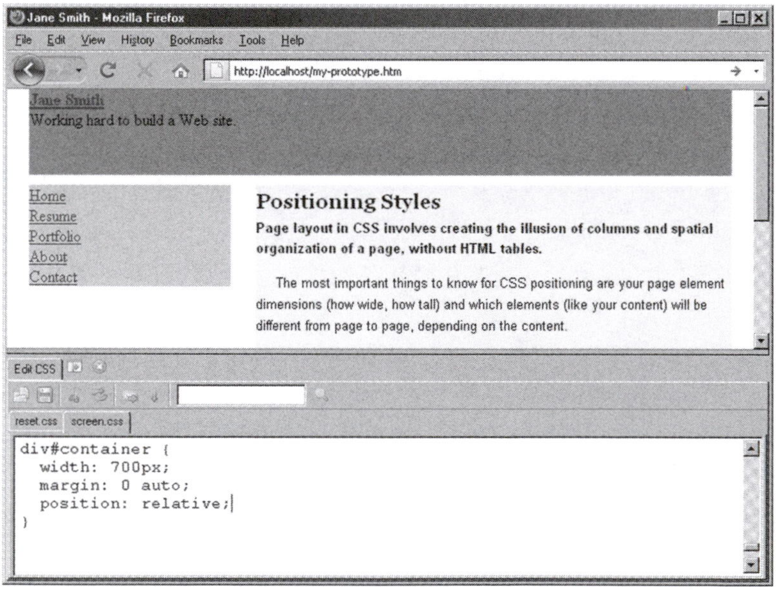

Jane Smith - Mozilla Firefox
File Edit View History Bookmarks Tools Help
http://localhost/my-prototype.htm
Jane Smith
Working hard to build a Web site.
Home
Resume
Portfolio
About
Contact
Positioning Styles
Page layout in CSS involves creating the illusion of columns and spatial organization of a page, without HTML tables.
The most important things to know for CSS positioning are your page element dimensions (how wide, how tall) and which elements (like your content) will be different from page to page, depending on the content.
Edit CSS
reset.css
screen.css
div#container {
width: 700px;
margin: 0 auto;
position: relative;
}

Figure 17.8. The navigation positioned absolutely, but with the container division as its positioning context.

Designing the Content Area

Suppose someone wanted to design this page's supporting content as a second column within the content area, by making another 200-pixel-wide column for the supporting content and positioning it absolutely (see Figure 17.9).

While it would be possible to position the supporting content 95 pixels from the top, a more easily modified design would come from setting the content area itself as a positioning context:

```
div#content { position: relative; }
```

That way, any changes to the content area's design (particularly its width and distance from the top of the page) would be reflected on the supporting content as well; see Figure 17.10.

A corrective measure to the supporting content spilling over the footer would be to add more text or media content to the content area. But assuming some pages might need to be short, a designer could

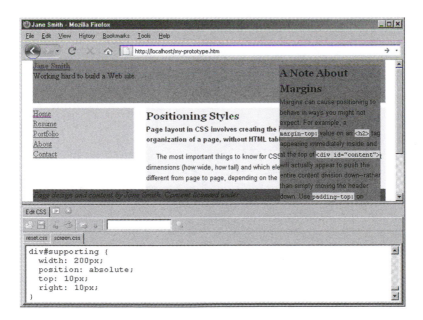

Figure 17.9. Supporting content positioned absolutely; its positioning context should be the content area, rather than the page.

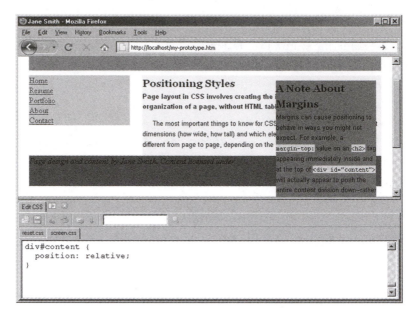

Figure 17.10. Supporting content positioned absolutely, but with the content area as its positioning context. Note that the supporting content now spills over the footer.

add a minimum height of 500 pixels to the main content area in this design:

```
div#main {

 padding-right: 210px;
  /*Move content out of the way of supporting,
   but use padding to keep background color*/

 min-height: 500px;
  /*The main content area should be
   at least 500 pixels tall*/

}
```

Figure 17.11 shows the page with the spill-over problem corrected. If there is more than 500 pixels worth of content, the area will automatically expand.

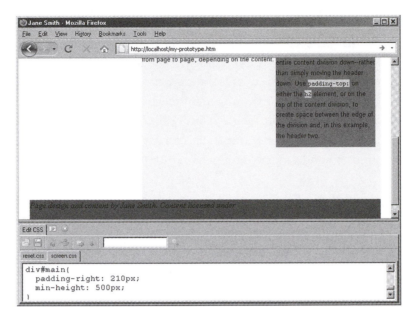

Figure 17.11. A minimum height on the main content area keeps supporting content from spilling over the footer. Additional content in the main area would have the same effect.

CONDITIONAL COMMENTS

Internet Explorer has a feature, known as conditional comments, that enables you to target XHTML markup to particular versions of IE. If, for example, you need to load a style sheet that corrects some of the idiosyncrasies of IE, conditional comments enable IE to load it; other browsers will see the content as just another XHTML comment. The form of conditional comments looks something like:

```
<!--[if IE]>
<link rel="stylesheet" type="text/css"
 href="screen-ie.css" />
<![endif]-->
```

Visit QuirksMode.org* for additional information on targeting IE using conditional comments.

*QuirksMode.org, "Conditional Comments," http://www.quirksmode.org/css/condcom.html

Note that because of a problem with `min-height` in Internet Explorer (IE) prior to version 8,[1] you would have to add `div#main { height: 500px; }` to an IE-only style sheet loaded via conditional comments (the RPK details their use in its `screen-ie.css` file; see also the "Conditional Comments" sidebar). IE expands the value specified for `height` to fit longer content, but other browsers, such as Firefox, cut the content off. But that is an acceptable workaround for IE's inability to understand the `min-height` property.

FINISHING TOUCHES WITH BACKGROUND IMAGES

Background images help to make a design really shine beyond simple boxes. Once your positioning is more or less in place, you can begin to experiment adding in background images.

Figure 17.12 shows the positioned page along with the branding and navigation styles from previous chapters. The design looks very boxy and does not seem to fit together very well.

One of the easier ways to pull a design together is to tile an image on the background that anticipates, for example, the content area. The

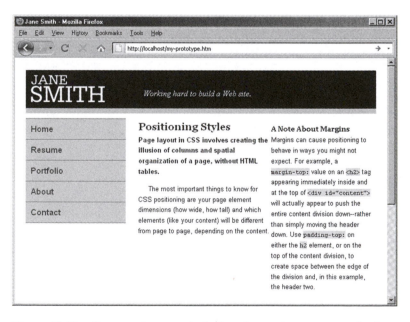

Figure 17.12.   Positioned page with the branding and navigation styles from previous chapters.

use of gradients, or areas of color that shift from one color to another, is just one means for bringing one area (such as the header) into a polished-looking relationship with another area (such as the content); Figure 17.13 shows the background image that will tile horizontally on the example design in this chapter.

Remember that, by default, background images tile horizontally *and* vertically; to limit an image tiling on the horizontal axis only, be sure to include `background-repeat: repeat-x;` in your CSS style declarations that use tiled images (to tile vertically, use the `repeat-y` value). This one background image addition helps pull the design together, as in Figure 17.14.

Fixing What Doesn't Work

The major problem with Figure 17.14 is the supporting content; the content area itself is too narrow to accommodate a second column. With a few revisions to the CSS (including another background image with a gradient on the content area), the supporting content now appears beneath the main content (see Figure 17.15).

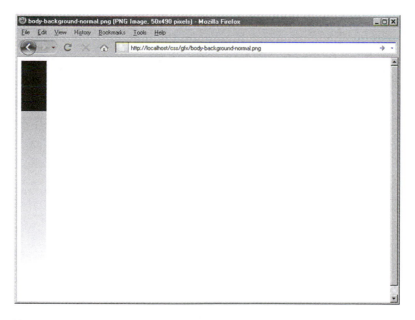

Figure 17.13. A background image to tile on the body to help pull the design together. (The space around the image is due to how Firefox displays images directly.)

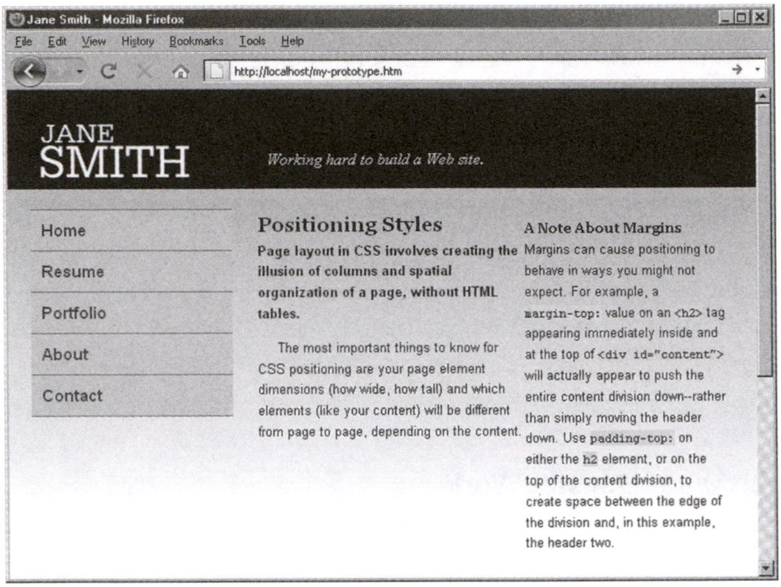

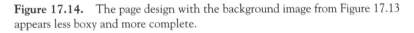

Figure 17.14. The page design with the background image from Figure 17.13 appears less boxy and more complete.

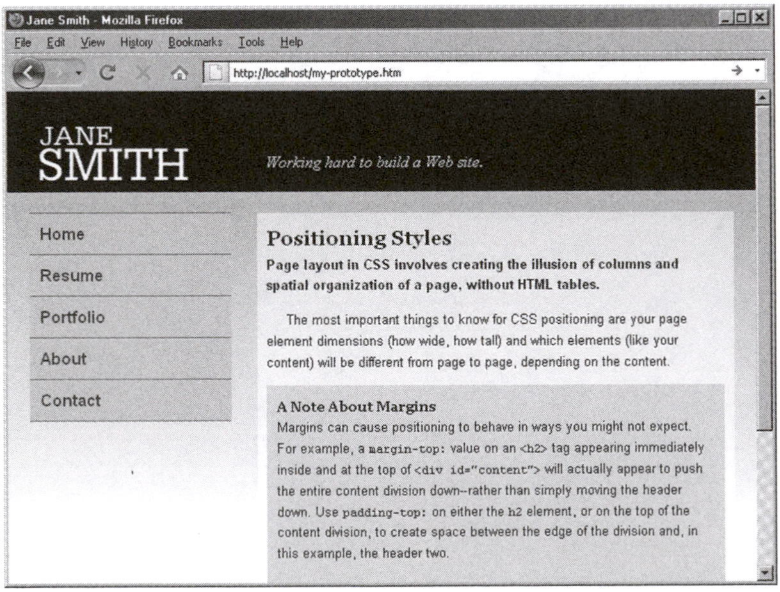

Figure 17.15. A revised layout on the content area, plus a gradient on the content area itself and a darker background color on the supporting content, further improve the page.

That is a strength of CSS-based design: it's possible to experiment with these kinds of revisions without ever touching the XHTML of a page. Tools like Chris Pederick's Web Developer Add-on for Firefox also let you experiment with the design right in your browser window.

The footer also looks unfinished still; like the header before the addition of the background image on the body, it still looks boxy in Figure 17.16.

Remember that there can only be one background image loaded per element in CSS 2; while one has been added to the `<body>` tag, the `<html>` tag has none. So here's a bit of CSS trickery to get the same effect from the header and body to work on the footer.

First, position the footer absolutely:

```
div#footer { position: absolute; }
```

All this does is pull the footer out of the document flow, and in this case, cause the `<body>` area to behave as though the footer no longer exists. Because of that, the footer now appears over the `<html>` area of the page.

Next, we can add a background image—actually the same background image as the original footer—to the `html` selector in CSS, and

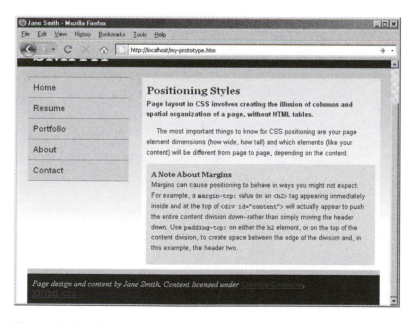

Figure 17.16.   The footer as styled in previous chapters; it looks unfinished.

have the image positioned at the bottom of the `<html>` element and repeated on the horizontal, filling the entire page width just like we did for the header (see Figure 17.17). (Once that's been done, remove the background image from the `div#footer` style declaration.) To make sure the image on `html` displays on longer pages, it's necessary to put some padding on its bottom. The complete style looks like:

```
html {
 background-image: url('gfx/footer-
  background.png');
 background-repeat: repeat-x; /*Tile horizontally*/
 background-position: left bottom;
  /*Show image at bottom of html element*/
 padding-bottom: 110px;
  /*Make room for the footer, and ensure that the
   html area always displays, even on longer
   pages*/
 }
```

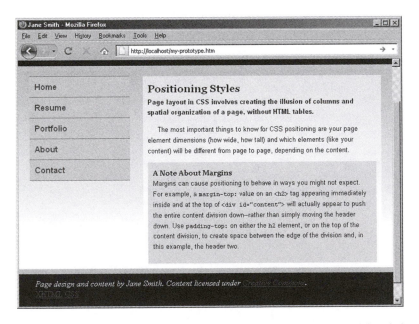

Figure 17.17. The footer positioned absolutely puts it over the top of the tiled image on the html area.

The Large-Screen Problem

When designing CSS layouts, it is important to test them on a variety of screen sizes. As Figure 17.18 shows, the page looks incomplete on larger screens, as the bottom of the page is white.

The fix for this is an easy one. Although we could use the trick from earlier and set a min-height on the page, effectively pushing the `html` area to the bottom of even very large screens, that would cause scroll bars to appear on smaller screens—falsely suggesting content below (when in fact only empty space would appear). So a better fix here is to set a background color of black on the `html` selector, so the entire page background matches the black on the tiled background image. Just to be safe, add a different background color (in this case, white) to the `body` selector, as the majority of the body area should be white (see Figure 17.19):

```
html { background-color: black; }
body { background-color: white; }
```

Chapter 19 will look at how DOM scripting can be used to alter your design for larger screens.

Figure 17.18. The page looks incomplete because of the white area at the bottom.

Figure 17.19. A simple background color fix makes the page look more complete, even on large screens.

NEXT STEPS

Using CSS to position elements into a layout is a matter of creating the illusion of columns and boxes. Remember, also, when you work with background images that they sometimes work better on elements other than the element you're actually trying to style, as with the header and footer examples in this chapter. You can find additional positioning techniques and solutions at the book's companion Web site, http:// sustainablewebdesign.com/book/.

The next chapter looks at adding images, video, and other media to your pages. But expect to return to your page layout often to make adjustments, particularly as you work to include media like images and video that might need a wider area than your layout accounts for.

NOTE

1. Microsoft Developer Network, "CSS Compatibility and Internet Explorer," http://msdn.microsoft.com/en-us/library/cc351024(VS.85).aspx

CHAPTER 18

Multimedia Content

Chapter 3 provided an overview of gathering and preparing multimedia content, including images, audio, and video. This chapter looks at how to display those media elements and integrate them with the design of your page. Particularly for audio and video, there are many different ways to load media elements on your page; this chapter will suggest only the most accessible and sustainable methods for doing so. But because the precise details of those methods change frequently and are a little too complex to go into here in the book, they are available at the book's companion Web site, `http://sustainablewebdesign.com/book/`.

The Rapid Prototyping Kit (RPK) includes a media folder with sub-folders for images, audio, and video, as well as for Flash movies and Portable Document Files (PDFs). If you decide to host media content on your own server (versus, for example, using YouTube for video hosting, as this chapter recommends), take advantage of the RPK's folders or a structure like them to keep your media content organized and manageable.

CONTENT IMAGES

All content images—that is, all images that appear on your pages when you mean, "Have a look at this!"—should be loaded in the XHTML image tag, `<img />`. In addition to the `<img />` tag being self-closing, there are two important attributes that it must include, `src` and `alt`.

- `src`: the path to and name of your image file; remember that Web-friendly formats include JPEG files (`.jpg`, sometimes

OUTSOURCING MEDIA HOSTING

While it is possible to host all of your multimedia content on your own site, you might consider outsourcing your media hosting—particularly video—to a third-party service such as YouTube. The benefit to this is not limited to reduced load on your server for transferring big video files. By using YouTube or some of the other services listed below, you also establish an account that provides yet another way to build your identity on the Web, and another place to link back to your Web site.

Explore these and other video-hosting sites (just do a Google search for *video hosting*), and try them out for picture, quality, sound sync, video length or size limits, and, most important, the ability to load videos into your own Web pages:

- Viddler, `http://www.viddler.com/`
- Vimeo, `http://www.vimeo.com/`
- YouTube, `http://www.youtube.com/`

Always check the terms of service for these and other video sites; some sites prohibit commercial uses for free accounts—meaning that you probably cannot promote your business using them.

.jpeg), PNG files (.png), and GIF files (.gif, though usually .png is preferable to .gif). Never try and load TIFF files, or the native files from your image editor (e.g., the .psd files from Adobe Photoshop).

- alt: the short alternate text for your image; I prefer to include the text "A photo of . . . ," or "An illustration of . . . ," or even "A pie graph showing . . ." to describe the nature of the image, as well as a few words to describe its content. Web accessibility guidelines suggest that alt text be less than 100 characters, so do keep it brief. Also, it is good practice to include descriptive text somewhere on your page, such as in captions, to clarify the purpose of your images. Markup such as:

```
<p class="caption">
      <span class="access-label">Photo caption:
      </span>We took this photograph of the Thomas
      Jefferson memorial during our visit to
      Washington, D.C. in November of 2010.
</p>
```

and accessible CSS for hiding the access label, such as:

```
.access-label {
  display: block;
   /*Display as a block for positioning*/
  position: absolute; /*Pull from document flow*/
  left: -10000px;
   /*Move way left of the screen*/
}
```

can provide additional image descriptions for all users, while hiding (if you'd like) the obvious "Photo caption" label that would be made clearer in your design.

The `<img />` tag should also include height and width attributes for your images. The values are in pixels, but you do not put the pixel unit in the value. For example, a 200-pixel-wide by 300-pixel-tall image would be specified with `width="200" height="300"`. While height and width attributes are not required, they tell the Web browser to save the space for your images, even before the image is done loading. That can keep your page content from moving around as the images load.

Note that you should never resize images with the height and width attributes; do that with your image editor's resize or resample function instead. The height and width attributes on your `<img />` tags should always match the actual pixel dimensions of the images that they load.

Developing a Consistent and Attractive Image Presentation

The `<img />` tag must appear in some sort of block-level element; that is, according to the XHTML specification, `<img />` cannot be a child of the `<body>` tag. The content divisions in the RPK address this issue, but you can go a step further to structure and display your images with an attractive, consistent design.

One approach to designing around your images is to create a little chunk of XHTML markup for reuse each time you want to present an image. For example:

```
<div class="photograph">
    <img src="" height="300" width="400" alt="Add
    alt text"/>
```

```
<!--Note the space before </span>:-->
<p class="caption"><span class="access-label">
 Photo caption: </span>

 Image description....

</p>
</div>
```

A little bit of CSS can turn that chunk of markup into a design that complements the photograph and its caption. This example (see Figure 18.1) uses the CSS float: property to enable caption text to appear alongside and, if the text is long enough, wrap around the image:

```
div.photograph {
      background: #333; /*Photos often show up well
      against darker backgrounds.*/
      color: #FFF; /*White text*/
      width: 678px; /*Allow for padding and border
      to total 700px*/
      padding: 10px; /*Add a bit of padding*/
}
div.photograph img {
      border: 1px solid black; /*Give definition to
      lighter edges of photos*/
      float: left; /*Float image to allow text to
      appear alongside of it*/;
      margin-right: 10px; /*Keep text away from the
      image*/
      margin-bottom: 10px; /*Also away from the
      bottom, should the text wrap around.*/
}
div.photograph p.caption {
      font-size: medium;
      font-weight: bold;
}
```

As with video, images and their presentation elements (a containing division, a caption) must be sized to work with page layout; this particular

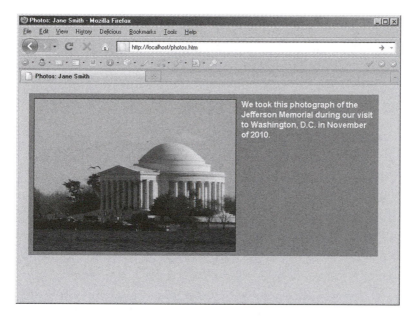

Figure 18.1. Even minor design enhancements, such as background colors and borders, can improve the presentation of photographs and other media—especially if they are used consistently.

example image presentation would require at least a 700-pixel-wide content area. For this reason, work with your images as you develop your page design (see Chapter 17) until you have reached a design and an element-sizing scheme that are in harmony with each other. Images should be large enough to be worth loading and looking at—while text content in the same area should not be so wide as to be difficult to read.

Additionally, it is essential to provide accessible, alternative content on all forms of media, usually in the form of descriptive text but also, in the case of sound and video, transcripts of any narration or dialogue. There are examples of embedding accessible content in the `<object>` tag (for audio and video, covered next) at this book's companion Web site, `http://sustainablewebdesign.com/book/`.

SOUND

Perhaps more than any other media element, sound must be treated with care if you're not going to drive your audience away with it. For that reason, here is a list of the Three Deadly Sins of misusing sound on the Web:

- **Deadly Sin #1: Sound that plays automatically when someone loads a page.** People view Web sites at work, in their offices, or other places where sound would be embarrassing or unwelcome if it started playing unannounced. Other people prefer to have music playing on their computers while browsing the Web. If sound starts automatically, it creates either embarrassment or an unnerving field of sonic chaos—introducing the potential for people to justifiably hate your site.

- **Deadly Sin #2: Sound that cannot be stopped once it begins playing.** If the only way to stop sound on a Web site is to close it or go to another site, that is exactly what site visitors will do. And they will be very wary of listening to any sound on your site in the future, should they ever come back. It's also best to provide some mechanism to pause sound, rather than just stop it, in case someone needs to step away from the computer but would want to pick up where the sound left off.

- **Deadly Sin #3: Sound that is recorded at low levels.** Sound that is recorded at low levels (that is, sound that is very quiet relative to other sounds, including music and system sounds) will force visitors to turn up their speakers as high as they can. Such an accommodating move can just about send people out of their minds with fright when music or operating-system sounds—like a new email alert—play at their higher levels. Pretty self-explanatory; computers will play other sounds besides yours, and with the audio cranked, poor old Uncle Ed's ticker doesn't stand a chance if he receives a new email or logs off his computer. Refer to the audio section in Chapter 3 and this book's companion Web site at `http://sustainablewebdesign.com/book/` to learn more about ensuring proper sound levels when you record and edit sound files.

There are many different plugins and players for sound (see "Audio Players" sidebar), but the best players will build unobtrusively over

AUDIO PLAYERS

Somewhat remarkably, there is no reliable way to play audio natively in most Web browsers (however, HTML5 will eventually change that; see the book's companion Web site at `http://sustainablewebdesign.com/book/`). But in addition to enabling your users to download your audio for use on their own MP3 players, you can try out a number of audio players for your site that work using ordinary links to audio files. All of these players require the Flash player and JavaScript, but they also leave links to your audio intact, so that JavaScript-less users can still download your audio files and listen to them on their own players:

- Yahoo! Media Player, `http://mediaplayer.yahoo.com/`
- WordPress Audio Player, `http://wpaudioplayer.com/`
- 1 Bit Audio Player, `http://1bit.markwheeler.net/`

Even as HTML5 continues to gain in popularity, it will likely be necessary to provide audio players such as those for users of older Web browsers.

links to your audio files. That is, to include sound on your page, just link to the file, for example, `<a href="/media/audio/mysound.mp3">`. That will, at the very minimum, allow someone to download the sound file and play it on whatever media player the person has available.

Going a step further, there are a few good choices for unobtrusive JavaScript-based audio players that use Flash: the Yahoo! Media Player is probably the easiest to add. You only have to link to it from the `<head>` area of your XHTML pages, and it will detect all of the audio files you link to, put a play button next to them, and add a playlist and customizable player to the bottom of your page.[1]

VIDEO AND FLASH

Depending on the region of the world, Flash is reportedly installed on more than 90 percent (and up to 99%) of all desktop computers.[2] That has made Flash a very popular platform for delivering video; not surprisingly, YouTube, Viddler, Vimeo, and many other video-hosting services use Flash to deliver video content. However, new mobile devices are challenging the use of Flash, so it is likely that other methods for delivering video—probably coupled with HTML5—will become more important to learn in the future. Again, refer to this book's companion site for the latest information.

As with images, you'll need to determine the dimensions that you want your videos to appear at; sites like YouTube will give you different options along these lines, but note that there are two different aspect ratios that are common to video. The old ratio is 4:3, which is shared with older television sets; the newer ratio is 16:9, sometimes 16:10, which is the ratio of widescreen televisions. The aspect ratio matters because a 4:3 video run at 640 pixels wide will be 480 pixels tall, whereas a 16:9 video that is 640 pixels wide will appear only 360 pixels tall. That matters if you are adding additional XHTML structure and CSS, including background images, to increase the visual appeal of your videos.

You can also, if you have access to the proper software, author your own Flash animations for inclusion in your Web pages. (However, as Chapter 19 shows, you can accomplish animation by using JavaScript and a library such as jQuery, especially for interface elements such as the navigation.) Regardless of whether you're loading Flash-based video or a Flash movie of your own construction, SWFObject is one of the better open-source JavaScript libraries for embedding Flash content in a way that is browser-neutral and standards-compliant. SWFObject is included with the RPK.

The SWFObject markup is too involved to show here in the book, but there are excellent tutorials available on, for example, using SWFObject to load YouTube videos.[3] I also have provided examples and detailed instructions at this book's companion Web site.

NEXT STEPS

This chapter has covered some of the core concepts and challenges of loading media content into your Web pages. The next chapter looks at page performance and interaction enhanced by unobtrusive JavaScript.

NOTES

1. Yahoo! Media Player, "How to Link," http://yahoomediaplayer.wikia .com/wiki/How_to_link

2. Adobe, "Flash Player Version Penetration," http://www.adobe.com/ products/player_census/flashplayer/version_penetration.html

3. Heidi Cool, "Embedding YouTube Videos the Standards Compliant Way—SFWobject 2.0" [sic], http://www.heidicool.com/blog/2008/04/20/ embedding-youtube-videos-the-standards-compliant-waysfwobject-20/

CHAPTER 19

Performance and Interaction

Enhancing the performance of your Web pages by adding behavior and interaction using JavaScript and the **Document Object Model (DOM)** is known as **DOM scripting.** DOM scripting is one of the more complex areas of Web design, but it makes possible the sort of rich Web applications and functionality that users have come to expect from sites like Facebook and Gmail. This chapter covers only the most introductory, general approaches to working with DOM scripting; to go deeper in this area, I encourage you to read Jeremy Keith's *DOM Scripting* and other DOM-scripting materials listed in "Resources for the Future."

To help you begin to understand the capabilities of DOM scripting, this chapter explains the principles of unobtrusive JavaScript through approaches to writing with the jQuery JavaScript library (which is included with the Rapid Prototyping Kit, RPK). The chapter introduces three basic but useful tasks that DOM scripting can be used for on your site: manipulating the DOM when JavaScript is present, enhancing pages for wide screens, and handling external links on your site differently from internal links. Additional and more complex examples can be found on the book's companion site at `http://sustaina blewebdesign.com/book/`.

In each of the chapter's examples, however, all of the relationships that this book emphasizes remain the same: XHTML still structures content and CSS handles all design matters; JavaScript performs minor adjustments to the structure of the XHTML, via the DOM. In more advanced uses of DOM scripting, JavaScript may play a more active role in controlling CSS; we will see a small example of this by using jQuery to animate the margins on a site navigation's links in response to the mouse hovering and leaving the links.

DOM SCRIPTING WITH A JAVASCRIPT LIBRARY

Some books, like Keith's *DOM Scripting*, will teach you to write unobtrusive JavaScript completely from scratch.[1] JavaScript by itself provides a number of language features for writing scripts to enhance your pages, but it requires writing a lot of code for some of the more common things that Web designers often want to do, such as selecting some unique element from your page. Additionally, while there is a standard form of JavaScript, known as ECMAScript, certain Web browsers implement it differently. For that reason, scripts written from scratch

JAVASCRIPT LIBRARIES

There are a number of high-quality JavaScript libraries available under permissive open-source licenses. While jQuery (`http://jquery.com/`) is the library I refer to in this book and in the RPK, there are other libraries out there that you might wish to explore:

- MooTools: `http://mootools.net/`
- Prototype: `http://www.prototypejs.org/`

A key benefit of using a JavaScript library (sometimes also called a *framework*) is that it does the heavy lifting for the scripting of your site, leaving you to write leaner, high-level code. Libraries that are updated frequently can also improve the performance of your site over time.

Also, you can elect to host your own copy of your library at your site, or you can use a service like the Google Libraries API* and pull in the library that the service hosts. While it is usually beneficial to have your own copy of the library while you're doing Web development on your computer (if only because you can work without an Internet connection), using the Google Libraries copy may make your live site load faster if someone has already visited another site that also loads the library. And depending on how you load the script from Google,* they can manage updates to the library for you, too.

*Google Code, "Google Libraries API— Developer's Guide," http://code.google.com/apis/libraries/dev guide.html often have to employ certain tricks to get all browsers to interpret the JavaScript the same way.

While writing JavaScript entirely from scratch is a useful skill, for the purposes of this book, we will skip ahead to writing DOM scripts that are built using a JavaScript library called jQuery.

Libraries like jQuery simplify DOM scripting because they are developed and tested extensively on many different browsers. That usually makes cross-browser compatibility much easier to achieve in your scripts. Additionally, JavaScript libraries simplify DOM scripting by offering an application programming interface (API) to build your own custom scripts.

If you think of a library as being something like a DVD player, the library's API is like the buttons on a DVD player: you probably don't need to know how, for example, the play or pause buttons on the player work—but you know what they should do when you press them. You also know that buttons only work in certain situations or under certain conditions: if a DVD is stopped, for example, the pause button will not do anything. And just as a DVD player comes with an owner's manual that documents its functionality, the jQuery library's general documentation is at `http://docs.jquery.com/` and its API is thoroughly documented at `http://api.jquery.com/`.

ANATOMY OF DOM SCRIPTING

The DOM is how a Web browser represents the structure and contents of an XHTML document to itself. JavaScript can then manipulate the browser's representation, or model. Take a familiar example: when you write CSS styles, particularly more complex selectors like `div#header h1`, you rely on the browser to have a model or representation of `<h1>` inside of `<div id="header">` so that the style you write in the CSS appears correctly when the browser displays the page.

jQuery scripts work best when run as soon as the DOM has finished loading; jQuery provides a method for doing that called the ready event, which is attached to the `document` object:

```
/*JavaScript*/
$(document).ready(function()
```

```
    {
                /*Scripts are written here to run
                once the DOM has been loaded*/
    }
);
```

Those lines translate as, "When the document object is ready, do all of the things listed here." Using that event and keeping JavaScript out of your XHTML are the most important factors in keeping your JavaScript unobtrusive. (The examples in the remainder of the chapter must appear inside the ready event.) If JavaScript isn't available in a visitor's browser, the script never runs, but the site must still be accessible to the JavaScript-less site visitor.

jQuery makes certain DOM scripting functions possible using selectors that are identical, or at least very similar, to CSS. If, for example, we wanted to use DOM scripting to put the text "DOM Scripting Is Awesome" in the <h1> tag inside of <div id="header">, we could use jQuery and write a line of JavaScript like this, inside the ready event shown in the source above:

```
/*JavaScript inside the ready event*/
$('div#header h1').html('DOM Scripting Is Awesome');
```

What that would do in the browser is first select all matching elements from the document (thanks to the jQuery dollar function, $();). It completes the match using a descendant selector that we know from CSS (div#header h1), which will find all of the <h1> elements inside of <div id="header">. (However, there should be only one match for <h1> on pages constructed according to the guidance in this book.) The <h1> tag's text will then read "DOM Scripting Is Awesome," regardless of what text the tag contained before.

Provided that that structure appears in your XHTML, the element selected by $('div#header h1') is returned as an object by jQuery and the Web browser. In computer languages, objects have two basic features: methods and properties. Methods are particular things that either object can do or can have done to it: by passing text to the html() method, we can set (rather than just read) the <h1> element's contents. Properties are information about the object—the example above refers to the html() method; used by itself, that method will read a specific property: the text and any XHTML tags that `<h1>` contains.

Under most circumstances, we would not use DOM scripting to set the text of XHTML elements; you would write the text as you'd want it to appear directly in the XHTML itself. In the more practical examples that follow, DOM scripting will be limited to manipulating classes on XHTML elements, which are then styled differently according to rules in the CSS. In one example, we will also preview the animation capabilities of JavaScript by progressively enhancing the link states on site navigation.

This may be all a bit much and confusing. But whether or not you are ready to agree that DOM scripting is awesome, the concepts should become clearer in the working examples below.

DOM SCRIPTING: IS JAVASCRIPT AVAILABLE?

In most of my sites that use DOM scripting, I write a simple function that adds a class of `hasjs` (short for *has JavaScript*) to the `<body>` tag (again, this line goes inside of the ready event):

```
/*JavaScript inside the ready event*/
$('body').addClass('hasjs');
```

That line uses the dollar-sign function to select the `<body>` tag on a page (In a compliant page, there should be only one `<body>` tag, of course.) The script then uses jQuery's `addClass` method to add the `hasjs` class to `<body>`.

Assuming that JavaScript is available and that the user's browser understands the DOM (which jQuery checks for automatically), the `<body>` tag of that document will have the `hasjs` class once the script has run. (You can check that the class has been added by choosing the View Generated Source menu from the Pederick Web Developer Add-on for Firefox.)

Used alone, that line of JavaScript is not very exciting; because it's only adding a class, you'd not even notice that the script has done anything—unless the class then becomes a hook for any advanced CSS styles that should appear in JavaScript environments. For a purely illustrative example with little practical value, if I wanted all paragraph text to appear in red when JavaScript is available, but black otherwise, my CSS file would include:

```
p { color: black; } /*Display paragraphs black*/
body.hasjs p { color: red; } /*Display paragraphs as
 red if JavaScript is available*/
```

DOM SCRIPTING FOR USER CONDITIONS: WIDE SCREENS

A native object in almost all Web browsers is `window`, which can be used to determine—among other things—how large a visitor's browser view-port is. (Of course, that depends on the visitor having JavaScript enabled.)

As was discussed briefly in the layout chapter (Chapter 17), a problem with wide fixed layouts is that they create an irritating horizontal scroll-bar on low-resolution screens. A parallel problem presents itself for wide screens when it comes to liquid layouts, which may not be easy to read on very wide screens because lines of text run out over very long lines.

One solution to designing for both screen sizes is to develop two different layouts: one either a liquid (with widths specified as percentages) or narrower fixed layout (with widths specified in pixels) for small screens, and another a fixed layout for wide screens. Then, using a little progressive enhancement in JavaScript, style the widescreen layout for large screens by using another hook on the `<body>` to deliver the widescreen layout via CSS.

The low-resolution layout should be the default; it seems safe to assume that someone with a low-resolution screen may be less likely to have JavaScript. Beyond that, a low-resolution layout (particularly a fixed one) will obviously be fully visible on a high-resolution screen. In other words, it would be a poor choice to have the default site layout geared for wide screens and use JavaScript to prepare a small-screen version.

This little function, available in the `sites.js` file in the RPK, determines the width of the browser's viewport using the `window` object and jQuery:

```
/*JavaScript*/
function rpkwidescreen() {
var rpkwidth = $(window).width();
```

```
if(rpkwidth>1100) { $('body').addClass('widescreen'); }
else { $('body').removeClass('widescreen'); }
}
```

We can then refer to that function inside of the ready event by writing:

```
/*JavaScript inside the ready event*/
rpkwidescreen();
```

What that function does is determine the width of the window (`width`), in pixels; if it is greater than 1100 pixels, the script manipulates the DOM to add a `widescreen` class to `<body>`. Coupled with the "has JavaScript" function, widescreen views of the site will have a body tag that looks like `<body class="hasjs widescreen">` once the page is loaded and the lines of the script have run.

Perhaps the site specified a default layout, using the `div#page` selector in CSS, that is 700 pixels wide, as in the example from Chapter 17 (see Figure 19.1):

Figure 19.1. The layout as it would appear without JavaScript active (or JavaScript enhancement).

```
/*CSS*/
div#page { width: 700px; }
```

Just below that style, one could write a widescreen style, using the `widescreen` class as a hook:

```
/*CSS*/
body.widescreen div#page { width: 1000px; }
```

Depending on how the rest of the page is designed in CSS, that simple addition may be enough to improve the site's appearance. In the case of the example from Chapter 17, the style declaration on the descendant selector with the `widescreen` hook is indeed all it takes to change the design (see Figure 19.2).

There is one problem, however: in its current form, the `rpkwidescreen();` function is run only once, when the page is loaded. Suppose someone changes the size of his browser window while looking at the site—either using the maximize button or dragging the corner of the browser window to make it larger or smaller. Either way, the window size has changed—perhaps to a wide screen size, perhaps to

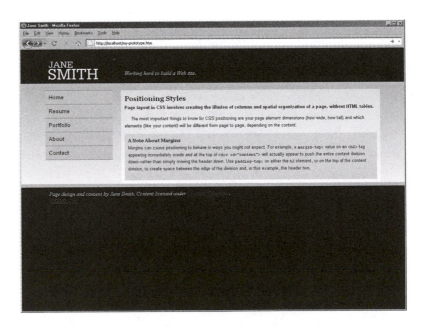

Figure 19.2. Using the `widescreen` class that a bit of DOM Scripting adds to the body, the layout can be adjusted in the CSS to suit larger screens.

a small screen size. To account for changes in the browser window size, an additional line of JavaScript would be necessary:

```
/*JavaScript inside the ready event*/
rpkwidescreen(); /*Check the window size when the
 DOM is ready*/
$(window).resize(rpkwidescreen);
/*Check again, whenever the window is resized*/
```

Using another event (resize), the rpkwidescreen(); function will run every time the browser window changes size. Resizes that are greater than 1100 pixels wide will result in the widescreen class being added to <body> (or being left on, if it already was added). If the window is *less* than 1100 pixels wide, the widescreen class will be removed if it had been added previously. The browser should automatically redraw the layout, if there is a change in size/class, using the appropriate instructions in the CSS.

DOM SCRIPTING FOR PAGE CONTENT: EXTERNAL LINKS

Suppose you wanted to use CSS to style contextual links differently when they point to pages outside of your Web site. That can be done manually with each external link by giving it a class like ext in the XHTML. However, that is time-consuming and tedious work. (CSS 3 has a selector for this, but it is not well supported on all browsers; although jQuery will let us use that selector, as we will see below.) So a DOM scripting solution might be worth exploring.

One thing that distinguishes external links from internal links is that external links must all be prefixed with the HTTP protocol string, http://; without that, Web browsers will actually ask the Web server for a file on your site. For example, <a href="www.google .com"> will cause a browser to look for a *file* named www.google .com on your site; to write the external link correctly so that it points to the Google home page, the href attribute-value would need to be href="http://www.google.com/".

DOM scripting excels at looking for and sorting out values in attributes; jQuery simplifies that process by supporting selectors found in CSS 3—even in browsers (such as Internet Explorer) that don't yet support them for use in CSS. So rather than write a special class for each external link in the XHTML, we could write a bit of DOM scripting that looks for all anchor tags whose `href` attribute begins with `http://`, and then add the `ext` class to each external link the script finds. Because contextual links are probably limited to the main content area (`div#content`), this script will use the descendant selector coupled with an attribute selector that looks for `href` values beginning with `http://`:

```
/*JavaScript inside the ready event*/
$('div#content a[href^=http://]').addClass('ext');
```

Adding a style declaration to the CSS could then color external links red by referring to the `ext` class that DOM scripting adds:

```
/*CSS*/
a.ext { color: red; }
```

Users without JavaScript will not experience any difference in your links, so if you think that it is critical for all users to be able to visually distinguish between internal and external links, the manual route of putting `class="ext"` on your external links in your XHTML source would be the better way to go.

DOM SCRIPTING AND ANIMATION

The uses of jQuery we have seen so far have show only a little of the library's ability. This final example will preview a bit more of its ability in handling simple animations. (To go even further with animation, you should investigate the official jQuery UI library.[2])

What we will do in this example is animate the `margin-right:` property on a navigation area's links to make them appear wider when moused over. A pure CSS approach to this would have a simple `:hover` selector that reduces the `margin-right:` from, for example, 30 pixels to 0 pixels, resulting in the effect of the navigation item expanding when it's moused over:

```
ul#navigation a { margin-right: 30px; }
ul#navigation a:hover { margin-left: 0px; }
```

In fact, to progressively enhance your pages, you would want to leave that in place, so that JavaScript-less users would see an indication of which link they're hovering over.

But to enhance the hover effect, we can use the hover(); and an-imate(); methods in jQuery to provide a smooth animation. Rather than the CSS jumping from 30 pixels to 0 pixels of righthand margin in the blink of an eye, we can tell jQuery to make the transition over a period of time, using either keywords such as fast or slow, or a specific time value in milliseconds (one second is equal to 1,000 milliseconds). The DOM scripting for this looks like:

```
/*JavaScript inside the ready event*/
$('ul#navigation a').hover(
function() {
        $(this).animate( { "margin-right": 0 } ,
        "slow");
},
function() {
        $(this).animate( { "margin-right": 30 } ,
        "slow");
        }
);
```

What those lines accomplish are first to select all of the anchor tags inside of <ul id="navigation"> and then add a hover event to them. The hover event in jQuery can take two functions: the first specifies what happens when a mouse moves over the element and the second specifies what happens when the mouse moves out and away from the element. The $(this) selector refers to the element selected origi-nally (ul#navigation a), and it takes the animate(); method, which can animate any numerical property in CSS (such as widths, heights, margins, padding, and opacity but not—importantly—colors; you'd need to use the jQuery UI library or another plugin to animate colors).

With that script in place, anyone mousing over the elements in this navigation who also has JavaScript will see the navigation buttons slowly become wider when they are moused over and slowly shrink

FINDING SCRIPTS

You can find all kinds of freely downloadable JavaScript code on the Web. But be very cautious of using just any old JavaScript, as many use outdated practices. A safer way to search for scripts is to look for ones that run with your JavaScript library of choice. Certain libraries, including jQuery, even host plugin libraries that you can browse.* But be judicious and test any plugins well on multiple browsers; the quality of scripts written by others varies widely.

*jQuery.com, *jQuery Plugins*, http://plugins.jquery.com/

back to normal when the mouse moves away. Have a look at the working example at `http://sustainablewebdesign.com/book/`.

NEXT STEPS

This chapter concludes the strategies for success for building individual pages. The next steps are for you to build in the rest of the pages of your site and prepare it for going live—topics that are covered in the next section, "Problems and Solutions."

NOTES

1. Jeremy Keith, *DOM Scripting: Web Design with JavaScript and the Document Object Model* (Berkeley, CA: Friends of Ed/Apress, 2005).
2. jQuery UI, "jQuery UI," http://jqueryui.com/

PART IV

PROBLEMS AND SOLUTIONS

This section of the book covers the problems and possible solutions that impact the architecture and launch of your live site. It also introduces some of the dynamic approaches and systems (specifically Word-Press) that you can use to help build and maintain your Web site. The section concludes with a chapter on tracking visitors to your site and making it easier for them to share and repurpose your content in order to establish your reputation further across the Web, beyond the borders of your own site.

CHAPTER 20

Site Architecture

The architecture of a Web site is the organization of all its pages, and how the pages relate to one another. A good site architecture matters to you as a site's designer, as it helps you to easily locate and edit your pages, and link them to one another.

Site architecture is equally important to your site's visitors. A sensible URL structure and a site navigation that reveals the general contents of your site increase the likelihood that users will understand what's on your site, how to find it, and where they are relative to the rest of your site.

To build a manageable Web site involves developing a thoughtful, scalable architecture for its pages—and a Web-like environment to test it in. This chapter looks at some of the choices you will have to make in developing your site's architecture once you have a local Web server running to test it in.

SETTING UP XAMPP FOR LOCAL DEVELOPMENT

If you open a Web page directly in a browser using File > Open, you'll see the address bar display a long URL like this one, on Windows:

```
file:///C:/Documents%20and%20Settings/username/
website/htdocs/index.htm
```

That causes serious problems for root-relative links (described below), which will go all the way back to the hard drive, `C:/`. The file URL also makes things needlessly confusing when it comes to designing your URLs. And if you are using any PHP (see Chapter 21), you also cannot test it in the simple file view, because running a Web server is required to interpret PHP in your pages.

The solution to those problems is to set up a little Web server that runs on your computer—or even on a USB drive. One of the easiest ways to set up your own Web server for development and testing is to install XAMPP.[1] XAMPP is a distribution of the Apache Web server, as well as MySQL and PHP (which are necessary for running WordPress). Although the word *server* may bring to mind a gigantic computer, a Web server is actually software, like XAMPP, which can run on your own computer while you work up your site's architecture as well as its design and content. (XAMPP is not designed to host your live site, however.)

I have posted on this book's companion Web site instructions for setting up XAMPP (see `http://sustainablewebdesign`.`com/book/`), but on Windows you basically only need to download XAMPP, unzip it to a USB drive, and click the `xampp_start` application in the `xampp/` folder to have a fully operational local Web server. You can then access your pages from your Web browser using a special URL, `http://localhost/`, provided that you put your site in XAMPP's root web folder, `htdocs`, which is inside of the `xampp/` folder. (There is an `htdocs/` folder that comes with XAMPP; you can just rename it to `htdocs-original/`, in case you need it later, before creating your own `htdocs/` folder or copying the `htdocs/` folder from the RPK.)

When you go to upload your site (see Chapter 23), your actual domain's URLs should function the same when you, for example, click on your links as the `http://localhost/` URLs in your XAMPP installation. You can think of `localhost` as a placeholder for your actual domain name.

SITE ARCHITECTURE

Chapter 5 and the Rapid Prototyping Kit (RPK) offer a folder structure for the different design and media components of your site. But the pages that make up your site require an architecture, too.

There are three types of architectures that are commonly used on Web sites:

- **File-oriented architecture,** which places all of the XHTML pages of a site in the root Web folder
- **Folder-oriented architecture,** which places related pages into separate folders off of the root Web folder
- **Data-driven architecture,** which typically relies on databases and the Web server to mimic file and folder references

Each of these types of architectures has its benefits and appropriate applications, depending on the size and type of site that uses them.

Simple: File-Oriented Architecture

The most basic site architecture is created by saving all of your XHTML files right into the root of your Web folder. This keeps your URLs short and simple, in a pattern like `http://example.com/mypage.htm`.

Having all of your XHTML files located in the root of a site may not be a problem if there are only a dozen or so pages on your site. But if the site grows to several dozen or more, having a massive list of all of the `.htm` files may make it difficult to find the page you want to edit.

Scale presents another problem for a designer who dumps all pages into the root of a site, regardless of the site's size. Pages that are related to one another, such as pages for individual portfolio items, will not necessarily be grouped together in file listings, which are ordered alphabetically or by modification date.

With a file-oriented architecture, users may become needlessly disoriented as well. That is, if all of your pages are kept in the root Web folder, but there are distinct areas of your site, a file-only URL does not reveal anything about the user's location within the larger structure of your site—or the context of a given page. (Navigation might help suggest context—but you shouldn't put everything in the navigation, either.) Consider the difference between `http://example.com/fruit.htm` and `http://example.com/paintings/fruit.htm`; which page can you better guess the contents of? The latter provides more than a hint and is the product of a folder-oriented architecture.

Complex and Scalable: Folder-Oriented Architecture

One alternative method for controlling the clutter of individual files in your root Web folder while also helping users orient themselves within your site is to create folders for each of your major site areas.

For example, rather than having a portfolio overview located at `http://example.com/portfolio.htm`, your portfolio can be located at `http://example.com/portfolio/`, thanks to the magic of the index file (see "The Index File" sidebar). Then, all of your portfolio items, like a company newsletter that you designed, can be stored in the portfolio folder, and accessed at URLs like `http://example.com/portfolio/company-newsletter.htm`.

The benefit of folders is that users can cut down the URLs to move up to higher levels in a site. In other words, visitors to your site can go to the address bar in their browsers and delete the file name off of

THE INDEX FILE

Most Apache Web servers are configured to serve `index.htm` when either the root of a site or a folder is requested (e.g., `http://example.com/` or `http://example.com/contact/`). If you save a file named `index.htm` in your root, but still see a listing of files, you may need to configure your Web server by adding a line that looks something like this to your `.htaccess` file:

```
DirectoryIndex index.htm index.html index.php
```

If the server finds `index.htm`, it will display that; otherwise, it looks for the `.html` or `.php` versions of `index`.

If you do not create your own index file, your Web server might list all of the files and folders in a given directory. To prevent your Web server from doing that in indexless folders (such as your `media` folder), add this line to your `.htaccess` as well:

```
Options -Indexes
```

That should prevent people from snooping the files on your site, in case you forget to save an index file in a folder where you have files that aren't quite ready for the world. There are additional `.htaccess` directives available at this book's companion site, `http://sustainablewebdesign.com/book/`.

the end of the URL and come upon, for example, an overview page at `http://example.com/portfolio/`.

And that is what is meant by a shallow architecture and navigation: a long URL like `http://example.com/portfolio/design/newsletters/` represents a deep architecture, presumably (or ideally) with overviews or landing pages at each level. Representing those in navigation or promotional links becomes a challenge—as does sharing URLs in email and elsewhere. Being selective of materials for a site and coming up with a shallow architecture help prevent a site from becoming needlessly complex.

That being said, even for areas of your site that might have only one page, you can still use a shallow folder-style architecture. You might save your resume, for example, as `index.htm` and place it in a `resume` folder, resulting in a URL for the resume like `http://example.com/resume/`.

Dynamic: Data-Driven Architecture

If you decide to build a site using WordPress or another blogging or content management system (CMS), your site's architecture with that system can be entirely dynamic. For example, `http://example.com/resume/` on a WordPress site would not point to a `resume` folder; instead, WordPress uses the `resume/` part of the URL to pull your resume out of its database. (See Chapter 22 for information about configuring WordPress and your Web server to use these so-called pretty URLs.)

However, if you're not yet ready to make the leap to WordPress, opting for a consistent, folder-oriented structure may make it easier for you to transfer your site to WordPress or another CMS's control later. To Google and to your users, a URL is a URL, whether it points to actual files and folders, or later to an abstract reference in a database.

ARCHITECTURE, PATHS, AND NAVIGATION

Site architecture matters also when it comes time to start linking your pages together, whether through site navigation or contextual links in your site's content. To link to resources within your site requires an understanding of URL paths, which instruct the browser to load different resources from your site onto a page (images or other media, as well as CSS and JavaScript files), or to take visitors to different pages.

Absolute, Relative, and Root-Relative Paths

There are three types of paths that you can write for your links: absolute, relative, and root-relative. To keep Web sites portable and to make their development easier (especially using an XAMPP installation's `http://localhost/` URL), it's generally preferable to use relative or root-relative links.

Absolute Links

Absolute links (sometimes called absolute URLs or absolute paths) include your full domain name and the name of the page/resource. For example, the absolute link to your resume might be `http://exam ple.com/resume.htm`. Absolute URLs are what people commonly share in email and what must be used to link one Web site to another.

However, aside from the absolute link to your Web site's home page in the header area of your pages (see Chapter 14), it's usually not a good idea to use absolute links to pages within your own site: not only are they longer, but if you should switch domain names or set up archives of your site at a subdomain, for example, `http://archive .example.com/resume.htm`, any absolute `http://example.com/` URLs in your links will no longer refer to items within the same version of the site.

Relative Links

To make sites more portable, you can use relative links, which are links created relative to the current document's place in the site architecture.

In a site with a file-oriented architecture, where all files exist directly in the root Web folder, relative links are very easy to write: to link from any page in the site to, for example, your resume, you would just write `<a href="resume.htm">view my resume</a>`.

But if your portfolio were in one folder and your resume in another (and saved as `index.htm`), to link to your resume from a page in your portfolio folder, you would have to write `<a href="../resume/">` or `<a href="../resume/index.htm">`. The `../` tells the server to move up one folder (out of `portfolio/` and up to the Web root) and then down into the `resume` folder. To move up two folders would be `../../`, three would be `../../../` and so on. It gets confusing pretty quickly; so let relative links serve as another argument against a deep architecture, and perhaps against relative links themselves.

Root-Relative Links

I prefer to write root-relative links in most situations; root-relative links always begin with a slash (`/`), representing the root Web folder, and proceed to the full path relative to the root of the site. Root-relative links will work from anywhere in a site, even if you have a very complex architecture: `<a href="/resume/">` can be used anywhere; because it starts from the root, it can always be found—provided that `resume/` is in the root Web folder. (However, root-relative links will only work during the development and testing of your site if you use something like XAMPP to run a Web server on your local computer.)

There is one case where you cannot write root-relative links beginning with a slash, though. If you are using a Web account like you might get through your school or business and it has a URL structure like `http://university.edu/~yourusername/`, you'd need to prefix all of your links with `/~yourusername/` to make them root-relative—otherwise, the root-relative links will point to (nonexistent) files and folders off of `university.edu/`. And, of course, once you have added `/~yourusername/` to your links, they will no longer be portable if you decide to purchase your own domain name. So add the root-relative link issue to the list of reasons why Chapter 5 urged you to buy your own domain name, rather than relying on hosting from your school or employer.

NEXT STEPS

As you begin to build a site architecture and test your pages using XAMPP, you move closer to creating a site that is ready for posting to the open Web. The next two chapters look at PHP and WordPress; if you aren't interested in those for the time being, skip ahead to Chapter 23, which talks about transferring your Web site to the server space that you've purchased from your Web host.

NOTE

1. Apache Friends, "XAMPP," http://www.apachefriends.org/en/xampp .html

CHAPTER 21

Reusing and Dynamically Generating Content

One advantage to styling your Web site using a single CSS file is that your design instructions are shared over multiple XHTML pages, which all load the same CSS file in the `<link>` tag. A change to one CSS file changes the design of your entire site.

But what about content? If you have a site with 20 pages, and you need to make a change to your navigation, you face the unhappy task of changing your navigation 20 times. While you could try and use a search-and-replace function across your files, you're still left with uploading all 20 files to your live Web site (not to mention placing a lot of faith in search and replace).

As you begin to develop your site's pages, you will no doubt notice that there are many structural features in addition to the navigation—the `<head>` area of your XHTML and your branding, for two examples—that are the same or almost the same from page to page.

Rather than rewriting the same content on every page, an alternative solution is to have a file that contains the repeated content and share it with all pages. Such content reuse, however, would require a different kind of design from the static XHTML pages that we have looked at so far. Static XHTML files (plus CSS and JavaScript) are rendered directly in the browser. To reuse content or otherwise make your pages more dynamic involves some kind of preparation on the server, otherwise known as **server-side scripting.**

When you purchase Web hosting, you're not just purchasing storage space: you're purchasing access to a Web server, which can do much more than simply transfer files down to a visitor's Web browser. The metaphor that I like to use is that Web sites made up of static XHTML pages are sort of like vending machines, whereas dynamic sites are more like fast-food restaurants. If you post an XHTML file to your Web site, and someone accesses it, the page on their machine is identical to the one on your server—not unlike when you see a candy bar in a vending machine, put in your money, and hit the button for the candy bar. Nothing changes about the candy bar when it falls from its little slot and into your hands.

Dynamic pages, however, are prepared by the Web server; it's a process that's instantaneous, but what lives on your server is not the complete file as it will be seen by visitors, but rather some mix of dynamic and static content. When you go to a burger joint, they don't (I hope) hand you a bun, ketchup, and a wad of raw meat; they take those ingredients, prepare them, and then hand them to you. Take that example to a Web server offering dynamic content: the server can assemble dynamic content from a number of different files before sending what appears to be a complete, static page to your visitors.

From the visitor's point of view, there is no difference between a dynamic page and a static one: a dynamic page still appears in the browser as XHTML, CSS, and JavaScript. And that's important to remember, and why this book has looked at XHTML, CSS, and JavaScript so closely: no matter what you have going on behind the scenes on your server, you are still offering XHTML, CSS, and JavaScript for users to experience your Web site.

PHP, a recursive acronym that stands for **PHP Hypertext Preprocessor,** is a widely used open-source server-side scripting language.[1] PHP is great for building simple dynamic XHTML Web pages. In fact, it is the language that WordPress (see Chapter 22) and many other open-source Web software packages are written in. In this chapter, we will look at some basic uses of PHP that will prepare you to learn how to create and modify your own WordPress templates.

WRITING PHP

By default on most Web servers, any files containing PHP must be named with a `.php` file extension (though see the "Parsing PHP in `.htm` Files" sidebar).

To call PHP into action requires using PHP tags; these are not the same as XHTML tags. PHP tags open with `<?php` and close with `?>`, and they allow you to jump in and out of static XHTML. The server will interpret, or parse, the PHP code appearing between the PHP tags. For example, to output the current year, a file might contain:

```
<p>The current year is <?php echo date('Y'); ?>.</p>
```

which during the year 2011 would appear in the browser's source view as

```
<p>The current year is 2011.</p>
```

Again, from the visitor's point of view, the page is nothing but XHTML. Unless there is something wrong with the Web server,

---

PARSING PHP IN `.HTM` FILES

By default on most Web servers, any files with PHP that you want the server to parse must have a `.php` extension.

If you have a site with lots of `.htm` or `.html` pages, but you decide to include PHP in them, you don't have to rename the file extensions from `.htm` to `.php`. Different Web hosts require different instructions for parsing PHP in `.htm` or `.html` pages, but usually you must edit the `.htaccess` file in your site's root Web folder so that it contains a line such as:

```
AddHandler application/x-httpd-php .php .htm .html
```

(This line is included in the RPK's `.htaccess` file; remove the hashes in front of it to use.)

Check the specific documentation for your Web host as to what lines you must put into `.htaccess` for this purpose. This is an example of why Chapter 5 suggested purchasing Web hosting from hosts that enable configuration with `.htaccess` files; there will be other examples of `.htaccess` in the chapter on WordPress.

visitors will never be able to detect which parts of your pages are static XHTML and which parts are created dynamically by PHP. (As you will see when you begin to work with WordPress templates, you can jump in and out of PHP as many times as you'd like. Just be sure to open and close your PHP tags.)

Anatomy of PHP

The majority of basic PHP involves writing or working with functions. Functions are made up of the function name, followed by open and closing parentheses where you would write any information, known as arguments, that the function needs. For example, if we had a function called `greet();` and it took the argument of the name of someone to greet, say Tom, we would write `greet("Tom");`, which might output `Hello, Tom!`, depending on how the function itself was written. PHP has both built-in functions, like the `date();` function above, and mechanisms to write your own functions. We will look at examples of both below.

PHP also has what are known as language constructs; they are sort of like functions, but use a different syntax—one that doesn't use parentheses. The most common construct is `echo`, which outputs any text you'd like, as though you'd typed it into your Web pages

---

PHPINFO

PHP has a special built-in function that will give you all sorts of information about your Web server. Simply write this in a blank text file:

```
<?php phpinfo(); ?>
```

and save it as `mysiteinfo.php`. Pull it up in your Web browser (e.g., at `http://localhost/mysiteinfo.php`), and you'll see all kinds of information about your Web server or XAMPP development environment (see Chapter 20).

That page can help you determine what your server has installed and whether it meets the requirements for running software like WordPress. PHPInfo doesn't make for thrilling reading; just know that it's there if you have a question about your Web server's environment or configuration.

yourself. (You will sometimes see a practically synonymous construct, `print`; the differences between the two are subtle, but for me it comes down to laziness: "echo" is faster to type than "print." It's one less character, and I don't have to inconvenience my pinky to type "p.")

In XHTML, you would type:

```
<h1>Site Overview</h1>
```

In PHP, you could write something similar to this:

```
<?php
echo "<h1>Site Overview</h1>";
?>
```

Their appearance in a user's browser would be identical.

Escaping

`echo` relies on quotation marks (single or double) to specify the contents of a string, which is just a collection of characters, as far as PHP is concerned. However, when writing plain old English prose, it's common to use quotation marks and apostrophes. When quotation marks appear inside of a string marked by quotation marks, for example, they need to be escaped with a backslash, \.

```
<?php
echo "I've just read \"The Road Not Taken\" by
Robert Frost.";
?>
```

In the browser, someone will see

```
I've just read "The Road Not Taken" by Robert Frost.
```

Escaping the quotation marks just keeps PHP from being confused that the string is ending earlier than you intend.

Sometimes, as when you are writing your own functions, you need to insert the contents of a variable into an echo statement. To do this, you need to use concatenation, a very fancy word for the unfancy task of simply joining strings and variables together. In PHP, you concatenate using dots. For example, if a script had a variable called `$username` (variables in PHP always begin with a dollar sign), it could be output as part of a greeting by writing:

```
<?php
$username = "Tom";
echo "Hello there, " . $username . "! It is good to
see you again.";
?>
```

Viewed in a browser, that short PHP script would output

```
Hello there, Tom! It is good to see you again.
```

The include(); Function

One of the most basic but useful features in PHP is its include(); function, which will add the contents of any file you include to the page where you call include(); from. If the file you include is a .php file, any PHP instructions in it will also be executed by the server.

The trick with include(); is that by default, it looks for paths relative to your server root, not your root Web folder. For this reason, it's convenient to put files you want to include in their own folder, perhaps off of the Web root, called includes. Then, in your include function, you'd use a PHP variable called $_SERVER["DOCUMENT_ROOT"], which contains the location of your root Web folder, followed by the includes folder and the file you wish to include. So, for example, if you had a folder called includes/ with a file that contained only your navigation, navigation.php, you'd write

```
<?php
    include($_SERVER["DOCUMENT_ROOT"].
    "/includes/navigation.php");
?>
```

wherever you want your navigation to appear.

That looks a little ugly, but by using the PHP document root variable, your include instructions should transfer easily from your development environment to your live Web site.

WRITING YOUR OWN FUNCTIONS

`include();` will go a long way to making your sites more manageable by repeating shared content. However, used the way it was above with the navigation file, it can only output the complete content of the file. To repeat content without including multiple files, as well as offer content that is slightly different from page to page, you can write a single PHP file that contains your own custom functions for each piece of repeated content.

You'll still need to use `include();` to load your functions file, but you'll only need to use the include function once, probably at the very top of your page. An important part of functions is that, unlike simple included files, they allow you to specify **arguments**, or bits of unique information, to use the function in a custom way on your pages. For example, let's say you wanted to write a function to display the <head> area on all of your pages. (You could write this function in a file you name `functions.php`.) To write custom functions in PHP, you must write `function` followed by the name you want to give the function. The contents of the function itself are written between curly braces. To prevent your custom functions from conflicting with the functions built in to PHP, prefix the names of your custom functions with your initials, or perhaps initials of your domain, and an underscore. I have written some custom functions in the RPK, all of which are prefixed with `rpk_`.

One of the elements in the head area of every page is the <title> tag, which should have text that provides a unique title for each page of your site. That can be handled by specifying an argument, `$title`, that must be specified when you actually call the function in your pages:

```
/*PHP*/
function rpk_head($title) {
echo "<head>
      <meta http-equiv=\"Content-Type\" content=
      \"text/html; charset=utf-8\" />
      <title>" . $title . " - Example.com</title>
      </head>";
}
```

Then, to actually call the `rpk_head();` function on your XHTML page, you'd write something like:

```
<!DOCTYPE html PUBLIC "-//W3C//DTD XHTML 1.0
Strict//EN" "http://www.w3.org/TR/xhtml1/DTD/
xhtml1-strict.dtd">
<html>
<!--The <head> gets loaded in a dynamically in
PHP-->
<?php
include($_SERVER["DOCUMENT_ROOT"] . "/includes/
functions.php");
rpk_head("Overview");
?>
<!--End PHP; resume static XHTML-->
<body>
```

A more complete function might also output the DOCTYPE declaration and any other repeated elements as part of the function rather than in the static XHTML as in the example above; the very basic `<head>` area here is only intended as a simplified example.

You can find additional functions in the RPK; see `http://sustainablewebdesign.com/book/`.

PHP AND SUSTAINABILITY

PHP is an open-source language and, while not as consistent or elegant as some other languages that are gaining popularity on the Web, particularly Ruby,[2] PHP is widely used and can contribute to your site's overall sustainability.

However, it is important that you review any custom PHP that you have written from time to time, and check any functions you've used against the reference at PHP.net. Functions occasionally become deprecated, meaning that they are no longer advisable to use, and may eventually be removed from the language entirely. However, other functions will take their place—and the PHP.net documentation is very good about making replacement functions clear. That being said, you can pretty much count on `echo` and `include();` to be around well into the future.

NEXT STEPS

This chapter has only scratched the surface of PHP, but it is enough to help you start work with the content in the next chapter on Word-Press. WordPress is written in PHP and has many of its own functions available that you can use to build or edit a WordPress template.

NOTES

1. PHP.net, http://php.net/
2. Ruby Programming Language, http://www.ruby-lang.org/en/

CHAPTER 22

Dynamic Sites in WordPress

As we have seen, Web sites can be a collection of XHTML files, perhaps enhanced with PHP. One benefit of keeping a site as a collection of files like that is that the site's content will require minimal maintenance, as it is delivered more or less as-is to site visitors.

But there are drawbacks to sites that are collections of files: you have to have access to an FTP or SFTP client to upload changed files to your site, and that's not always possible to set up on computers that aren't your own. The required FTP or SFTP access to a site may also complicate collaboration, if you are building a site together with other people—unless you trust them with your SFTP password (and you shouldn't; they'll goof something up and it'll be your problem to fix).

Collections of files also become more difficult to revise and improve if a site grows to hundreds or thousands of pages; file- and folder-based architectures have trouble supporting that kind of growth. Finally, unless you are using PHP or another server-side language to include repeated page elements, such as site navigation, even minor changes to all of your site's pages can become needlessly time-consuming.

This chapter looks at WordPress, a popular open-source blogging and content management system (CMS). While WordPress's primary function is as a blogging system, it can also be used to create, manage, and revise the kinds of pages found on many different kinds of portfolio, organizational, or business sites.

OPEN-SOURCE PROJECTS

WordPress is an example of an open-source software project.

A key idea behind open-source software is that its source is available for viewing and, if released with a permissive license, also for modification and extension.

In the case of WordPress, not only is the source available, but there is a large community of people who are actively working on the software. That means that WordPress is more reflective of the blogging community that uses it, and also that bugs and potential security issues are usually found and fixed very quickly.

Even as a user of WordPress, you can contribute to the community by reporting problems, contributing to the documentation, or even—if you get good enough—working on the WordPress source itself. The techniques for WordPress templating in this chapter are a good first step in that direction.

To read more about the open-source movement, visit the Open Source Initiative at `http://opensource.org/`. You might also want to read Eric Raymond's book *The Cathedral and the Bazaar.**

---

*Eric S. Raymond, *The Cathedral and the Bazaar: Musings on Linux and Open Source by an Accidental Revolutionary,* revised and expanded ed. (Sebastopol, CA: O'Reilly Media, 2001).

One word of caution, though: if you opt to run your Web site with WordPress, you need to make a commitment to regularly update your copy of WordPress so that you always have the latest, most secure version. You should also check before you purchase Web hosting that your hosting company regularly updates its PHP, MySQL database, and Apache Web server and that the hosting company's advertised versions meet the current WordPress requirements for PHP, MySQL, and Apache.

UNDERSTANDING WORDPRESS AND SITE ARCHITECTURE

Like many content management systems, WordPress does not store your content in separate files (as you do when you create XHTML pages). Instead, WordPress keeps your content organized in a database. In addition to storing site content, WordPress also uses its database to store configuration settings and site preferences. The only exception to that is the `wp-config.php` file, which is where it stores information about connecting to your database and some other information about your Web server and Web site (`wp-config.php` is set up the first time that you install WordPress, although you can edit it in your text editor later, if necessary).

So when people access blog posts or pages in WordPress, the URLs are actually instructing WordPress to retrieve records from a database. By default, WordPress has a URL scheme that looks like `http://ex ample.com/?q=21`, where "21" refers to some record in the database. But if your Web host has enabled Apache's mod_rewrite module (most do, but check before you purchase hosting),[1] you can set up WordPress to generate "pretty" URLs, like `http://example.com/about/`. (See the sidebar "PHPInfo" in Chapter 21 for determining your Web host's server configuration.)

Understanding that URL scheme requires a bit of a conceptual shift, though. So far, we have seen that a pattern like `http://example.com/about/` usually indicates the presence of a folder called `about/` in your root Web folder. Not so with WordPress and mod_rewrite, which let you write URLs that are independent of files and folders. You can

THE DOCUMENTATION: WORDPRESS CODEX

The documentation for WordPress is called the Codex, and it is available at `http://codex.wordpress.org/`. Although the Codex includes a search function, I often find it easier to search the Codex using Google, using Google's `site:` syntax and the Codex URL. For example, to search for pages in the Codex that talk about template tags, I'd go to Google and search:

```
template tags site:codex.wordpress.org
```

Here are some other tips for reading the Codex:

- Have PHP.net open to consult on the particulars of PHP.
- Use your browser's Find function (`Ctrl` or `Cmd + F`) to wade through long pages.
- If you are working to fix a problem with your site or template, do not ignore posts in the WordPress forums; the odds are that someone has had the same problem or question as you at some point.

even configure WordPress to automatically generate URLs according to particular patterns for different types of content, although you still retain the option to edit the URLs on each blog post or page that you create.[2]

INSTALLING WORDPRESS

WordPress is constantly revised and improved, so in addition to the installation suggestions at `http://sustainablewebdesign.com/book/`, be sure to consult WordPress's instructions.[3]

However, here are some general points to consider when installing WordPress:

- If you only want to use WordPress for a blog, and not for the rest of your site's pages, consider installing WordPress in a dedicated folder, such as `blog/`, so that your WordPress blog would be accessed at `http://example.com/blog/`.
- If you want to use WordPress to manage your entire site, you can install it in the site's root Web folder. However, I have found that it is much easier to later update WordPress when it's stored in its own folder off of the site root, such as `wp/`. You'll have to move the WordPress `.htaccess` and `index.php` file into your site root, but keeping the core WordPress files in their own directory makes updates easier, and keeps your site root folder more tidy.
- If you set up WordPress so that you can upload images and other media, consider using the `media/` folder from the RPK, perhaps with a `wp/` subfolder where WordPress can keep your media uploads organized. By default, WordPress stores uploads inside of the `wp-content` folder, but that can make upgrading WordPress tricky if you want to start with a clean installation on each upgrade (discussed at the end of this chapter).
- If you allow comments on your blog, be sure to obtain an API Key from Wordpress.com (the hosting site of Wordpress.org),[4] which will let you set up the Akismet plugin that comes with WordPress.[5] It does an outstanding job of catching spam comments, saving you the headache of filtering literally thousands of spam comments by hand.

TEMPLATING WORDPRESS

WordPress has a system for building custom templates. I have also created a starter WordPress template based on the Rapid Prototyping Kit (RPK). It uses the same structural blocks as the XHTML version of the RPK, so the good news is that if you have used the RPK for designing your XHTML pages, building a WordPress template from your design may be very easy: you may not have to touch the PHP templating files at all; simply copy your CSS files into the correct place in the RPK template folder. (The complete details of the RPK WordPress template are at this book's companion site, `http://sustainablewebde sign.com/book/`.)

The Template File Hierarchy

To customize the content and look of your WordPress site, it's important to understand WordPress's template hierarchy, which is the order of files that WordPress checks in your theme folder to decide which template to display for a given page. The hierarchy moves from specific to general. For example, if WordPress is trying to display a page, it looks for the specific `page.php` file; absent that, Word-Press will simply use the generic `index.php` fallback as it does for all pages.

There is a "Visual Overview" of the template hierarchy at the Codex,[6] but here is a basic description of what you will find in the WordPress version of the RPK:

- `page.php`, for displaying individual pages
- `single.php`, for displaying individual posts, with comments and a comment form
- `archive.php`, for displaying per-date, per-category, or per-tag listings of posts
- `search.php`, for displaying the results of searches
- `404.php`, for alerting users to a missing page
- `index.php`, for displaying the home page of your site

The template hierarchy provides mechanisms for specifying additional templates, but this is the basic set for a baseline template.

Additionally, there are files that are used to build the header, footer, and sidebar across all templates and display a custom comment form when necessary:

- `header.php` includes the head area and header branding. Some of the information, such as the site title and URL, will be pulled from your WordPress database; the rest you can copy from your RPK prototype file.
- `footer.php` includes the footer area, which uses essentially the same XHTML markup from the footer area of the RPK's `prototype.htm` file.
- `sidebar.php` includes the navigation and room for any widgets you'd like your site to include.
- `comments.php` handles the list of blog post comments and the comment form.
- `functions.php` handles any miscellaneous custom site functions in PHP that you wish to include (see Chapter 21).

As you will discover by working with the files, templating for WordPress is not a whole lot different from working with the regular RPK—except that there is PHP intermingled throughout. It's also helpful to enter a few blog posts in WordPress and/or a few pages, and compare their output in the browser (using View > Source) with the template files as they appear in your text editor. You may also find it useful to open the WordPress Edit Post page to edit an already-published post, so you can see where the items in the WordPress Edit Post interface (the post title, the post body, the date, and so on) appear in the published post as viewed in the browser.

Editing and designing the CSS is no different from editing the CSS for static pages (although the RPK WordPress template does include some additional `<div>` tags for you to work with). Remember that, no matter what system is running on the Web server, the browser still receives XHTML that you can experiment styling using the Pederick Web Developer Add-on or other in-browser development tools. And because the RPK WordPress templates use the same structure as the plain XHTML version, your CSS from a static site built in the RPK should transfer quite easily.

UPGRADING WORDPRESS

If you run WordPress or another blog/CMS package to power your Web site, it is essential to keep your site updated with the latest version. Although WordPress has an automated upgrade system, I find it preferable to upgrade manually so as to retain control over and see firsthand the changes to my WordPress sites. See the next chapter, "Going Live," to learn about connecting to your hosting account and uploading files.

Assuming you followed the recommendation above of keeping WordPress in its own directory and the suggestions at the book's companion site, upgrading WordPress is not too painful of a process.

First, you want to go to your administration panel in WordPress and disable all of your plugins.

Second, back up your `wp-content` folder; this is where, among other things, your file uploads may appear (although if you specify an alternate location for the uploads, outside of the WordPress directory, this is not an issue). Pull a copy of `wp-content` down from your Web site using your FTP or SFTP client for archival purposes (that allows you to restore your WordPress installation, should something go wrong with the upgrade). You should also be sure to download copies of your `wp-config.php` file and `index.php` where you modified the path to WordPress.

Third, it's important to back up your database. If you have SSH access, you can do this by running

```
mysqldump -umyusername -pmypassword wpdatabase >
wpdatabase.sql
```

replacing `myusername` and `mypassword` with your database username and password (though keep the `-u` and `-p`) and `wpdatabase` with the name of your WordPress database. If you don't have SSH access, locate the database administration tool provided by your Web host to dump/export your database for backup.

Finally, I prefer to delete all of the WordPress files on my server before uploading fresh copies. Using your FTP program, you can delete the remote folders `wp-admin` and `wp-includes`, as well as all of the `.php` files that begin with `wp-`. You can also delete `xmlrpc.php`; a new copy will be uploaded with your upgrade.

Download a new copy of WordPress to your computer and drag in your custom theme, plugin, and upload folders (if they are not stored outside of the WordPress folder) to their appropriate locations in `wp-content`. Copy over your `wp-config.php` and `index.php` files, too. Then, upload the whole set of files to your server.

NEXT STEPS

WordPress enables you to maintain a dynamic, database-driven Web site. But it requires you do regular maintenance and upgrades over time, including uploading copies of the WordPress site to your hosting space. The key details on moving your site—whether it's a collection of static files or a WordPress installation—are covered in the next chapter, "Going Live."

NOTES

1. Apache HTTP Server Version 2.0, "Apache Module mod_rewrite," http://httpd.apache.org/docs/2.0/mod/mod_rewrite.html

2. Wordpress.org, "Using Permalinks," http://codex.wordpress.org/Using_Permalinks

3. Wordpress.org, "Installing WordPress," http://codex.wordpress.org/Installing_WordPress

4. Wordpress.com, "API Keys," http://en.wordpress.com/api-keys/

5. Wordpress.org, "Plugins/Akismet," http://codex.wordpress.org/Plugins/Akismet

6. Wordpress.org, "Template Hierarchy," http://codex.wordpress.org/Templates_Hierarchy

CHAPTER 23

Going Live

Once you have designed and tested your site locally using XAMPP (see Chapter 20) and it's working to your satisfaction, it's time to publish your site to the Web by copying the files from your computer or USB drive to the space provided by your Web host. Assuming that you have been thoughtful in developing your site architecture by keeping everything in your htdocs/ folder, going live should be a relatively painless task of copying the contents of htdocs/ to the root Web folder provided by your host. This chapter offers some checklists to run through before and after you upload your site.

BEFORE YOU UPLOAD: A CHECKLIST

Before you upload your site to your Web server, here is a list of things to check in all of the files that make up your site:

- **Check that you haven't written any links that refer to your testing URL, http://localhost/:** Make sure that you have no domain names in links that point to your own pages (except for the link to your home page in the `<div id="header">` area of your document, which should be your actual domain name and not `http://localhost/`, if you have been using that for testing purposes.
- **Check for links or images loaded from folders outside of your Web root folder and its subfolders:** When you're working on your own computer, you can link to pages or images anywhere

on your computer. These links, however, will not work on the open Web, so be sure that you have moved all of your images into a folder inside of your Web root, and that links from your pages point there.

- **For WordPress sites:** Make sure that you have specified your actual URL inside of the WordPress administrative interface and that you have also made any necessary changes in `wp-config.php` to refer to the database that you have set up with your Web host, including the database's name and the username and password to access it.

Also, if you have purchased your domain name from someone other than your Web host (as was recommended in Chapter 5), you will need to go to your domain-name registrar's Web site and log into the control panel they provide for managing your domain. Once logged in, you will enter your Web host's nameservers for your domain (nameservers are usually in the form of `ns1.example.com` and `ns2.example.com`; additionally, some registrar's require each nameserver's IP address, which your host should provide for your information). That's how you ensure that your domain name points to your site at your hosted server space. Google for "nameservers" and the name of your Web host and "specify different nameservers" and the name of your domain provider to determine how to do this. Once you have changed the nameservers that your domain uses, it may take some time (around 24 hours) before your domain points to your actual site.

Locating FTP/SFTP Instructions for Your Web Host

Every Web host is a little different in terms of how you access your account to upload files. Make sure that you find, read, and follow the host's instructions carefully. Some require setting a "passive" FTP mode, for example, so you'll need to select an FTP client that supports passive mode. Do a Google search.

If you have a host that offers SFTP, use that rather than FTP (even if the host offers both); FTP transfers your password without any encryption, which makes it easy for someone to break into your site. Make sure, also, that you select a client that supports SFTP (see the "Selecting an FTP/SFTP Client" sidebar).

SELECTING AN FTP/SFTP CLIENT

It is essential to select an FTP/SFTP client that meets the requirements of your Web host. Here are some flexible clients that you might try to use; they are all free and open source.

- **WinSCP** (`http://winscp.net/`) is an excellent choice for Windows users and can handle almost any kind of FTP/SFTP connection that your Web host requires.
- **CyberDuck** (`http://cyberduck.ch/`) is a very versatile FTP/SFTP client for Mac OS X. Better still, it acts just like another OS X folder window, so copying files from your computer to your server is no harder than copying files from folder to folder on your computer itself.
- **FileZilla** (`http://filezilla-project.org/`) offers a free and open-source FTP/SFTP client for Windows and Mac, as well as Linux.

Finally, you need to check the address you need to upload your files to. Sometimes this is a generic address for your host (such as `ftp.webhost.foo`), but that passes your files to your account based on your username. Sometimes you get an FTP address in the form of `ftp.example.com` that uses your own domain name. If you're using SFTP, though, you usually just specify your domain name for the address: `example.com`. You will need to specify the correct address in your FTP/SFTP client.

GETTING YOUR FILES TO THE RIGHT PLACE

Every Web host specifies a root Web folder where you must place your files in order for them to be viewable at your URL. You'll need to check your host's documentation to determine where that folder is; just like `htdocs/` was the root Web folder in your XAMPP Web server (see Chapter 20), different hosts may specify `www/`, `http-docs/`, or even `html/` as their root Web folder. You want to make sure that you transfer your files from `htdocs` to your host's root Web folder. (But do not transfer `htdocs` itself, unless you want people to access your Web site at `http://www.example.com/htdocs/`. And nobody wants that.)

FILE AND FOLDER PERMISSIONS

Early in the book, I suggested purchasing Web hosting from a company that uses Linux servers and that grants you secure shell (SSH) access. Setting file and folder permissions is one area where SSH access is essential. It offers a straightforward mechanism for seeing and changing which users on a system, including the user the Web server runs as, can read and write files.

There are two parts to permissions: the username of the file or folder's owner and the owner's group and what the file or folder's owner, associated group, and everyone with server access can do to the file (read, write, and/or execute). In order to enable browser uploads in WordPress, for example, you may have to change the permissions on your uploads folder to allow the Apache Web server user to write files there. And sometimes, you also have to make sure that your own user, the one you access the server with to transfer files, can in turn download browser-uploaded files over FTP/SFTP.

Details on determining and setting file permissions are available at this book's companion site, http://sustainablewebdesign.com/book/.

AFTER YOU UPLOAD: A CHECKLIST

Depending on how large your site is, and how fast your Internet connection speed is (even high-speed connections are usually slower for uploads than they are for downloads), it may take a little while to upload your site.

But once your FTP/SFTP client indicates that your files have been uploaded, it's time to check out your live site for the first time by pointing your browser to your actual domain name's URL in the form of `www.example.com` or `example.com`, depending on whether you've elected to use `www.` or not (see the "WWW, or No WWW?" sidebar).

Check your live site for the following potential problems:

- **Do your pages load?** This is the most obvious check; you want to see your own work when you go to your own domain name. If you do not see your own work there, try reloading the page. Many Web hosts will put a temporary `index.html` file in your root Web folder, so you may need to use your FTP client to delete that if your own `index.htm` file does not appear. Also, if you see a page that appears to be from your domain registrar,

WWW, OR NO WWW?

Some Web sites, like `http://www.google.com/` force the use of `www.` in their URL (if you try to go to `http://google.com`, Google's server will add the `www.` onto the URL for you).

My attitude, shared with the people behind http://no-www.org/ is that www. is superfluous for Web sites. That's why my site forces http://karlstolley.com. Anyone using www. to access the site will be automatically sent to the correct, www-less URL.

However, there is an alternate view, expressed by the community at http://www.yes-www.org/ who urge the use of `www.` in Web URLs.

Whether you use `www.` or not, or allow users to use both, is up to you; just make sure that, `www.` or not, people can access your site at either one. Here are some instructions to put in an `.htaccess`; these are available in the RPK `.htaccess` file; uncomment the lines to use no-www or www on your Web server (these may cause problems on an XAMPP installation):

- Force no www:

```
RewriteEngine On
RewriteCond %{HTTP_HOST} ^www\.(.+)$ [NC]
RewriteRule ^(.*)$ http://%1/$1 [R=301,L]
```

- Force www:

```
RewriteEngine On
RewriteCond %{HTTP_HOST} !^www\.(.+)$ [NC]
RewriteRule ^(.*)$ http://www.%1/$1 [R=301,L]
```

you will have to set up your domain to use your host's name-servers as described above. If you've done that already, try your site again in a few hours.

- **Do your images and CSS files load?** If you are seeing your XHTML pages, but not your design, you need to first check that the files were uploaded. This can be as easy as pointing your browser to, for example, `http://example.com/css/screen.css` and seeing if your CSS file's source displays. If it doesn't, go back to your FTP client and upload it again. If the CSS file's source does display, you need to check the paths that load it in your XHTML file (see Chapter 20).

- **Are your XHTML pages and CSS files validating?** Particularly if you've included validation links in the footer, try them out and make sure that everything is validating. If they fail to validate, make the necessary corrections and re-upload any problem files.

UPDATING FILES

Unless you do a major overhaul of your site, it's usually only necessary to upload your entire site once. Thereafter, you only need to upload files that you've made changes to. That should be as easy as finding your computer's copy of the file, and uploading it to the proper location on your Web server with your SFTP client. Always keep both a local and a remote version of your site; CD-ROM or other backups are also smart to maintain in the event that both your own computer and your Web server crash. You don't want to lose your work!

Making Copies of Browser Uploads

If you use WordPress or another content management system, you likely also have the ability to upload files via your Web browser. It is important to regularly download copies of these files using your FTP/SFTP client. Be sure to preserve the same folder structure the files are stored in on the server (WordPress, for example, will create its own set of folders to keep things organized) so that you can restore your site in the event of a server crash.

NEXT STEPS

"Going live" sounds a lot more interesting than it actually is! Copying files is pretty yawn-worthy—though it should be exciting to see your site at your own URL that you can share with the rest of the world. You'll use these same steps into the future, editing files on your own computer, checking them, and then uploading them before checking them again on the live site. (If changes don't appear after you upload them, try clearing your Web browser's cache.) The final chapter of the book will help you learn how to develop a picture of who's visiting your site and how you can share your content to increase the reach of your identity across the Web.

CHAPTER 24

Tracking Visitors, Sharing Content

To monitor and improve the growth of your site and online identity, you will want to track your site's usage over time after it's been uploaded and indexed by Google and other search engines. This chapter looks at some of the popular tools for tracking site visits. But tracking visits is only part of the picture of building your identity on the Web. To maximize the reach of the content you post on your site, you should make it possible for users to access your content away from your site, and perhaps even allow them to republish your site's content.

TRACKING VISITORS

You can hang a poster up someplace but not have any idea who, if anyone, has looked at it. The Web is very different in this way. Each time someone accesses a page on your site, most Web servers record certain information about the visit: the page being accessed, the visitor's IP address (a unique number that identifies each computer on the Internet), the Web browser the visitor used, and the date and time of the visit.

In addition to your Web server's logging activity, you can set up third-party services—such as Google Analytics—to track visits to your site.[1]

Before you get too invested in site statistics, though, realize that visit numbers and page views are only one metric—and it some ways, the *least* important metric—of the impact your site has on your identity. A well-designed site with few visitors but that helps to land someone a job is much more rhetorically successful than a site that boasts tens of thousands of visitors but has little impact on them.

Nevertheless, it does not hurt to have a picture of who is accessing your site, and what they are looking at and even clicking on while they are there.

Hosted Statistics Programs: Webalizer

Many Web hosting companies will provide you with Web site statistics programs; one common program hosts install is Webalizer, which is free and open source.[2] (These programs can be tricky to set up yourself, so if you're very concerned about statistics, be sure to purchase hosting from a Web host that provides a statistics program for you.)

Webalizer automatically analyzes the log files on your server, as often as every day. The log files are written to by your Web server each time someone tries to access something on your Web site. Webalizer reports users by their IP address and uses that information to try and determine, among other things, the country from which the visitor accessed your site. It also reports search engine terms people used to arrive at your site, and the top pages that people enter and exit on.

Webalizer also reports hits, files, and pages on your site. The difference between these three can be somewhat confusing. But essentially:

- **A hit** is any request for a file from your site. If you have a page XHTML (one hit) that loads one CSS file (one hit) and three image files (three hits), one person's access of that one page will be recorded as five hits. So "hits" should not be confused with number of visits, visitors, or page views, but rather the total number of files requested. (Even more confusing, if someone tries to access something on your server that doesn't exist, that, too, will be recorded as a hit.)
- **A file** is counted the same way as a hit, except that the file count does not include attempts to access files on your server that do not exist. So hits are all of the requests; files are only the successful requests.
- **A page** differs depending on how Webalizer is configured, but generally all .htm, .html, and .php files are treated as pages (depending on the configuration of Webalizer, word processor

or PDF files may also be counted as pages, though not necessarily). The number of pages accessed, then, is the closest metric to actual pages that are looked at on your site.

But it's not even that simple: Part of the problem with Webalizer—as with most statistics packages—is that it is limited in its ability to distinguish between an actual human being visiting your site and a search engine robot crawling your site to index it. That makes it difficult to know whether you are racking up visits from people or search engines.

Remote Statistics: Google Analytics

Google Analytics is one remote alternative to hosted statistics programs, such as Webalizer. To use Google Analytics, you only need to have an account with Google (such as for Gmail); once you set up your site with Google Analytics, it will provide you with a small piece of JavaScript to place at the very bottom of each of your pages. (This is one more reason why using WordPress or PHP with includes makes managing your site easier—you can just add the Google Analytics code to your template or include file; see Chapters 21 and 22.) One limitation to Google Analytics is that it only works when JavaScript is enabled; so any visitors coming to your site with JavaScript disabled will not appear in your Google Analytics reports.

Google Analytics reports are growing more interesting and complex all of the time; Google provides documentation for them, and you can find additional information about Google Analytics on this book's companion Web site, `http://sustainablewebdesign.com/book/`.

Tracking User Interaction

Both Webalizer and Google Analytics provide information *that* users are visiting your site. However, they do not provide information *about* *what* their activity looks like. For example, you might know that people are visiting your resume page, but how are they arriving there? A button in your navigation bar? A contextual link in your home page text?

One solution to answering those kinds of questions are services that track the geographic location of clicks on pages of your Web site. There is a for-pay service called CrazyEgg that does this,[3] though there are open-source alternatives that you can run yourself, including ClickHeat.[4] (Also, shortly before this book went to press, Google Analytics added a beta version of a limited click-tracking service called In-Page Analytics; however, at that time, it only listed click percentages in little balloons next to particular hyperlinked items on a page, as opposed to the heat maps provided by Crazy Egg and ClickHeat.)

What these types of services do is offer you a visual map of where on your page users are clicking. Over time, a picture emerges of where in your design users seem most likely to click—your navigation, contextual links, and other areas. One of the more useful things you can learn through click tracking are elements that *aren't* clickable but that users are clicking on anyway. That kind of information is helpful in improving a design: either make the element (photographs especially seem to draw clicks) clickable, or come up with a design that does not invite clicking on nonclickable elements.

How to Use Visitor Tracking Information

Whether you're running Webalizer, Google Analytics, ClickHeat, or some combination of all three (and others), it's important to remember that statistics are not the whole picture of the impact your site has. Still, here are some things to watch for:

- **What pages are drawing the most visits?** Pages that are getting a lot of attention are worth looking at closely. Did you write some interesting content that others are finding useful? Is there something unusual about the design or visual content of the page? There are often lessons to be learned about your audience by popular pages. Consider what might make those pages attractive, and use those observations to think about how you might revise and improve your other, less popular pages.
- **What happens when you post new content?** That 537 people visited your site on January 10 is interesting; but what happened on January 8 and 9 (and 11)? Did you add some new content or make a blog post? Did you self-promote on Twitter? Keeping a log of your activity (or using the annotation feature on Google Analytics charts), and watching how that activity impacts site

visits, can be very helpful to making your site grow—and help you to reach more of your potential audience.

- **Where are people coming from?** Webalizer and Google Analytics both track where your visitors came from; if someone has linked to your site, go check out their page. Why are they referring to your site? You might also notice that users are arriving from Facebook, Twitter, and other social media sites.

- **Are people coming back?** Google Analytics offers some very helpful tools to help you track return visits (though these are limited to visits from the same computer; a single public computer at a library may actually represent many different visitors, each of whom came to your site for the first time). Try and determine whether people are coming back to the same content, or to new content—such as blog posts—and use that information to reward return visits to your site by regularly posting new material.

SHARING CONTENT

Knowing more about who's visiting your site is interesting and helpful, but the reach of your identity on the Web should be about more than page views on your site itself. Enhancing your online identity is something you can do by making it easy for visitors to share your content.

At first glance, that may seem counterintuitive: people who write Web sites should greedily want as many visits to their own site as possible, right? Not necessarily. Think back to the first chapter of this book, when you did Google searches on your name. One of the ideas there was to use Google to establish a picture of who you are on the Web. Your site is one part of that, but if you make it easy for others to use your content (and give you credit for the content, and a link back to your site), your reputation extends across the Web—even if visits to your site do not increase measurably (though they certainly might).

Once your site is live on the Web, you can start to take advantage of the ability to share content. Part of sharing content is a matter of content licensing, perhaps under Creative Commons licenses, which allow people to repost, and perhaps modify, your content. But the other part of sharing content is publishing it to your site with enhancements that makes it easy to share on social media Web sites.

Licensing Content

One way to share content is a legal move: licensing your content under some form of content license. Creative Commons licenses are one option to alert your visitors as to what they can and cannot do with your content.[5]

The basic idea behind Creative Commons is that you gain more by being more permissive with your content. If you take a great photograph, or write some interesting text, and someone wants to use it, by licensing your content under Creative Commons, you can give people specific guidelines as to how your content may be used. In the words of the Creative Commons Web site, the licenses "help you keep your copyright while allowing certain uses of your work—a 'some rights reserved' copyright."[6]

All Creative Commons licenses specify that people republishing or building on your work must give you attribution; on your Web site, you might additionally specify that they need to provide a link to your site. Additional Creative Commons license permissions include the ability to remix or alter your content, and to do so for commercial purposes.

There are four basic features of Creative Commons licenses, and you can pick and choose which features accompany how you license your work using the Creative Commons licensing tool:[7]

- **Attribution:** All Creative Commons licenses require that someone using your work give you credit for your work. You can specify how you would like attribution given to you (e.g., with your name hyperlinked back to your Web site) somewhere on your Web site.
- **Derivative Works:** You can license your work so that it can be used only in its original form (no derivatives) or that people can alter, remix, or build upon your work.
- **Share Alike:** You can specify that anyone using or building upon your work (if you allow them to make Derivative Works) must, in turn, license that derived work under the same license as your original work.
- **Commercial Use:** Finally, you can specify whether your content may be used for commercial purposes, for example, to sell goods and services or to be sold itself.

So the most restrictive Creative Commons license would stipulate that nobody is allowed to make derivatives of your work, and that it may not be used for commercial purposes. The most permissive Creative Commons license would allow derivative works and allow your work to be used for commercial purposes.

If you have questions about Creative Commons or other licenses, however, you should speak to an attorney.

Metadata for Sharing Content

Another way to make your content shareable involves particular technological moves. Really Simple Syndication (RSS) is one form of this and is often a feature built into CMSs such as WordPress. To be maximally flexible, you should license the content in your RSS feed under Creative Commons. RSS enables other sites to repost or aggregate your content or individuals to read your content from a centralized location, like Google Reader.[8]

But RSS is not the only option for sharing content. You can also enable your visitors to share your pages, or links to them, on Facebook and other social media services. A de facto standard of sorts has emerged for this, called Facebook Share.[9] Facebook Share specifies a few additional meta tags added to the <head> of your XHTML document: one for the title of the page (which should probably match the contents of the <title> tag in your <head>), a description tag, and an optional <link> tag that refers to a thumbnail image of your page or, more simply, of your site.

So Facebook Share metadata on a page titled "Please Share This" whose description reads "I want you to share this page" and has a thumbnail of thumbnail.jpg would look like:

```
<meta name="title" content="Please Share This" />
<meta name="description" content="I want you to
  share this page." />
<link rel="image_src" href="http://example.com/media/
  img/thumbnail.jpg" />
```

Someone can then easily post your page to Facebook, or a social bookmarking service like Magnolia (which uses Facebook Share), and the shared or bookmarked item will have exactly the title, description, and thumbnail that you specify. (These metatags are available in the RPK; just uncomment to use them. The RPK WordPress template pre-populates the title and description, though you must add your own thumbnail.) You can even add a Facebook Like button to each of your pages for sharing content directly on Facebook.[10] Other sites, such as AddThis,[11] provide buttons for your site that enable one-click sharing of your content on a variety of different social media Web sites.

FINAL STEPS? THERE ARE NO FINAL STEPS

This is the end of the book, but only the beginning of your own activity developing an identity on the Web. As has been stressed throughout this book, building a Web site is an ongoing process—and the material covered here only scratches the surface on any given topic. Be sure to consult the "Resources for the Future" section of this book for suggested materials to learn more about Web design, and watch the companion site to this book, `http://sustainablewebdesign.com/book/`, for updates and changes.

NOTES

1. Google Analytics, http://www.google.com/analytics/
2. The Webalizer, http://www.mrunix.net/webalizer/
3. CrazyEgg, http://crazyegg.com/
4. Labsmeida, "ClickHeat," http://www.labsmedia.com/clickheat/index .html
5. Creative Commons, http://creativecommons.org/
6. Creative Commons, "What Is CC?," http://creativecommons.org/about/ what-is-cc
7. Creative Commons, "License Your Work," http://creativecommons.org/ choose/
8. Google Reader, http://www.google.com/reader
9. Facebook Developers, "Facebook Share," http://developers.facebook .com/docs/share
10. Facebook Developers, "Like Button," http://developers.facebook.com/ docs/reference/plugins/like
11. AddThis, http://www.addthis.com

Resources for the Future

There are countless books and resources on Web design, but it can be difficult to know which are worth your time to read. Below is a list of my favorites, many of which I consult regularly in my own Web writing and design work. Most are written for advanced audiences, but the techniques and approaches in *How to Design and Write Web Pages Today* will prepare you to engage with these additional resources.

CSS DESIGN GALLERIES

There are many excellent CSS design galleries available on the Web; do a Web search for "CSS design galleries" to find more.

CSS Elite: CSS Gallery and Website Development Resources, http://www .csselite.com/

CSS Elite is one of many CSS galleries that is updated quite regularly; it has a browsable showcase of the latest designs, and also provides tags in categories such as "colorful" or "clean" to help you browse other designs for inspiration.

CSS Zen Garden: The Beauty in CSS Design, http://www.csszengarden .com/

The CSS Zen Garden is not updated much anymore, but it is a rich and inspiring example of the design possibilities of changing only the CSS over an HTML page.

Unmatched Style, http://ww.unmatchedstyle.com/
Another fine CSS gallery that also features audio podcasts and a good blog.

WEB DESIGN MAGAZINES AND BLOGS

The best way to stay current in your Web design and writing practices is to read magazines and blogs by leading Web designers. A Web search for "web design blog" will turn up more like these.

A List Apart, http://www.alistapart.com/
A List Apart is one of the finest Web magazines out there; issues are published on the Web every other week. Topics range from standards documents to design practices.

Shea, Dave. *Mezzoblue*, http://www.mezzoblue.com/
Shea is one of many excellent designer-bloggers; he is also the caretaker of the CSS Zen Garden.

37 Signals. *Signal vs. Noise*, http://37signals.com/svn/
Signal vs. Noise is a very influential blog on work practices, industry, and the big picture of Web design and development activity.

COMMUNITIES

Before posting to any community forums, be sure you familiarize yourself with their posting policies—and that you've done your research (including searching their forums for a same or similar question as yours someone might have posted previously.

CSS Beauty, *SkillShare Forum*, http://cssbeauty.com/skillshare/
A quiet and generally welcoming community of Web professionals and amateurs.

SitePoint, *SitePoint Forums*, http://cssbeauty.com/skillshare/
A large and active community, covering topics from hardcore development to design basics; do your homework before posting a question.

WordPress.org, *WordPress > Support Forums*, http://wordpress.org/support/
The best community to turn to in all matters for WordPress installation, use, and templating.

WEB STANDARDS

Cederholm, Dan. *Bulletproof Web Design*. 2nd ed. Berkeley, CA: New
    Riders, 2007.

A favorite of beginning and advanced Web designers, this book looks at
building sites that work best under a wide range of conditions.

Keith, Jeremy. *HTML5 for Web Designers*. New York: A Book Apart, 2010.

A compact but complete introduction to HTML5 that will be immediately
accessible for anyone with knowledge of XHTML.

Zeldman, Jeffrey. *Designing with Web Standards*. 3rd ed. Berkeley, CA:
    New Riders, 2009.

The defining, classic book on standards-based Web design.

ACCESSIBILITY AND USABILITY

Clark, Joe. *Building Accessible Websites*. Berkeley, CA: New Riders/
    Peachpit Press, 2002.

A classic text in accessible Web design; the principles are good, although
some of the examples are aging a bit.

Krug, Steven. *Don't Make Me Think! A Common Sense Approach to Web
    Usability*. 2nd ed. Berkeley, CA: Peachpit Press/New Riders, 2006.

An extremely popular and useful book on Web usability.

Pilgrim, Mark. *Dive into Accessibility*. http://diveintoaccessibility.org/

A book, also available as a free PDF or set of HTML files, that covers a
range of approaches to accessibility.

SITE ARCHITECTURE

Morville, Peter, and Louis Rosenfeld. *Information Architecture for the
    World Wide Web*. 3rd ed. Sebastopol, CA: O'Reilly Media, 2006.

A classic work in information architecture and a must-read for creators of
large Web sites.

Walter, Aaron. *Building Findable Websites: Web Standards, SEO, and
    Beyond*. Berkeley, CA: New Riders, 2008.

Covers a range of topics in site architecture as related to search engine
optimization (SEO) and findability.

CSS DESIGN

Clarke, Andy. *Transcending CSS: The Fine Art of Web Design.* **Berkeley, CA: Peachpit Press/New Riders, 2007.**

A follow-up, in some respects, to Shea and Holzschlag's Zen of CSS Design, this book pushes the envelopes of CSS design and is one of the best for exploring the practices behind CSS positioning.

Shea, Dave, and Molly E. Holzschlag. *The Zen of CSS Design: Visual Enlightenment for the Web.* **Berkeley, CA: Peachpit Press/New Riders, 2005.**

An excellent (if advanced) guide to CSS design, using examples from the CSS Zen Garden.

JAVASCRIPT AND DOM SCRIPTING

Castledine, Earle and Craig Sharkie. *jQuery: Novice to Ninja.* **Collingwood, Australia: SitePoint, 2010.**

A thorough introduction to jQuery, including the jQuery UI library.

Keith, Jeremy. *DOM Scripting: Web Design with JavaScript and the Document Object Model.* **Berkeley, CA: Friends of Ed/Apress, 2005.**

One of the very best introductions to DOM scripting and object-oriented uses of JavaScript.

Resig, John. *Secrets of the JavaScript Ninja.* **Greenwich, CT: Manning Publications, 2010.**

An advanced and thorough treatment of JavaScript by the author of the popular jQuery JavaScript library.

TEACHING AND LEARNING

Opera Software, *Opera Web Standards Curriculum,* **http://www.opera.com/company/education/curriculum/**

A free, thorough curriculum in standards-based Web design.

Web Standards Project (WaSP) Interact, *Curriculum,* **http://interact.web standards.org/curriculum/**

Another free curriculum that goes into advanced topics of server-side development and user science—from the perspective of Web standards.

VISUAL DESIGN

Elam, Kimberly. *Grid Systems: Principles of Organizing Type*. New York: Princeton Architectural Press, 2004.

A treatment of grid-based design, specifically aimed at typography.

Lidwell, William, Kritina Holden, and Jill Butler. *Universal Principles of Design*. Gloucester, MA: Rockport Publishers, 2003.

The title says it all: a treasure of different, essentially universal design principles.

Samara, Timothy. *Making and Breaking the Grid: A Graphic Design Layout Workshop*. Gloucester, MA: Rockport Publishers, 2002.

An outstanding treatment of grid-based design in print and digital media.

Wilde, Judith, and Richard Wilde. *Visual Literacy: A Conceptual Approach to Graphic Problem Solving*. New York: Watson-Guptill, 2000.

A fun book of different visual design problems, with discussion and principles of visual design.

Glossary

Here are brief definitions of the most frequently used technical and design terms used in the text. Additional terms can be found at the book's companion Web site http://sustainablewebdesign.com/book/.

attribute: In XHTML, attributes provide metadata on tags; common attributes include `class` and `id`.

attribute-value: In XHTML, values assigned to attributes can be called attribute-values; in `<div id="navigation">`, *navigation* is the attribute-value.

byte: A measurement of file size; usually as kilobytes (about 1,000 bytes), megabytes (about 1,000 kilobytes), and gigabytes (about 1,000 megabytes).

child: The immediate tags nested inside a parent XHTML tag. In `<p><strong>Example</strong></p>`, `strong` is a child of `p`.

class: An XHTML attribute for adding additional structure that can be shared among a group of elements.

client-side scripting: Scripting languages, such as JavaScript, that run in a Web browser (the client side, versus the server side).

CSS, Cascading Style Sheets: Standards-based Web design's design language, which the browser builds over the top of structural XHTML.

descendant: Any tag nested inside of any other tag, no matter how deeply; a more generic version of child.

DOM, Document Object Model: The browser's representation of an XHTML page, which is often manipulated and enhanced through JavaScript (see Chapter 19).

DOM scripting: JavaScript that manipulates the DOM, versus older uses of JavaScript that were inserted directly into XHTML.

element: The alphabetic contents of an XHTML tag, which can also be a selector in CSS; in the `<p>` tag, p is the element (and a valid CSS element selector).

id: An XHTML attribute for adding additional structure to a unique element, once per page.

JavaScript (ECMAScript): A common scripting language for adding enhanced features to Web pages; can be combined with the DOM and referred to as *DOM Scripting*.

method: A function that an object in object-oriented programming is cable of performing or being the target of.

object: The primary unit in object-oriented programming; objects have both properties and methods.

parent: The immediate tags in which others are nested. In `<p><strong>Example</strong></p>`, p is the parent of `strong`.

PHP, PHP Hypertext Preprocessor: A common server-side language for creating dynamic Web content (see Chapter 21).

pixel: A common unit of measurement in Web design; refers to an individual square of light on a monitor.

positioning context: In CSS, the positioning context determines what an element is positioned with regard to. By default, the positioning context is the browser window, but parent elements that are positioned absolutely or relatively become the positioning context for any descendant elements.

property: In CSS, a property is the visual aspect that a style will change; `color`, `font-family`, and `width` are all examples of properties.

root Web folder: The folder on a Web host that holds the site files; a file named `mypage.htm` in the root Web folder can be accessed at `http://example.com/mypage.htm`.

selector: In CSS, a selector is what the CSS style will affect; to change all list items inside of the navigation list, the selector would be `ul#navigation li`.

server-side scripting: Scripting languages, such as PHP and Ruby, that run on the server before being sent to the browser (client).

sibling: In XHTML, siblings are any adjacent tags that share a parent.

source order: In XHTML, source order refers to the arrangement of contents in the source, for example, header, followed by content, followed by navigation, followed by a footer.

style declaration: A unit of CSS including the selector to be styled, and the properties and values the selector will be styled as.

syntax highlighting: An essential function of good text editors, which colorize the text of different components of a language (and any textual content) to make source easier to read.

validator: A service for checking XHTML and CSS files against the rules for their use.

value (CSS): The setting for a given property; for example, to set text color to red, the `color` property should be set to the `red` value: `p { color: red; }`.

viewport: The part of the browser window where a Web page displays.

Web standards: A collection of technological specifications issued by the World Wide Web Consortium, ECMA International, and the International Organization for Standardization (ISO) used to guide the design of accessible and sustainable Web sites.

XAMPP: An open-source, portable Web server for testing purposes (see Chapter 20).

XHTML, Extensible Hypertext Markup Language: A common, standard language for structuring content on the Web.

INDEX

About the Author

KARL STOLLEY earned his doctorate from the Rhetoric and Composition program at Purdue University in West Lafayette, IN, where he was Webmaster of the world-renowned Purdue Online Writing Lab (OWL). As assistant professor of technical communication at the Illinois Institute of Technology in Chicago, IL, he teaches graduate courses on Web design, information architecture, and the rhetoric of technology. He also directs Gewgaws Lab (http://gewga.ws), an open-source design and development research group. His publications have appeared in such journals as *IEEE Transactions on Professional Communication*, *Journal of Business and Technical Communication*, and *Kairos: A Journal of Rhetoric, Technology, and Pedagogy*. He has also served as interface editor for *Kairos* and led its redesign, which was awarded the Council of Editors of Learned Journals' Best Journal Design Award in 2009—the first Web-based journal to receive such a distinction.

Stolley maintains a Web presence at http://karlstolley.com/ and is on Twitter @karlstolley.